Working with Communities and Society

WORKING WITH COMMUNITIES AND SOCIETY

Ajit K. Singh

CENTRUM PRESS
NEW DELHI-110002 (INDIA)

CENTRUM PRESS

H.O.: 4360/4, Ansari Road, Daryaganj,
New Delhi-110002 (India)
Tel: 23278000, 23261597, 23255577, 23286875

B.O.: No. 1015, Ist Main Road, BSK IIIrd Stage,
IIIrd Phase, IIIrd Block, Bengaluru-560085 (INDIA)
Tel: 080-41723429

Email: centrumpress@gmail.com
Visit us at: www.centrumpress.com

Working with Communities and Society

First Edition, 2012

ISBN 978-93-81293-61-4

PRINTED IN INDIA

Printed at Tarun Offset, Delhi

Contents

Contents

Preface

Community work has been an integral frontline method of professional social work. It has been primarily concerned with enabling people to develop collective responses to shared needs. During the last few years, however, human rights approaches have gained more attention in the development discourse. In sociology, the concept of community has led to significant debate, and sociologists are yet to reach agreement on a definition of the term. There were ninety-four discrete definitions of the term by the mid-1950s. Traditionally a "community" has been defined as a group of interacting people living in a common location. The word is often used to refer to a group that is organized around common values and is attributed with social cohesion within a shared geographical location, generally in social units larger than a household. The word can also refer to the national community or international community.

A community usually was already existing when all of its residents were not yet born, and it will likely continue to exist when all of the people in it have left. It is something that is beyond its very components, its residents or community members. A community may have members who have temporarily moved to other locations. They may wish to eventually return, but not all do. A "*community*" in some senses may not even have a physical location, but be demarcated by being a group of people with a common interest. In the training material here, however, the "*community*" which is the object of a mobiliser's attention is usually one with a physical geographic location.

The profession of Social Work is an odd mixture of many things. It is usually practised by government civil servants in the west (Europe and North America) while many international NGOs have social workers on their staff. The clientele of social work are often called the vulnerable, i.e people whose special conditions or circumstances put them in positions of weakness or vulnerability in comparison with the mainstream of a society. Generally they include members of society who need some help. Typically, these include those with physical or mental disabilities, persons who are not able to work for a living or not able to care for themselves. In special cases, these may include battered women (those who have been physically or emotionally assaulted – e.g by their spouses –and can not escape dangerous situations on their own), frail elderly persons, children without parents to support them, or who are being mistreated.

The tasks of a social worker mainly include administration and counselling, along with a little bit of medical (usually psychological) intervention and advocacy. The social worker provides her or his clients with little bits of wisdom, advice, information, counselling, as needed. Every case is different. The government (or NGO) social worker in a western country (Europe and North America) provides services that are usually provided by elders and family members in other countries. Social work services are too expensive for governments in the least developed countries.

This book makes an ideal text for a wide range of disciplines including Working with Communities and Society.

—Editor

1

Introduction

COMMUNITY WORKING GROUP

The Community Working Group Inc. (CWG) is a nonprofit organization that emerged as a community response to homelessness in the Midpeninsula of the San Francisco Bay Area. The mission of the Community Working Group is to serve the needs of the homeless and those at-risk of becoming homeless in the Midpeninsula area (Palo Alto, East Palo Alto and Menlo Park) through the development and operation of housing and services, and through strategic alliances with community partners who are likewise committed to the promotion of human dignity.

WORKING WITH COMMUNITY

It is important to be clear about the longer term impacts of working with social groups in health. Communities and different organs of civil society have experienced waves of state-or NGO-led social mobilization, often issue-specific. Such interventions can leave them as isolated and powerless at the end as they were at the beginning. Powerful state or non-state actors can affect civic movements in contradictory ways. On the one hand, they can-even with benevolent intent-coopt and take the energy out of civic movements, and water down their positions or relations with their members.

On the other hand, they can also provide new skills, forms of interaction with authorities and benefits that strengthen the confidence of civic groups and their members and their interaction with the state. The consciousness and capacities that grow with civil involvement are important, as is the need to respect the terms and interests that civic groups bring to programmes (identified in the stakeholder analysis) Social action theory is really a view about social change and the ability of communities to mobilize themselves against injustice. Social action is intrinsically about community life and people's ability to resist the consequences of social inequality. Using social action to move a community to action is about mobilization and motivation.

DIFFICULTY: CHALLENGING

Instructions

- Select the proper issue for mobilization. This issue must affect the community as a whole and have strong resonance throughout the group. Health care, policing, income and investments are all central issues for most communities. Selecting a single, powerful issue can bring a community together in ways that a more abstract set of ideas cannot.
- Use media to build a critical consciousness. Critical consciousness is that sense of mind that there is something wrong and we need to take action. Use of all media, from newspapers, to internet, to flier distribution, is central for building that frame of mind that can later respond to mobilization.
- Speak to community leaders about both the capacity of the area for mobilization and the nature of the social capital available. The capacity of a community refers to its ability to fight an injustice and its specific resources, from money to political representation. Social capital is an important concept because it refers to capacity in more quantitative terms: the availability of leadership and the ability to withstand the counter-mobilization of the broader society. The key element here is the ability to alter a critical consciousness from a passive to an active state. Many communities know that there are severe problems, but either do not know how to fight them or are afraid to. Changing this is the job of the proper use of social action.

- Study the community thoroughly. Recognize the change mechanisms within a community. Change mechanisms are the built-in means that a group might have to change society. Its voting strength is clearly one, its abilities to demonstrate and bring the message to those in power are others.
- Analyse the issue in terms of social context. The issue must be centrally relevant to the community under review. If public health is a major issue, then the context must be local governments, scientific analysis and the ability to influence a state legislature or local committee to spend the money and administer the program in a way relevant to the community.

RURAL AREAS AND TOWNSHIPS

Working poor communities, it is relevant to get into a mutually supportive relationship with the local people. Since unemployment levels are high, communities are in dire need of job-creating businesses. At the same time, it is relevant that your business is well accepted and embedded in the community and does not disregard local values and customs.

Mutual respect is one of the building blocks of a good working relationship, and this requires the ability to listen to people and be sensitive to what is ethical and useful for the community. On a very practical level, you may need the buy-in from the leadership in the area, and this involves both the political and traditional leadership. In rural areas, the traditional leadership is usually more influential than the political authorities. You should however consult and involve both to achieve broad acceptance of your business plan. When you enter a rural community, visit both the traditional and political leaders.

If your work stretches beyond the community, you may want to speak to the District Municipal Manager (DMM) and Local Municipal Managers (LMM). At Ward level, you will need to consult the Councillors. Ask the DMM to put you in contact with the LMM, and then further with the Councillor. He or she can then also refer you to the Community Development Workers (CDWs) in the area. Be aware that there might be gatekeepers involved, or that at times the leaderships tries to take ownership of the idea. Also note that each community may have several Wards, so there may be more than one councillor to talk to. At the same time, at community level you should contact the local chiefs.

This can be done through the House of Traditional Leaders at Provincial and District level. In rural areas, chiefs are often more powerful. So if you can convince them to call a community meeting on your behalf, there is a strong likelihood that all community members will appear. Alternatively, the councillor and CDWs can call a community meeting. You can use such a meeting to present your business idea and consult the community regarding their concerns and suggestions. Once they support your idea, the chances of success are higher. You should however be conscious that it is not simply about 'selling' your idea to them, but also about listening and taking their concerns into consideration.

Note: Most rural people in South Africa live under some type of common property regime or group ownership system. This is likely to continue into the foreseeable future for three main reasons. Firstly, the titling and registration of individual freehold remains unaffordable for the majority of South Africans. Secondly, land reform policy allows programme applicants to choose to live under communal property associations. Thirdly, traditional authorities will remain an important institution in managing land and access of the rural poor to land.

When working with communities in townships, you will also need to consult the political authorities as when working in rural areas, but there is usually not a strong traditional leadership. You should further contact civil society organisations active in various sectors in the community (rural community as well as townships). Try to find them through the Prodder Directors, the database of the South African NGO Coalition (SANGOCO), as well as databases from other networks in the area. Civil society organisations are generally divided into larger Non-governmental Organisations (NGOs) and Community-based Organisations (CBOs). While NGOs are more formal and operate funded programmes, CBOs are informal organisations made up of local community members. Involving them may be helpful, as they are already groups of people who support their communities and may be wiling to cooperate if they see the benefit for the people. They can also be important intermediaries between you and the community, as they are often well known and trusted.

You can also use the media to reach community people, such as newspapers or community radio stations.

THE NATURE OF COMMUNITIES

Like most things in the social sciences, community does not fit into a nice neat package.. We use the word a lot, but in this training it is important to ask more seriously what it is. First, let us note that a "*community*" is a construct, a model.. We can not see a whole community, we can not touch it, and we can not directly experience it.. Like the words "*hill*" or "*snowflake*," a community may come in one of many shapes, sizes, colours and locations, no two of which are alike.. More importantly, a community is not just the people who are in it.

A community usually was already existing when all of its residents were not yet born, and it will likely continue to exist when all of the people in it have left. It is something that is beyond its very components, its residents or community members.. A community may have members who have temporarily moved to other locations.. They may wish to eventually return, but not all do. A "*community*" in some senses may not even have a physical location, but be demarcated by being a group of people with a common interest. In the training material here, however, the "*community*" which is the object of a mobiliser's attention is usually one with a physical geographic location.

Sociological : Not only is the concept of a community a "*construct*" (*model*), it is a "*sociological construct.*". It is a set of interactions, human behaviours that have meaning, and expectations between its members. Not just action, but actions based on shared expectations, values and beliefs, and meanings between individuals.. To understand how a community operates, and how it changes, it is necessary to learn a little bit about sociology the science.. The mobiliser is an applied scientist; social scientist. While a pure scientist is interested in how things work, the applied scientist is interested in taking that knowledge and getting useful results.

Fuzzy Boundaries: When an identified community is a little village, separated by a few kilometres from other villages, in a rural area, its boundaries appear at first to be very simple.. That pattern of human interaction may be seen as consisting only of the residents living inside that location, inside that village.

But its residents interact also with people outside the village.. They marry persons from near and far, and may move or bring a spouse in to live with them.. At any one time, those village residents may have sisters, brothers, cousins, parents and extended relatives living elsewhere.. The boundary of that community is not so precise.

COMMUNITIES WITHIN COMMUNITIES

There may be communities within larger communities, including districts, regions, ethnic groups, nations and other boundaries.. There may be marriages and other interaction that link villages on both sides of national borders.

Communities May Move: Furthermore, where technology is not based on local horticulture, the community residents may be physically mobile.. They may be nomadic herders walking long distances with their cattle.. They may be mobile fishing groups who move from time to time as the fish are available.. They may be hunters who move to follow the game.

Urban Communities are Special: In urban areas, a community may be a small group of a few homesteads of people from a common origin.. That community in turn, may be part of a neighbourhood community or a barrio or other local urban division. As the boundaries become wider, there is more heterogeneity (differences in origin, language, religion or other features that can form a common identity).. It may be in turn, a part of a wider municipality, which in turn may be part of a conglomeration comprising a large city.

In general (with exceptions) an urban community has more fuzzy boundaries, is more difficult to demarcate, is more heterogeneous (varied, mixed), more complex, and more difficult to organise using standard community development methods, and has more complex and sophisticated goals, than rural communities.

SOCIAL PERSPECTIVE OF HUMAN SETTLEMENTS

A human settlement, or community, is not merely a collection of houses. It is a human (social and cultural) organisation.. (The houses, which are cultural products of humanity, belong to one of the six dimensions of society or culture, the technological dimension, as explained below). Also, it is not just a collection of human individuals; it is a socio-cultural system; it is socially organised.. This means that you need to know some things about society — things learned in sociology.

The community has a life of its own which goes beyond the sum of all the lives of all its residents. As a social organisation, a community is cultural. That means it is a system of systems, and that it is composed of things that are learned rather than transmitted by genes and chromosomes.. All the social or cultural elements of a community, from its technology to its shared beliefs, are transmitted and stored by symbols.

Social Animation (promoting community participation or self help) mobilises and organises a community.. This means that the social organisation of the community is changed, however slightly or greatly. The mobiliser or animator, therefore, is a social change agent, or catalyst.. Understanding the nature of social change, its social nature, in a community, should be among the inventory of a mobiliser's tool box.

An Animator Must Know About Society: It may be dangerous to dabble in changing something you know nothing about. It is therefor the responsibility of the animator to learn something from the sciences of anthropology and sociology.

A mobiliser is an applied sociologist, so must know some important features of the subject. Although the science of sociology is usually taught at the university level, and a social scientist needs a PhD nowadays, you do not need all that formal education.. Starting from here, perhaps doing a little private literature research on your own as well, you can learn what you need about sociology to understand the social nature of communities.

The most important thing to learn was mentioned already, that a social organism such as a community has a life of its own that goes beyond the lives of the residents in it.. Those individuals have their own changes while they develop as human individuals. They are born, they get older, they become adults, they marry, they get jobs, some become recognised leaders, they have children, they die.. All of these personal changes in individuals do not, in themselves, change society or a community.. In fact, as they are recognised, they contribute to the stability of society, and to the continuation of the community. The second thing to learn was briefly mentioned also.. All things social and cultural are transmitted by symbols rather than by genes. Community development, which is a form of social change, requires changes in the messages of symbols rather than genetic surgery.

Keep the Essential Elements of Society in Mind

While sociology in itself can be interesting, the mobiliser needs to know more about it so as to be a better mobiliser.. Since the notion of "community" is a social construct, the nature of "social" is important to understand. What, for example, is the "glue" that holds a community (or any social organisation) together?. How can individuals be interdependent upon each other, even while they believe they are independent organisms?

Do such beliefs, even if they are not accurate, serve some purpose in sustaining or supporting social organisation?. It is important for the animator to note the inter-connections between the cultural dimensions (described below) which comprise a community.. While social scientists may disagree about the precise nature of those inter-connections, all will agree that the basic characteristic of society (and thus of the communities within a society) is that they are interconnected.

A community, like other social institutions, is not merely a collection of individual persons; it is a changing set of relationships, including the attitudes and behaviour of its members. Remember that your goal is community empowerment. Knowing what a community is, and its social and cultural nature, will help you to know what it is that is becoming empowered by your efforts.

Culture is Learned

We mentioned above that a community is a cultural organism, and that it was something that went beyond those individual human beings that make it up.. Culture in the social sciences is something far more than opera and ballet; so what is it? Culture consists of all those things, including actions and beliefs which human beings (as physical animals) learn, which make them human.. Culture includes learned behaviour, but not things which are determined genetically.. Culture is stored and transmitted by symbols; never by chromosomes.

While some culture is learned in childhood (like how to talk, for example), other is learned by adults. When the animator is engaging in promoting social change, she or he is promoting the learning of new ideas and behaviour. When culture is learned first, by a child, to become human, the process is called enculturation or socialization.. When it is re-learned, as when a person moves to a different society, or when a community changes around the individual, it is called acculturation.

Since you as a mobiliser are much involved in stimulating social change in a community, then you will come face to face with acculturation. Adult educating skills are therefore needed. This sociological definition of "culture," which means "sociocultural system," which is society itself, is not the common everyday definition of culture, where people usually think only of drumming and dancing, or only the arts (those belong to only one of the six dimensions of culture, the aesthetic).

Culture Transcends its Humans

Culture is superorganic (and a community is cultural).. Understanding this concept, "superorganic," is important in understanding a community. Just as the organic level is based on inorganic (living cells are made up of non living atoms, etc.; a dog or a tree is not a cell even though it is made up of cells), so the superorganic is based on the organic (society is not a human being even though it is made up of human beings).. This means that, during animation (mobilisation and organisation) of a community, the animator must always be able to separate what is happening to the overall community itself, in contrast to what is happening to particular individuals.

We use the word "transcend" here to mean "go beyond.". It does not have a religious connotation in this use. Just as a tree, as a living organism, transcends its atoms, molecules and cells which make it up, so a community, or any social organisation in culture, transcends the individual human beings which make it up.. The tree or dog would not exist without its atoms or cells, nor would a community exist without its individual human beings.

The principles which affect an atom or a cell (in a dog or a tree), are not the same as those which affect the dog or tree.. The forces which affect an individual human being (in a community) are not the forces which affect the development of a community. A good mobiliser must understand the nature of social change in a community, and be able to distinguish that from the changes undergone by individuals in that community.. To do that, you the mobiliser must develop a social perspective, and see how a community transcends its residents.

SUPERORGANIC ORGANISM OR SYSTEM

A community can be seen as being something like an organism (i.e it is organised; it has organs). It lives and functions even though its human members come and go, are born or die. Just as a living cell, plant or animal, transcends its atoms, so an institution, a behaviour pattern, or a community, transcends its individual humans.. The behaviour of an atom or the life cycle of a molecule happens according to a different set of forces than the living plant or animal in which the atom or molecule is found.

So, too, an individual human being is subject to a different set of forces than a social organisation (such as a community) where it is found.. A belief, for example, is believed by living persons, but that belief may live on through other persons long after the first ones die. The same with an institution such as marriage, an organisation such as an air force, a town such as Kumasi, a custom such as shaking hands, a tool such as a hoe, or a system such as marketing. All of these transcend the individual human beings which carry them.

A society, then, is a system — not an inorganic system like an engine, not an organic system like a tree, but a superorganic system built up of learned ideas, expectations and behaviour of human beings.. Think of three levels of organisation: inorganic, organic and superorganic. Although a community is a cultural system (in that it transcends its individual persons) do not assume that a community is a harmonious unity.. It isn't.. It is full of factions, struggles and conflicts, based upon differences in gender, religion, access to wealth, ethnicity, class, educational level, income, ownership of capital, language and many other factors.

In order to promote community participation and development, it is the task of the animator to bring these factions together, encourage tolerance and team spirit, and obtain consensus decisions. For you to promote social change in a community, it is necessary to know how that system operates, and therefor how it will respond to changes. Just as an engineer (an applied physical scientist) must know how an engine operates, the community facilitator (an applied social scientist) must know how a community operates.. To know how a community operates one must not anthropomorphise a community. To "anthropomorphise" means to assume and ascribe human characteristics to a non human thing (e.g thinking that ducks and bears have "families" when "family" is a human institution).. A community does not talk, does not think, can not feel, and does not act like a human being.. It is a superorganic entity, and therefore moves, responds, grows and behaves through different principles, forces and mechanisms than a human being does.

DIMENSIONS OF CULTURE AND COMMUNITY

When we say a community is not the same thing as a human being, we say it does not have emotions, a head, thoughts, legs, or a hobby.. It does, however, have different parts to it, that apply to social organisations and culture rather than to individual human beings. One important way to analyse a community, break it into different parts, is to use the six cultural "dimensions.". We use "dimension" because these are analytical categories, made by us human beings, rather than being based upon observable parts (like parts of the body: head, arms, legs). In one of the training modules, Community Research, you will see that these six cultural dimensions (plus geography and demography) can be used as organising categories for you to research, observe, and understand the community where you intend to work.

In mathematics, an object has three dimensions, such as height, width, and depth, four if you include time.. No matter how small or in what ways you cut up that object, each piece will still have all four dimensions.. So too a socio cultural entity, like a community. No matter how small or in what ways you cut up a piece of culture, it will always have all six of its dimensions.

These dimensions of culture include:

- Technological,
- Economic,
- Political,
- Institutional (social),
- Aesthetic value, *and*
- Belief conceptual.

Each of these dimensions of culture are transmitted by symbols (not genes) and consist of systems of learned ideas and behaviour.. They are not "aspects" of culture; they are dimensions.

Cultural dimensions may vary in size but, by definition, permeate the whole. All of these are systems within every social (or cultural) system.. They are based on learned behaviour, which transcends the individuals who each learned parts of them.

If any one dimension of culture is missing, by definition, all are missing. You can not "see" a dimension of culture or society, as you can see an individual person.. Every individual manifests each of the six dimensions of culture.

To become socially aware, the animator must be able to analyse all six of the dimensions, and their interrelationships, even though s/he can only see individuals, not those dimensions.

THE TECHNOLOGICAL DIMENSION OF COMMUNITY

The technological dimension of culture is its capital, its tools and skills, and ways of dealing with the physical environment.. It is the interface between humanity and nature. Remember, it is not the physical tools themselves which make up the technological dimension of culture, but it is the learned ideas and behaviour which allow humans to invent, use, and teach others about tools.. Technology is much a cultural dimension as beliefs and patterns of interaction; it is symbolic..

Technology is cultural. This cultural dimension is what the economist may call "real capital" (in contrast to financial capital). It is something valuable that is not produced for direct consumption, but to be used to increase production (therefore more wealth) in the future; investment. In capacity development, it is one of the sixteen elements of strength that changes (increases) as an organisation or a community becomes stronger.. In the war against poverty, technology provides an important set of weapons.

For an individual or a family, technology includes their house, furniture and household facilities, including kitchen appliances and utensils, doors, windows, beds and lamps. Language, which is one of the important features of being human, belongs to the technological dimension (it is a tool).. This goes along with communication aids such as radio, telephones, TV, blackberries, books and typewriters (now computers).

In an organisation, technology includes desks, computers, paper, chairs, pens, office space, telephones, washrooms and lunch rooms.. Some organisations have specific technology: footballs, goalposts, and uniforms for football clubs, blackboards, desks and chalk for schools, alters, clerical garb, and pews for churches, guns, tasers, and billie sticks for police forces, transmitters, sound booths, and microphones for radio stations.

In a community, communal technology includes its facilities such as public latrines and water points, roads, markets, clinics, schools, road signs, parks, community centres, libraries, sports fields.. Privately owned community technology may include shops, factories, houses and restaurants. When a facilitator encourages a community build a latrine or well, new technology is introduced.. A well (or latrine) is as much a tool (and an investment) as is a hammer or computer.

In general (i.e there are exceptions) technology is perhaps the easiest of the six dimensions for introducing cultural and social change.. It is easier to introduce a transistor radio than to introduce a new religious belief, new set of values or a new form of family. Paradoxically, however, introduction of new technology (by invention or borrowing) will lead to changes in all the other five dimensions of the culture.

Remember there are always exceptions; in Amish society, for example, there is a conscious communal decision to resist the introduction of new technology.. They rely on the preservation of older technology (no tractors, no automobiles, no radios) such as horse drawn carts and ploughs, to reinforce their sense of cultural identity. Those changes are not easily predicted, nor are they always in desired directions.. After they happen, they may appear to be logical, even though they are not predicted earlier.

Through human history, technology has changed generally by becoming more complex, more sophisticated, and with a greater control over energy.. One form does not immediately replace another (although horse whips have now gone out of fashion after the automobile replaced the horse over a century of change).

Usually changes are accumulative, with older tools and technologies dying out if they become relatively less useful, less efficient and more expensive. In the broad sweep of history, gathering and hunting gave way to agriculture (except in a few small pockets of residual groups).. Likewise, agriculture has been giving way to industry.. Where technology is highly advanced (e.g in information technology, computers, the internet) it is practised by a very small proportion of the world population.

People still practising older less efficient technologies often find themselves marginalized and facing poverty (e.g gatherers and hunters). Technology that might be introduced by mobilisers may belong to medicine (clinics and medicine) and health (clean water, hygiene), school buildings or covered markets in rural areas.. There the residents are not usually unaware of them; they simply did not have them, before mobilising to obtain them.

The facilitator must be prepared to understand the effects on other dimensions of culture by the introduction of a change in the technological dimension.

The Economic Dimension of Community

The economic dimension of culture is its various ways and means of production and allocation of scarce and useful goods and services (wealth), whether that is through gift giving, obligations, barter, market trade, or state allocations. It is not the physical items like cash which make up the economic dimension of culture, but the ideas and behaviour which give value to cash (and other items) by humans who have created the economic systems they use.. Wealth is not merely money, just as poverty is not merely the absence of money.

Wealth is among the sixteen elements of community strength or organisational capacity.. When the organisation or community has more wealth (that it can control as an organisation or community) then it has more power and more ability to achieve the things it wants to achieve. Over the broad course of human history, the general trend in economic change has been from simple to more complex.. One system did not immediately replace another, but new systems were added, and less useful ones slowly died out.

In simple small groups, wealth (anything that was scarce and useful) was distributed by simple family obligations. When someone came home with some food or clothing, it was allocated to the other members of the family with no expectations of immediate returns. As society become more complex, and different groups came into contact with each other, simple trade through various forms of barter were acquired.. Distribution within each family group remained more or less the same.

As barter became more complex and extensive, new institutions were added to simplify the accounting: currency, accounts, banks, credit, credit cards, debit cards.. This did not immediately remove earlier forms, but gift giving and family distribution eventually became relatively smaller among the wide range of distribution systems, and barter became less important. Remember that currency (cash, money) itself has no intrinsic value.. It has value only because society — the community; the culture — has ascribed some value to it.. A hundred dollar bill, for example, may be used to start a fire or to wrap tobacco into a cigarette, but its face value is worth much more than for those.

In any community, you will find various forms of wealth distribution.. It is important for you to learn what they are, and what things can be given, what exchanged and what bought and sold. In many societies some things may not be allocated by purchase, such as sexual favours, spouses, hospitality, children, entertainment, and whatnot.. Learning how they are distributed and under what conditions and between whom is part of the research you need to do.

When a community decides to allocate water on the basis of a flat rate for all residences, or to allocate it on the basis of a payment for each container of water when it is collected, then a choice is being made between two very different systems of economic distribution. The animator should encourage the community to choose what it wants so as to be more consistent with prevailing values and attitudes.. (*A* good mobiliser will not try to impose her or his notion of what would be the best system of distribution; the community members, all of them, must come to a consensus decision).

The Political Dimension of Community

The political dimension of culture is its various ways and means of allocating power, influence and decision making.. It is not the same as ideology, which belongs to the values dimension (shared ideas about what is good and bad). It includes, but is not limited to, types of governments and management systems.. It also includes how people in small bands make decisions when they do not have a recognised leader. Political power is among the sixteen elements of community power or organisational capacity.. The more political power and influence it has, the more it can do the things it desires.

An animator must be able to identify the different types of leaders in a community.. Some may have traditional or bureaucratic authority; others may have charismatic personal qualities.. When working with a community, the animator must be able to help develop the existing power and decision making system to promote community unity and group decision making that benefits the whole community, not just vested interests. In the broad sweep of human history, leadership (power and influence) at first was diffuse, temporary and minimal.. In a small band of gatherers and hunters, a leader might be anyone who suggested and organised a hunt.

In small bands, there were no chiefs, elders or kings, and these groups are named by anthropologists as "acephalous" (headless). As history progresses, political systems become more complex, and power and influence increased and affected larger numbers of people.. Levels of political sophistication, and hierarchy, ranged from acephalous, band, tribe, through kingdom to nation state.

In the simplest band, there is very little difference between the amount of power and influence of the leader and the lowest member of the band.. Compare that with the difference in amount of power and influence of the President of the USA and some janitor cleaning toilets in a Washington slum hotel. Communities, including the ones where you work, all have some political system, and some distance between the most and least levels of power between individuals and groups.. It is your first task to understand how it works, how power and influence are distributed (not always the same way) and what changes are occurring.

You will have some influence on that power arrangement as you stimulate the formation of a development committee.. And you will be responsible for encouraging an increase of political complexity if that is the first such committee in that community.

The Institutional Dimension of Community

The social or institutional dimension of culture is composed of the ways people act, interact between each other, react, and expect each other to act and interact.. It includes such institutions as marriage or friendship, roles such as mother or police officer, status or class, and other patterns of human behaviour. The institutional dimension of society is what many non sociologists first think about when they hear "sociology.". It is only one of six dimensions of social organisation (culture), however.

The dimension has to do with how people act in relation to each other, their expectations, their assumptions, their judgements, their predictions, their responses and their reactions.. It looks at patterns of relationships sometimes identified as roles and status, and the formation of groups and institutions that derive from those patterns. A "mother-in-law," for example, is both a role (with a status) and an institution.. In a community, the social organisation of the community is the sum total of all those interrelationships and patterns. The level of organisation (or organisational complexity), the degree of division of labour, the extent of division of roles and functions, is another of the sixteen elements of community strength or organisational capacity. The more organised, and the more effectively organised, it is (and you as mobiliser can help it to become more so), the more capacity it has to achieve its communal or organisational objectives. As with the other dimensions, over history, the general movement has been from simple to complex. In early simple societies, the family was the community, and was the society.

The family defined all roles and status.. As societies became more complex, first the families became more complex, then new nonfamily relationships developed and were recognised.. Later the family itself declined in relative importance among all the many other kinds of relationships. Every time a new role is created, with its duties, responsibilities, rights, and expected behaviour patterns, then the society becomes more complex.. If you encourage the formation of a new development committee, with its official positions and membership, then the community has become that much more complex.

A small rural community with no clinic or school is very likely composed of residents who are all related to each other through descent and/or marriage.. If you stimulate that community to build a school or clinic, with paid teachers or health workers (usually outsiders), then you are increasing the social complexity of that community. In that sense, perhaps the social dimension is similar to the technological dimension in being less difficult (than the other dimensions, especially the last two) in introducing social change.. As with all six dimensions, a change in one such as the social dimension will have effects in each of the other five dimensions.

For the animator to be successful, she or he must know what are the local institutions, what different roles are played by men and women, and what are the main forms of social interaction.

The Aesthetic Values Dimension of Community

The aesthetic value dimension of culture is a structure of ideas, sometimes paradoxical, inconsistent, or contradictory, that people have about good and bad, about beautiful and ugly, and about right and wrong, which are the justifications that people cite to explain their actions. The three axes along which people make judgements are all dependent upon what they learn from childhood.. These include judging between right and wrong, between good and bad, and between beautiful and ugly, all based upon social and community values.

They are not acquired through our genes, but through our socialization.. That implies that they can be relearned; that we could change our judgements. Values, however, are incredibly difficult to change in a community, especially if residents perceive that an attempt is being made to change them.. They do change, as community standards evolve, but that change can not be rushed or guided through outside influence or conscious manipulation.

Shared community standards are important in community and personal identity; who one is very much is a matter of what values in which one believes.. The degree to which community or organisational members share values, and/or respect each others' values, is an important component among the sixteen elements of strength and capacity. Values tend to change as the community grows more complex, more heterogeneous, more connected to the world.. Changes in values tend to result more from changes in technology, changes in social organisation, and less by preaching or lecturing for direct changes.

It appears that there is no overall direction of change in human history, that judgements become more liberal, more tolerant, more catholic, more eclectic — or less — as societies become more complex and sophisticated.. Communities at either end of the social complexity spectrum display standards of various degrees or rigidity. In spite of that range, within any community there is usually a narrow range of values among residents.. Urban and heterogeneous communities tend to have a wider variation in values and aesthetics.

Prestige, one of the three elements of inequality, becomes more spread as societies move from simple to complex. The vast distance in prestige of the janitor versus the president in Washington would be incomprehnsible among equalitiarian societies such as the Pygmies. It is not easy to predict the value standards of any community before you go to live there and to find out how to operate within the community.. Because of their importance, however, it is necessary that you, the mobiliser learn as much as you can about community standards, and do not assume that they will be the same as your own.

While the introduction of new facilities and services in a community may eventually lead to changes in community standards, anything a mobiliser proposes must be seen to be within the prevailing sets of community values.. Whenever an animator introduces new ways of doing things in the community, prevailing values, however contradictory and varied, must be considered.

THE BELIEFS CONCEPTUAL DIMENSION OF COMMUNITY

The belief conceptual dimension of culture (world view) is another structure of ideas, also sometimes contradictory, that people have about the nature of the universe, the world around them, their role in it, cause and effect, and the nature of time, matter, and behaviour. This dimension is sometimes thought to be the religion of the people.. It is a wider category, and also includes atheistic beliefs, for example, that man created God in his own image.. It includes shared beliefs in how this universe came to be, how it operates, and what is reality.

It is religion — and more. When you drop a pencil onto the floor, you demonstrate your belief in gravity. When you say the sun comes up in the morning (it does not; the earth turns) you express a long gone world view. If you, the mobiliser, are seen to be some one who is attacking the beliefs of the people, you will find your work hindered, opposition to you and your goals, and failure as a mobiliser.. Whether or not you want to oppose local beliefs, you must be seen to be not wanting to change them.

In the broad sweep of human existence, the general trend of change has been for a decrease in the number of deities, and a reduction from sacred profane differences in space to secular space.. From local polytheism with many gods, humans moved to a polytheism with fewer gods, from that humans moved to monotheism (one god) and from there an increase in the proportion of people who believe in no god.

In humankind experience, it appears that those groups with local traditional gods tend to be more tolerant of other gods than are the so-called "universal" religions which each say they alone have the true answer.. Huge wars have been fought over religions (an irony in that most religions call for peace and tolerance), and this should be a warning to the mobiliser about the extent to which people fervently hold their beliefs.

The animator must learn, study and be aware of what the prevailing beliefs are in the community.. To be an effective catalyst of social change, the animator must make suggestions and promote actions which do not offend those prevailing beliefs, and which are consistent with, or at least appropriate to, existing beliefs and concepts of how the universe works.

All Six Dimensions are in Each Bit of Culture

The important thing to remember is that in any society, in any community, in any institution, in any interaction between individuals, there is an element of culture, and that includes something of each of those six cultural dimensions.. All of these are learned from birth.. The new-born child is like an animal, not yet a human being, but he or she begins learning culture (humanising) immediately (for example, when drinking from the breast) by interacting with other humans, and thus starts becoming human.. (Many say that this humanising process begins in the womb).

This process of learning, and thus of becoming human, continues until death. If you are not learning, you are dead. When you are at a community meeting, when you are in a classroom, when you meet someone face to face, wherever you are, you are part of culture, part of the sociocultural system, and you can find all six dimensions.. Sometimes, when we try to look objectively at culture in a scientific way, we forget that we are part of culture ourselves.

The tools we use, the interaction we are engaged in, the beliefs and values we hold, are all part of our culture, and part of our existence as social animals.. If we do our work as a mobiliser in a community other than where we grew up, our culture will differ from that of the residents.. We are not free of that obligation if we are trying to mobilise our own community.. A proverb that illustrates an anthropological principle is, "It is a strange fish that knows the existence of water."

Because our very existence, and our understanding of ourselves, is a product of our culture, and our socialization into it, we are not aware of the nature of that culture.. Like a fish that has never been out of water (and able to compare it with its absence) we can not and do not exist outside of culture.

Interconnectedness has a Practical Use

For the mobiliser, and for anyone who is engaged in any development activities, the important part of all this is the variety of interconnections between those cultural dimensions.. They may be causally and functionally inter-related.. Technology (in contrast to popularly held ideas), for example, both the tools and the skills to use them, is as much a part of culture or social system as are beliefs, dances, and ways of allocating wealth. To make changes in any one dimension has repercussions in each of the other dimensions. To introduce a new method of obtaining water, for example, requires the introduction of new institutions to maintain the new water system.

Learning any new ways of doing things will require the learning of both new values and new perceptions.. Changes in any dimension will start changes, like the ripples of water on a calm lake when you throw a stone into it, and ultimately all six dimensions will change. To ignore such interconnections while promoting technology transfer is to do so at your peril (unexpected and/or unwanted results may be produced).. You need to carefully observe changes in the community where you may be working, and look for the repercussions in change in each dimension as they affect the other dimensions.

THE INTERCONNECTEDNESS AFFECTS SOCIAL CHANGE

To change something in one cultural dimension not only requires changes in other dimensions, it causes changes in other dimensions.. That is why social impact assessment should be made of all projects, large and small. As you become more experienced, you will begin to see some changes that follow as a result of introductions of new ways of doing things.. The more you can predict such changes, the more you can be prepared for them.

The more you can predict changes in each dimension, the more you can modify your actions so that the community might be more likely to change in ways you desire.. Remember, however, that you are not a social engineer, and can not precisely determine how a community will respond to your work.

To be more effective as a mobiliser, to empower or strengthen communities, you need to know the nature of communities, and how they behave.. Communities are social or cultural organisations, and, as such, are characterised by the six cultural dimensions.. Communities are not the same as human individuals, but grow and change by their own sets of principles.

The key to understanding these characteristics and principles is to recognise that six dimensions of culture, and their inter-relationships.. The inter-connections between these cultural dimensions are neither simple nor easy to predict. The animator must be aware that they exist, and continually encourage observation, analysis, sharing of ideas, reading, and attending lectures or seminars.. By working with communities, the animator must learn more and more about their culture, and the dynamics of their cultural dimensions.

POVERTY AS A SOCIAL PROBLEM

We have all felt a shortage of cash at times. That is an individual experience. It is not the same as the social problem of poverty. While money is a measure of wealth, lack of cash can be a measure of lack of wealth, but it is not the social problem of poverty. Poverty as a social problem is a deeply embedded wound that permeates every dimension of culture and society. It includes sustained low levels of income for members of a community. It includes a lack of access to services like education, markets, health care, lack of decision making ability, and lack of communal facilities like water, sanitation, roads, transportation, and communications. Furthermore, it is a "poverty of spirit," that allows members of that community to believe in and share despair, hopelessness, apathy, and timidity. Poverty, especially the factors that contribute to it, is a social problem, and its solution is social.

We learn in these training web pages that we can not fight poverty by alleviating its symptoms, but only by attacking the factors of poverty. This handout lists and describes the "Big Five" factors that contribute to the social problem of poverty. The simple transfer of funds, even if it is to the victims of poverty, will not eradicate or reduce poverty. It will merely alleviate the symptoms of poverty in the short run. It is not a durable solution. Poverty as a social problem calls for a social solution. That solution is the clear, conscious and deliberate removal of the big five factors of poverty.

Factors, Causes and History

A "factor" and a "cause" are not quite the same thing. A "cause" can be seen as something that contributes to the origin of a problem like poverty, while a "factor" can be seen as something that contributes to its continuation after it already exists. Poverty on a world scale has many historical causes: colonialism, slavery, war and conquest. There is an important difference between those causes and what we call factors that maintain conditions of poverty. The difference is in terms of what we, today, can do about them. We can not go back into history and change the past. Poverty exists. Poverty was caused. What we potentially can do something about are the factors that perpetuate poverty. It is well known that many nations of Europe, faced by devastating wars, such as World Wars I and II, were reduced to bare poverty, where people were reduced to living on handouts and charity, barely surviving. Within decades they had brought themselves up in terms of real domestic income, to become thriving and influential modern nations of prosperous people. We know also that many other nations have remained among the least developed of the planet, even though billions of dollars of so-called "aid" money was spent on them. Why? Because the factors of poverty were not attacked, only the symptoms. At the macro or national level, a low GDP (gross domestic product) is not the poverty itself; it is the symptom of poverty, as a social problem.

The factors of poverty (as a social problem) that are listed here, ignorance, disease, apathy, dishonesty and dependency, are to be seen simply as conditions. No moral judgement is intended. They are not good or bad, they just are. If it is the decision of a group of people, as in a society or in a community, to reduce and remove poverty, they will have to, without value judgement, observe and identify these factors, and take action to remove them as the way to eradicate poverty. The big five, in turn, contribute to secondary factors such as lack of markets, poor infrastructure, poor leadership, bad governance, under-employment, lack of skills, absenteeism, lack of capital, and others. Each of these are social problems, each of them are caused by one or more of the big five, and each of them contribute to the perpetuation of poverty, and their eradication is necessary for the removal of poverty.

Ignorance

Ignorance means having a lack of information, or lack of knowledge. It is different from stupidity which is lack of intelligence, and different from foolishness which is lack of wisdom. The three are often mixed up and assumed to be the same by some people. "Knowledge is power," goes the old saying. Unfortunately, some people, knowing this, try to keep knowledge to themselves (as a strategy of obtaining an unfair advantage), and hinder others from obtaining knowledge. Do not expect that if you train someone in a particular skill, or provide some information, that the information or skill will naturally trickle or leak into the rest of a community.

It is important to determine what the information is that is missing. Many planners and good minded persons who want to help a community become stronger, think that the solution is education. But education means many things. Some information is not important to the situation. It will not help a farmer to know that Romeo and Juliet both died in Shakespeare's play, but it would be more useful to know which kind of seed would survive in the local soil, and which would not. The training in this series of community empowerment documents includes (among other things) the transfer of information. Unlike a general education, which has its own history of causes for the selection of what is included, the information included here is aimed at strengthening capacity, not for general enlightenment.

Disease

When a community has a high disease rate, absenteeism is high, productivity is low, and less wealth is created. Apart from the misery, discomfort and death that results from disease, it is also a major factor in poverty in a community. Being well (well-being) not only helps the individuals who are healthy, it contributes to the eradication of poverty in the community.

Here, as elsewhere, prevention is better than cure. It is one of the basic tenets of PHC (primary health care). The economy is much healthier if the population is always healthy; more so than if people get sick and have to be treated. Health contributes to the eradication of poverty more in terms of access to safe and clean drinking water, separation of sanitation from the water supply, knowledge of hygiene and disease prevention — much more than clinics, doctors and drugs, which are costly curative solutions rather than prevention against disease.

Remember, we are concerned with factors, not causes. It does not matter if tuberculosis was introduced by foreigners who first came to trade, or if it were autochthonic.&; It does not matter if HIV that carries AIDS was a CIA plot to develop a biological warfare weapon, or if it came from green monkeys in the soup. Those are possible causes. Knowing the causes will not remove disease. Knowing the factors can lead to better hygiene and preventive behaviour, for their ultimate eradication.

Many people see access to health care as a question of human rights, the reduction of pain and misery and the quality of life of the people. These are all valid reasons to contribute to a healthy population. What is argued here, further than those reasons, is that a healthy population contributes to the eradication of poverty, and it is also argued that poverty is not only measured by high rates of morbidity and mortality, but also that disease contributes to other forms and aspects of poverty.

Apathy

Apathy is when people do not care, or when they feel so powerless that they do not try to change things, to right a wrong, to fix a mistake, or to improve conditions. Sometimes, some people feel so unable to achieve something, they are jealous of their family relatives or fellow members of their community who attempt to do so. Then they seek to bring the attempting achiever down to their own level of poverty. Apathy breeds apathy.

Sometimes apathy is justified by religious precepts, "Accept what exists because God has decided your fate." That fatalism may be misused as an excuse. It is OK to believe God decides our fate, if we accept that God may decide that we should be motivated to improve ourselves. "Pray to God, but also row to shore," a Russian proverb, demonstrates that we are in God's hands, but we also have a responsibility to help ourselves. We were created with many abilities: to choose, to cooperate, to organize in improving the quality of our lives; we should not let God or Allah be used as an excuse to do nothing. That is as bad as a curse upon God. We must praise God and use our God-given talents. In the fight against poverty, the mobilizer uses encouragement and praise, so that people (1) will want to and (2) learn how to — take charge of their own lives.

Dishonesty

When resources that are intended to be used for community services or facilities, are diverted into the private pockets of someone in a position of power, there is more than morality at stake here. In this training series, we are not making a value judgement that it is good or bad. We are pointing out, however, that it is a major cause of poverty. Dishonesty among persons of trust and power. The amount stolen from the public, that is received and enjoyed by the individual, is far less than the decrease in wealth that was intended for the public. The amount of money that is extorted or embezzled is not the amount of lowering of wealth to the community. Economists tell of the "multiplier effect." Where new wealth is invested, the positive effect on the economy is more than the amount created. When investment money is taken out of circulation, the amount of wealth by which the community is deprived is greater than the amount gained by the embezzler. When a Government official takes a 100 dollar bribe, social investment is decreased by as much as a 400 dollar decrease in the wealth of the society.

It is ironic that we get very upset when a petty thief steals ten dollars' worth of something in the market, yet an official may steal a thousand dollars from the public purse, which does four thousand dollars worth of damage to the society as a whole, yet we do not punish the second thief. We respect the second thief for her or his apparent wealth, and praise that person for helping all her or his relatives and neighbours. In contrast, we need the police to protect the first thief from being beaten by people on the street.

The second thief is a major cause of poverty, while the first thief may very well be a victim of poverty that is caused by the second. Our attitude, as described in the paragraph to the left, is more than ironic; it is a factor that perpetuates poverty. If we reward the one who causes the major damage, and punish only the ones who are really victims, then our misplaced attitudes also contribute to poverty. When embezzled money is then taken out of the country and put in a foreign (e.g Swiss) bank, then it does not contribute anything to the national economy; it only helps the country of the offshore or foreign bank.

Dependency

Dependency results from being on the receiving end of charity. In the short run, as after a disaster, that charity may be essential for survival. In the long run, that charity can contribute to the possible demise of the recipient, and certainly to ongoing poverty.

It is an attitude, a belief, that one is so poor, so helpless, that one can not help one's self, that a group cannot help itself, and that it must depend on assistance from outside. The attitude, and shared belief is the biggest self justifying factor in perpetuating the condition where the self or group must depend on outside help. There are several other documents on this web site which refer to dependency. When showing how to use the telling of stories to communicate essential principles of development, the story of Mohammed and the Rope is used as a key illustration of the principle that assistance should not be the kind of charity that weakens by encouraging dependency, it should empower.

The community empowerment methodology is an alternative to giving charity (which weakens), but provides assistance, capital and training aimed at low income communities identifying their own resources and taking control of their own development –becoming empowered. All too often, when a project is aimed at promoting self reliance, the recipients, until their awareness is raised, expect, assume and hope that the project is coming just to provide resources for installing a facility or service in the community. Among the five major factors of poverty, the dependency syndrome is the one closest to the concerns of the community mobilizer.

These five factors are not independent of one another. Disease contributes to ignorance and apathy. Dishonesty contributes to disease and dependency. And so on. They each contribute to each other. In any social change process, we are encouraged to "think globally, act locally." The Big Five factors of poverty appear to be widespread and deeply embedded in cultural values and practices. We may mistakenly believe that any of us, at our small level of life, can do nothing about them.

Do not despair. If each of us make a personal commitment to fight the factors of poverty at whatever station in life we occupy, then the sum total of all of us doing it, and the multiplier effect of our actions on others, will contribute to the decay of those factors, and the ultimate victory over poverty. The training material on this web site, is aimed at poverty reduction on two fronts, (1) reduction of communal poverty by mobilizing community groups to unite, organize and take community action, and (2) reduction of personal poverty by the creation of wealth through the development of micro enterprise.

You, as a mobilizer, are in a key position to have an effect on the big five of poverty factors. By conducting your mobilizing and training for poverty reduction, you can ensure your own integrity, hinder those who would corrupt the system, and encourage all your participants to practice the attack on factors of poverty in the course of the actions they choose, when guided and trained by you. The big five factors of poverty (as a social problem) include: ignorance, disease, apathy, dishonesty and dependency. These, in turn, contribute to secondary factors such as lack of markets, poor infrastructure, poor leadership, bad governance, under-employment, lack of skills, lack of capital, and others. The solution to the social problem of poverty is the social solution of removing the factors of poverty.

COMMUNITY BASED SOCIAL WORK

This is another training document in the series of community mobilizing methods for results other than a physical construction such as a communal water supply, clinic or school. The product or output is a programme of services for vulnerable members of the community, many of whom can help themselves if only they are provided with a relatively small amount of help and encouragement.

What is Social Work?

The profession of Social Work is an odd mixture of many things. It is usually practised by government civil servants in the west (Europe and North America) while many international NGOs have social workers on their staff. The clientele of social work are often called the vulnerable, i.e people whose special conditions or circumstances put them in positions of weakness or vulnerability in comparison with the mainstream of a society. Generally they include members of society who need some help. Typically, these include those with physical or mental disabilities, persons who are not able to work for a living or not able to care for themselves. In special cases, these may include battered women (those who have been physically or emotionally assaulted – e.g by their spouses –and can not escape dangerous situations on their own), frail elderly persons, children without parents to support them, or who are being mistreated.

The tasks of a social worker mainly include administration and counselling, along with a little bit of medical (usually psychological) intervention and advocacy. The social worker provides her or his clients with little bits of wisdom, advice, information, counselling, as needed. Every case is different. The government (or NGO) social worker in a western country (Europe and North America) provides services that are usually provided by elders and family members in other countries. Social work services are too expensive for governments in the least developed countries.

The word "social" is a bit misleading because, in the west, where it is mainly practised, the social worker does not work with a whole society, or even with a community or a group in a social context. The social worker usually handles "cases," and a case is usually about an individual or lately increasingly, a family. This is even more ironical because where social work is taught, usually in a university in a department or a school of social administration or social work, often (where they are small) they are attached to sociology departments. Such schools or departments, in turn, are then usually also where community development (like much of the material on this web site) is also taught. Community development, in contrast, is an activity aimed at social institutions, such as communities or groups, rather than at individuals.

One of the many motivating facts pushing the development of this web site is that the empowerment of communities is important and highly needed in low income countries. Limiting the training of community workers to those who are studying in universities, limits the available number of potentially capable community workers; this should be taught to middle school level students (after they have been working out in the real world and have some life experience). This document will not teach you how to become a social worker (any more than the water module will teach you how to become a civil engineer), but will help you in initiating and developing a community based social work (CBSW) programme. The training on this web site is aimed at community workers who do not have to be educated to university level.

Where is CBSW Appropriate?

Rich countries can usually provide social work services (on an individual or family basis, not community based), and poor countries rely on the advice, experience and knowledge of elders and family members. So where would it be appropriate to place a community based social work programme? Community based social work services are needed where they can not be provided by elders and families, but where there is not enough finance available to provide it on an individual basis.

The situation which comes to mind most readily is where there are large displaced or refugee populations, in camps, in poor countries. Further to that, after the emergency is over, those same refugees may return home. Their lives will have been interrupted, losing many family members, including elders and family members, thus the need for social work services remains. So long as there is enough funding available for a professional social worker to supervise the community based work, keeping it up to required standards, the community itself can supply the energy, time and interest in making it work. Apart from refugee situations, wherever there is a large disaster that results in the removal of elders and family members, and/or which disrupts the normal and traditional social organization, are included among situations where it would be appropriate to set up a community based social work programme. Post disaster situations would be included in these.

Where there are large refugee populations, the basic services, food, water, shelter, elementary medical, are usually provided, often by UN agencies and international NGOs. Finance is not unlimited, however, so there may only be a token attempt at providing social work services, if any at all. This is a good situation in which to consider organizing a community based social work programme.

Community Perceptions

When a child is a witness to atrocities that destroy her world, she is affected. To watch your family members and/or neighbours being shot or bombed produces immense trauma if you are a child. In many cases, the experience results in the child withdrawing into herself, refusing to talk, and/or refusing to respond to daily interactions. The child who is traumatized by the same events which lead to refugee or displaced communities, may display behaviour that is often misinterpreted by her remaining family or care givers. Sometimes she is deemed as mentally retarded, and beyond recovery. Sometimes she is seen as affected by evil spirits. Sometimes her condition is seen as a punishment for previous misdeeds by her family members. In all these cases, there is much shame and secrecy associated with her behaviour. All too often her care givers do not understand that she is reacting to the terrible events of the disaster or civil war, and they do not know that the condition can be reversed by a few simple interventions.

Many times such children are hidden (even tied up) in darkened rooms away from public view. They can not dress or clean themselves, and often are found in their own filth and in poor health, hungry, dirty, sick, weak and helpless. Public announcements do not get the message across. Hands on intervention is needed to assess each child. If they are traumatized by atrocious events, and not retarded or otherwise disabled by other factors, they can show remarkable changes, learning to dress themselves, clean themselves and feed themselves. This requires patience, love and care, extended over several weeks and months. A stimulus or two in the form of a doll, and perhaps later a ball, are effective and useful tools for the job.

Here is a situation, repeated hundreds of thousand times around the world, where a community based social work programme is appropriate. This is a typical or classic situation for CBSW. A single, university educated, professional social worker can appraise the situation, prescribe appropriate interventions, and monitor. Community mobilizers can work with the community members to identify hidden and suffering children, recruit community level social workers, arrange for their training and supervision, organize CBOs to manage and operate the CBSW programme at community level, and ensure an effective flow of information. Local residents, on a volunteer basis or with some incentives, can provide the care and stimulation to the children in need, and keep the mobilizers informed about changing conditions and further needed training.

This is only one of many kinds of situations involving vulnerable refugees or displaced persons in communities disrupted by (but surviving) disasters caused by natural or human made events.

The PHC Principles

The "Primary Health Care" (PHC) policy promoted by WHO (UN World Health Organization), has several basic principles, perhaps the best known one being that prevention is better than cure. Another, that is particularly applicable here to community based social work, is the idea that resources should not be spent on expensive cures for a few people.

Underlying this is a public health policy in support of the greatest good for the greatest number. With a limited budget available, that means to concentrate on a few common diseases, to provide elementary training to persons educated at low levels, and reaching the most rural and remote patients. This gave rise to the popular (but slightly inaccurate) concept of "The Barefoot Doctor." If the PHC policy is transferred to the need for social services, then the idea is to give elementary training to persons without university level education, concentrating on the most common and easily treated conditions, and relying on a referral system for more complicated diseases or conditions. The goal in community based social work, then, is to organize a cadre of community members who can be given low level training (i.e not requiring university education) to treat a limited number of social conditions of vulnerable community members. Their interventions will not be as flexible or a sophisticated as those of social workers with university level education and extensive social work training, but they will be able to reach a wider proportion of the population than if only highly skilled and relatively costly professionals are employed. "The greater good for the greater number."

Structure

What is a possible structure for a CBSW programme? Where you have a population of refugees or others who have had severe disruptions in their community lives, where they are able to access support for their immediate needs (food, shelter, water, housing) but no social welfare. Where you may have a professional social worker or two for a population too large for them to reach everybody. Where you have a situation conducive to organizing voluntary community groups.

There you have the basis for CBSW. The professional social workers need to make a needs analysis to determine the limited number of conditions that can be addressed by community workers with low level training. They then need to train and to supervise the training of a cadre of community workers who have access to the client community or communities. Both the needs assessments and the training would not be once-off, but ongoing. They and the community workers (mobilizers) need to identify, recruit, and train community members, as community leaders of the programme, as practitioners of social work interventions in their communities, and as monitors of the changing situations in their respective communities.

Members of the community groups conduct the social work interventions. They need to be supported with training and guidance by the mobilizers and (more indirectly by) the professional social workers. What results in effect is like a social work pyramid, with the professional social worker(s) at the apex, possible social work trainers (temporary or long term) supervised by the social workers, mobilizers, community leaders and managers of the community groups (CBOs) and community and CBO members who conduct most of the interventions.

Training and Support

In general, community mobilizers should never be trained once-and-for-all, but need regular support, encouragement, and a forum in which to ask questions that arise in the field. In CBSW this is even more a requirement. First, mobilizers without formal training (the main audience for this web site) need continued support and professional inputs. Second, the tragedies witnessed in CBSW require field workers to meet with their colleagues to share experiences and to be re-energised and re-infused with enthusiasm and positive attitudes. A CBSW programme as described above needs a routine and predictable forum for getting mobilizers together to share experiences, to ask questions arising from the field, and to obtain inputs from more highly trained and educated social workers. A training unit could be an answer to this need. How it is to be set up depends upon available finances and circumstances.

An initial training programme for the mobilizers could use the first six training modules from this web site. They can be printed and handed out in the training programme. They can be easily adapted to developing a CBSW programme. The training for social work, in contrast, needs to be defined and generated by the professional social workers, after they make their initial appraisal of the situations, and will be modified as new information comes in.

Where there are only one or two highly trained professional social workers for a large population, perhaps involving several communities (as in refugee and similar situations), so that no social work interventions would reach the majority of the population, and where that population has extra need of such interventions following natural or human made disasters, CBSW may be the answer. It requires rearranging available resources, putting the available social workers into positions of appraisal, monitoring and guidance, using mobilizers to organize community groups to do the daily work, setting up a training programme, concentrating on a few of the most common situations that affect the greatest number of persons, and maintaining the training, encouragement and guidance of the mobilizers and community workers. In the appropriate situations, such a programme can be effective and useful.

COMMUNITY EDUCATION, COLONIALISM AND DEVELOPMENT

We explore in more detail the colonial nature of community education (and community development) and some important themes for practitioners in communitv organization and community participation.

The Indebted South

The vast majority of countries in the South have remained locked into positions in the international economic order which impose constraints on national decision-making of a quite different magnitude from those which affect most countries in the North. In the 1980s these inequalities in power and influence were brought into sharper focus by a global recession and a widespread debt crisis among developing countries. A study covering 107 developing countries, of which forty-one were categorized as 'least developed countries', found that between 1980 and 1990 there were significant falls for most 'developing countries' in gross domestic product, public expenditure and private consumption per head.

The latter decreased in 81 percent of the least developed countries and in 64 percent of other developing countries. The United Nations (2000) reports that more than 2.8 billion people, close to half the world's population, live on less than the equivalent of $2/day. More than 1.2 billion people, or about 20 percent of the world population, live on less than the equivalent of $1/day. South Asia has the largest number of poor people (522 million of whom live on less than the equivalent of $1/day). Sub-Saharan Africa has the highest proportion of people who are poor, with poverty affecting 46.3 percent or close to half of the regions' population (United Nations Briefing).

Debt service (the amount of money paid in interest and other charges on loans) increased to claim a greater share of export earnings in 87 percent of the least developed countries and in 84 percent of the other developing countries during the 1980s. For a number of states in Latin America, and for some in Africa, difficulties in repaying international loans had already started in the 1970s, with the 1973 oil price rises bringing the first major shock to more fragile economies.

Exhibit 1: Debt Increases and Decreases

Sub-Saharan Africa: For every $1 received in aid grants in 1999, the countries in the region paid back $1.51 in debt service. They owe $231 billion to creditors, that is $406 for every man, woman and child in Africa. Sub-Saharan countries spend over twice as much on debt service as on basic health care. They spend 6.1 % of GNP on education and spent 5.0 % of GNP on debt service. If Africa's debt were cancelled it could almost double its spending on education.

In sub-Saharan Africa, GDP per capita had grown at over 3 percent a year between 1965 and 1973 but had stagnated between 1973 and 1980. Between 1980 and 1988 it fell by about 25 percent. More recent figures (United Nations 2000) reveal that the top fifth (20 percent) of the world's people who live in the highest income countries have access to 86 percent of world gross domestic product (GDP). The bottom fifth, in the poorest countries, has about one percent. In 1998, for every $1 that the developing world received in grants, it spent $13 on debt repayment (United Nations Briefing).

Education in the South

Between 1950 and 1970, the numbers of those enrolled in schools rose dramatically on a global level, and literacy levels rose, though not as rapidly as had been hoped. Rural communities, and especially rural women, still missed out on educational opportunities. None the less, the hope was that access to education would deliver many benefits: for the nation, a skilled work force to contribute to economic development, national unity and social cohesion, and in some countries, popular participation in politics. For the individual, it promised an escape from poverty, greater social prestige and mobility, and the prospect of a good job, preferably in town. In practice these hopes were often unfulfilled, particularly among the least privileged social groups, but they remained powerful aspirations.

In many countries of the South the debt crisis of the 1980s ended an era of unprecedented growth for education. Countries severely affected by the economic crisis, often compounded by military and political conflict, saw the numbers of children enrolling in school fall, and a marked increase in dropout rates among children who do start school. They saw a decline in opportunities for young people and adults to participate in education. More recently, the situation has generally improved in a number of countries-although, most significantly, not in sub-Saharan Africa. The United Nations (2000) reports that worldwide:

The number of children in school has risen significantly, from 599 million in 1990 to 681 million in 1998. (However, there are major regional disparities-school enrolments went down in sub-Saharan Africa-from 60 percent in 1980 to 56 percent in 1996). Since 1990, some 10 million more children go to school every year, which is nearly double the 1980-90 average. East Asia, the Pacific, Latin America and the Caribbean are close to achieving universal primary education.

The number of out-of-school children decreased from 127 million in 1990 to 113 million in 1998. In Latin America and the Caribbean, for example, the number of out-of-school children was halved, from 11.4 million in 1990 to 4.8 million in 1998. (There are significant gender differences, however. Girls represent 60 percent of out of school children. In a similar fashion attendance tends to be lower in rural areas).

The number of children in pre-school education has risen by 5 percent in the past decade. Some 104 million children were enrolled in pre-primary establishments in 1998. The number of literate adults doubled from 1970 to 1998 from 1.5 billion to 3.3 billion. Today, 85 percent of all men and 74 percent of all women can read and write.

Some 87 percent of young adults (15-24 years olds) are literate worldwide. Despite progress in actual numbers, illiteracy rates remain too high: at least 875 million adults remain illiterate, of which 63.8 percent are women – exactly the same proportion as 10 years ago. United Nations Briefing-education.

Given the scale of indebtedness and the lack of internal funds for education and social programmes, Southern countries have become particularly dependent on assessments and perspectives made by key international and national agencies in the north. Here the various reviews and policy analyses undertaken or sponsored by the World Bank have been particularly influential. As King (1991) argued, the agency map of educational priorities became much more clearly profiled, but this often happened without a corresponding local attempt to analyse national educational requirements. The sheer comprehensiveness of the Bank's analysis of national education systems, and indeed the thoroughness of many of the education missions of other agencies, can sometimes suggest that there is nothing more for the local agencies to say. This is an exaggeration, of course, but it points to an imbalance between the weight of the external analysis of a country's educational needs and the country's own diagnosis. On some debates about education, the signals broadcast from the agency perspective are so powerful it is difficult to hear the local voices at all.

The problem is that the views of the Bank are borne of a particular perspective and their views on economies and on the education sector are open to considerable debate. The Bank's research insights and opinions are not ordinary research findings but are one significant part of a series of conditions and negotiations about loans to education in the South. Second, there is frustration at the sheer visibility and influence of the polices. Third, there is much indignation that the major Bank polices in education seem to rest so heavily on the work of foreign, Northern scholars and agency staff. The pervasive influence is relatively recent and borne of the economic crisis facing many Southern countries. One reason for the power of the Bank in this area is because their reports are easily available, cheap and well presented. This in a situation where there is relative little literature which looks across a continent or region.

The Question of Colonialism

Discussion of the dominance of external visions of education inevitably brings us to questions of colonialism and imperialism.

Colonialism in its most traditional sense involves the gaining of control over particular geographical areas and is usually associated with the with the exploitation of various areas in the world by European powers from about 1500 on. It is often used interchangeably with 'imperialism'. (Imperialism-as the extension of state power and dominion either by direct territorial acquisition or by gaining political and economic control of other areas-of course, has a longer history). Colonialism commonly involves the settlement of the controlling (often western) population in a territory; and the exploitation of local economic resources for metropolitan use. It has taken many forms ranging from models of assimilation e.g. France and Portugal where the occupying power has sought make the colony more formally part of their system and culture; to more segregational approaches such as that adopted by Britain.

Neo-colonialism is usually taken as referring to the economic situation of former colonies post-independence. Here the basic argument runs something like the following. Political de-colonization did little or nothing to alter the economic balance between states and the power of western (and now eastern) capital. International law, institutions such as the World Bank (and banks in general), corporate property rights and the operation of world markets has left control in the hands of the elites in the former metropolitan powers.

Under neo-colonialism, as under direct colonial rule, the relationship between the centre and the periphery... is said to involve the export of capital from the former to the latter; a reliance on Western manufactured goods and services which thwarts indigenous development efforts; further deterioration in the terms of trade for the newly independent countries; and a continuation of the process of cultural Westernization which guarantee the West's market outlets elsewhere in the world. the operations of transnational corporations in the Third World are seen as the principal agents of contemporary neo-colonialism since these are seen as exploiting local resources and influencing international trade and national governments to their own advantage.

The linkage of economic change and education; and the interest of the World Bank in such developments would appear to support the thesis that education initiatives can be the agent of colonialism. This is certainly the case for schools, argues Carnoy:... schools are *colonialistic* in that they attempt to impose economic and political relationships in the society *especially* on those children who gain least (or lose most) from those relationships. Schools demand the most passive response from those groups in society who are the most oppressed by the economic and political system, and allow the most active participation and learning from those who are least likely to want change. While this is logical in preserving the status quo, it is also a means of colonializing children to accept unsatisfactory roles. In its colonialistic characterization, schooling helps develop colonizer-colonized relationships between individuals and between groups in society. It formalizes these relationships, giving them a logic that makes reasonable the unreasonable.

This echoes the sorts of arguments put forward by Gandhi and Kenyatta with regard to schooling. It is also in this way that Freire characterizes colonialism as the culture of silence. The colonial element in schooling (or in informal and non-formal education initiatives) being the attempt to silence particular ways of speaking about the world. To this extent one class or group could be said to colonize another. Sometimes the term domestic or internal colonialism is used to describe such exploitative relationships between the 'centre' (the metropolis) and the 'periphery' (the satellite) of particular societies or nation states. There have been problems around such usage-especially as colonialism has tended to be used in relation to the exploitation of majority populations by minority groups. However, as a metaphor it remains a highly suggestive one-especially as it dramatizes the links with imperial powers.

As well as direct economic and political arrangements, colonialism also involves powerful cultural forces, in particular, language. Fanon (1952) has written graphically of the experience of being colonized by language. To speak... means above all to assume a culture, to support the weight of a civilization". An especially pernicious aspect of this is the way in which this entails taking on a restricting and demeaning sense of self. One of Fanon's main targets was the extent to which 'blackness' in French (or English for that matter) was associated with sin and evil.

In an attempt to escape the association of blackness with evil, the black man dons a white mask, or thinks of himself as a universal subject equally participating in a society that advocates an equality supposedly abstracted from personal appearance. Cultural values are internalized, or "epidermalized" into consciousness, creating a fundamental disjuncture between the black man's consciousness and his body. Under these conditions, the black man is necessarily alienated from himself. (Poulos 1996).

With the work of Said (1985), Spivak (1990) and others we now have a powerful set of under standings concerning the discourses of colonialism and the way in which it is imposed upon institutions and draws people into its net. (This body of literature is sometimes, confusingly, described as *post-colonial* theory. The 'post' here can be variously taken as a historical period after colonialism; as being concerned with those writers who opposed, and hence looked beyond, colonialism; and as somehow linked with the discourse of post-modernism or post-modernity. Education systems, in their different forms, are key carriers and promoters of the discourses of colonialism. They are also potentially significant weapons in the countering of such discourses.

2

Concept of Community

The term "community" is clearly defined by the book's authors, who use the word with a very specific meaning in mind. Whereas a community tries to be an inclusive whole, in celebration of the interdependence of public and private life and of the different callings of all, the term "lifestyle" is basically segmental and celebrates similarity, not differences, which is why the latter term is not favoured by the authors.

"Lifestyle enclaves" is an interesting term used in the book to denote what is essentially an outgrowth of the sectoral organization of American life, which has resulted from the emergence of the national market (due to industrialization). For a long time in American twentieth-century history, private life and leisure time and leisure consumption patterns were basically expressions of one's social status, which in turn was linked to social class and category, as happens in more traditional societies. However, the authors feel that as social status and class came to depend more and more on a national occupational system and less on the local community, a degree of freedom became possible in modern American private life that would not have been dreamed of in the small town or among the older, more traditional urban elite groups.

CHARACTERISTICS OF A COMMUNITY

In 2001 a study of 118 persons with different social and ethnic backgrounds defined community as "a group of people with diverse characteristics who are linked by social ties, share common perspectives, and engage in joint action in geographical locations or settings." One element of community was identified as a "sense of place,something that could be located and described, denoting a sense of locale or boundaries." A community is an identifiable area or location, such as a city, a village, a neighborhood, or even a workplace.

This study also identified "sharing common interests and perspectives" as part of belonging to a community. As members of a community, we share our values, norms, religion, interests, worries, needs, happiness, and suffering with the other members of our community. Many times these commonalities have existed for years, if not for centuries. Other identified elements of community were joint actions that bring people together or social ties such as family, friends, and diversity.

KEY CHARACTERISTICS OF THE COMMUNITY

The characteristics discussed below are some that may be useful in identifying incentives to good resource management in communities. The list in no way attempts to be comprehensive since there are innumerable characteristics that might in different circumstances play a role in communities' abilities to work together on resource management activities. Nor are the categories intended to be mutually exclusive.

One might list ethnicity or language under cultural factors just as well as under social factors, where they are placed in this analysis. The categories are simply a convenience that may help in thinking through some of the issues that are likely to be among the most important determinants of social cohesion and the ability to collaborate on forestry activities.

Historical Factors

Communities are a product of their past: current development activities take place against a historical backdrop. Historical factors may hinder or help the implementation of community forestry projects; what is undisputable is that they will have some impact on the success of those projects. Among the historical factors that play a key role in community cohesion and resource management are:

- population and settlement history; and
- conflict history.

The population history reflects the ancestral origins of the community. In some cases all present members of the village may be descended from a single ancestor or family. This may be an important factor in current social cohesion. In other cases families may have divided or new families may have joined the community. If so, it is important to try to understand the basis on which the more recent members were admitted into the community. The sequential arrival of families, lineages and clans may give rise to distinctions between founders and first settlers on the one hand, and later arrivals or even 'stranger' families on the other.

Alternatively some founding families can be subjugated by later, more numerous and more powerful arrivals. Whatever their relative status, the two groups often view public issues quite differently. Their resource use patterns often reflect attempts to overcome perceived injustices in the historical distribution of resources. Newcomers may attempt to use a community forestry project to gain access to resources otherwise denied them. Founding families may try to use the project to maintain their traditional dominance. These are examples of historically based incentives influencing certain behaviours that can affect the implementation of community forestry activities. The community's experience with conflict and the way it has managed conflict in the past greatly influence its present degree of social cohesion and its willingness to engage in cooperative resource management activities.

Old cases of land tenure disputes, violent confrontations and contested divorces or adultery may appear to have been settled, but they may leave a residue of resentment in the community. Past conflicts often determine trust levels between members of the community and the willingness of the population to delegate decisions or responsibilities to subgroups or individuals. Bitterness that has existed for decades, even centuries, may create strong disincentives to collective action. At the very least such old sources of conflict may make arriving at a consensus very time-consuming and may even make it impossible.

Social Factors

There are numerous issues related to the social structure

of the community that affect its cohesion and the kinds of interests different groups may wish to protect as they seek solutions to resource management problems. Some of the most salient include:

- ethnicity and language;
- family structure;
- caste and other social divisions; and
- gender relations.

While ethnicity is not necessarily a divisive factor in communities, it certainly can have a divisive effect. It may be compounded by other issues such as the ways different ethnic groups pursue their livelihoods. One ethnic group may make its living principally from herding, for example, while another practises cultivation or fishing.

Other potentially divisive factors include religion and language. In each of these cases a key question is whether a particular local population's allegiances lie primarily with the community in which it lives, or whether it identifies more closely with interests outside the community. A particular religious sect, for example, may be more readily prepared to follow directives of its religious leader than to follow.-directives from within the community. Some ethnic groups may feel greater affinity to people of their own ethnicity who live outside the community than to their immediate neighbours. In such cases community organization for the purpose of governing resources can be difficult. In other cases, however, this is not an issue and all the inhabitants of a community share overriding common interests despite their differences. Sometimes the divisive factors work primarily inside a community. Factions within the community may be organized according to affiliation with a religion, caste or ethnic group. Even when they do not have strong ties outside the village, these factions can have different interests and concerns that make collective action more difficult.

Family structures often play an important role in creating or limiting social cohesiveness. When intermarriage is common in a community, a vast network of relationships is created that may (but does not necessarily) contribute to a common sense of identity and purpose. This is less likely to take place when other factors such as caste, ethnicity, cultural taboos or family histories discourage such intermarriage. Gender considerations are also a key to understanding whether communities will be able to organize action in response to some of the more complex resource governance problems. It is clear that both men and women need to be integrally involved in resource management whenever, as is usually the case, both are active participants in the harvesting, transformation and use of tree products. If one group (more often women) feels that its interests are not represented when decisions are made about rules for resource access or use, it is less likely to follow the rules and to participate in enforcing them. Conversely if both men and women feel that their concerns are reflected in resource governance agreements, they will have a stronger incentive to participate in making the management plans work.

Economic Factors

The preceding section described several social factors that can affect whether members of a community are more willing or less willing to work together to solve their resource management concerns. Economic factors can also play a role in determining whether people have similar or divergent interests concerning how resources should be managed. Two salient issues are:

- differences or similarities in livelihood strategies; and.
- the degree of economic stratification in the community.

People's perceptions of resources and their attitudes toward those resources will differ depending on how resources fit into their individual livelihood strategies. Some people may depend almost entirely on tree and plant resources. This would be the case of someone who specializes in the preparation of medicines or teas from plants, for example, or a charcoal maker. For others tree products may be an important input into their activities if they use tree products to feed animals or to provide fencing or fuel-wood. Others, such as shopkeepers, may have relatively little direct use for tree products.

These economic interests provide various incentives to protect, invest in and exploit tree resources. As an agriculturist Maman had an incentive to protect and maintain trees in his field in order to promote crop productivity. On the other hand the herder who cut his trees had an incentive to lop off branches for animal feed and was not concerned with what happened to the soil under the *gawo* trees he cut. Both of them were trying to look out for their families' economic well-being, but with dramatically different effects on the sustainable use of resources.

People's interest in the resource base also varies depending on their level of economic well-being. There is now considerable evidence to suggest that poor people often depend more heavily on forest resources to meet their subsistence needs than do people who are more wealthy. Poor people, for example, may not be able to afford gas for cooking or modern pharmaceuticals. Instead they depend on forest products for fuel and medicine. Because of this they may face very different incentives for their own use of resources and they may have strong opinions about what the rules for access and exploitation should be. As with the gender considerations above, if these concerns are not reflected in the management plans devised by the community, the incentives for some groups *not* to comply with the regulations are likely to be strong.

The success of many collective community forestry activities depends on people's perceptions that they want to stay in a community and are willing to make investments in it. Conversely if they expect to leave (or think that their children will do so) their interests may be divergent from those of the rest of the community. In such cases they may even destroy forestry resources in order to finance their departure.

Cultural Factors

Many cultural factors affect the incentives people face in protecting and exploiting their tree and forest resources. Some of them are related to religion. People sometimes believe in the power of a religious item such as a fetish or the Quran or other holy book to seek out and punish transgressors of local rules regarding tree use or activities in forests. Such beliefs may reduce the need to monitor the behaviour of local people although there may still be a need to use other means to control access by people who do not accept these beliefs.

Cultural beliefs also play a profound role in people's sense of ownership of resources. In some communities it is unthinkable that an individual might be considered the owner of a tree or forest since people believe that those resources are only in the temporary stewardship of the current generation, which manages them on behalf of the ancestors and future generations. This creates incentives that are very different from those in another culture where people believe that trees can be property like anything else, and that the owner has absolute rights to decide what should be done with that property.

Community

In biological terms, a community is a group of interacting organisms sharing a populated environment. In human communities, intent, belief, resources, preferences, needs, risks, and a number of other conditions may be present and common, affecting the identity of the participants and their degree of cohesiveness.

In sociology, the concept of community has led to significant debate, and sociologists are yet to reach agreement on a definition of the term. There were ninety-four discrete definitions of the term by the mid-1950s. Traditionally a "community" has been defined as a group of interacting people living in a common location. The word is often used to refer to a group that is organized around common values and is attributed with social cohesion within a shared geographical location, generally in social units larger than a household. The word can also refer to the national community or international community.

The word "community" is derived from the Old French *communité* which is derived from the Latin *communitas* (*cum*, "with/together" + *munus*, "gift"), a broad term for fellowship or organized society.

Since the advent of the Internet, the concept of community no longer has geographical limitations, as people can now virtually gather in an online community and share common interests regardless of physical location.

PERSPECTIVES FROM VARIOUS DISCIPLINES

German sociologist Ferdinand Tönnies distinguished between two types of human association: *Gemeinschaft* (usually translated as "community") and *Gesellschaft* ("society" or "association"). In his 1887 work, *Gemeinschaft and Gesellschaft*, Tönnies argued that *Gemeinschaft* is perceived to be a tighter and more cohesive social entity, due to the presence of a "unity of will." He added that family and kinship were the perfect expressions of *Gemeinschaft*, but that other shared characteristics, such as place or belief, could also result in *Gemeinschaft*. This paradigm of communal networks and shared social understanding has been applied to multiple cultures in many places throughout history. *Gesellschaft*, on the other hand, is a group in which the individuals who make up that group are motivated to take part in the group purely by self-interest. He also proposed that in the real world, no group was either pure *Gemeinschaft* or pure *Gesellschaft*, but, rather, a mixture of the two.

Social Capital

If community exists, both freedom and security may exist as well. The community then takes on a life of its own, as people become free enough to share and secure enough to get along. The sense of connectedness and formation of social networks comprise what has become known as social capital. Social capital is defined by Robert D. Putnam as "the collective value of all social networks and species (who people know) and the inclinations that arise from these networks to do things for each other (norms of reciprocity)." Social capital in action can be seen in all sorts of groups, including neighbors keeping an eye on each others' homes. However, as Putnam notes in *Bowling Alone: The Collapse and Revival of American Community* (2000), social capital has been falling in the United States. Putnam found that over the past 25 years, attendance at club meetings has fallen 58 percent, family dinners are down 33 percent, and having fiiends visit has fallen 45 percent.

The same patterns are also evident in many other western countries. Western cultures are thus said to be losing the spirit of community that once were found in institutions including churches and community centers. Sociologist Ray Oldenburg states in *The Great Good Place* that people need three places: 1) the home, 2) the office, and, 3) the community hangout or gathering place. With this philosophy in mind, many grassroots efforts such as The Project for Public Spaces are being started to create this "Third Place" in communities. They are taking form in independent bookstores, coffeehouses, local pubs, and through many innovative means to create the social capital needed to foster the sense and spirit of community.

Sense of Community

In a seminal 1986 study, McMillan and Chavis identify four elements of "sense of community": 1) membership, 2) influence, 3) integration and fulfillment of needs, and 4) shared emotional connection. They give the following example of the interplay between these factors:

Someone puts an announcement on the dormitory bulletin board about the formation of an intramural dormitory basketball team. People attend the organizational meeting as strangers out of their individual needs (integration and fulfillment of needs). The team is bound by place of residence (membership boundaries are set) and spends time together in practice (the contact hypothesis). They play a game and win (successful shared valent event). While playing, members exert energy on behalf of the team (personal investment in the group). As the team continues to win, team members become recognized and congratulated (gaining honor and status for being members), Influencing new members to join and continue to do the same. Someone suggests that they all buy matching shirts and shoes (common symbols) and they do so (influence).

A *Sense of Community Index* (SCI) has been developed by Chavis and colleagues and revised and adapted by others. Although originally designed to assess sense of community in neighborhoods, the index has been adapted for use in schools, the workplace, and a variety of types of communities.

Studies conducted by the APPA show substantial evidence that young adults who feel a sense of belonging in a community, particularly small communities, develop fewer psychiatric and depressive disorders than those who do not have the feeling of love and belonging.

Anthropology

Cultural (or social) anthropology has traditionally looked at community through the lens of ethnographic fieldwork and ethnography continues to be an important methodology for study of modern communities. Other anthropological approaches that deal with various aspects of community include cross-cultural studies and the anthropology of religion. Cultures in modern society are also studied in the fields of urban anthropology, ethnic studies, ecological anthropology, and psychological anthropology. Since the 1990s, internet communities have increasingly been the subject of research in the emerging field of cyber anthropology.

Archaeology

Archaeological studies of social communities. The term "community" is used in two ways in archaeology, paralleling usage in other areas. The first is an informal definition of community as a place where people used to live. In this sense it is synonymous with the concept of an ancient settlement, whether a hamlet, village, town, or city. The second meaning is similar to the usage of the term in other social sciences: a community is a group of people living near one another who interact socially. Social interaction on a small scale can be difficult to identify with archaeological data. Most reconstructions of social communities by archaeologists rely on the principle that social interaction is conditioned by physical distance. Therefore a small village settlement likely constituted a social community, and spatial subdivisions of cities and other large settlements may have formed communities. Archaeologists typically use similarities in material culture—from house types to styles of pottery—to reconstruct communities in the past. This is based on the assumption that people or households will share more similarities in the types and styles of their material goods with other members of a social community than they will with outsiders.

SOCIAL PHILOSOPHY AND COMMUNITARIANISM

Communitarianism as a group of related but distinct philosophies (or ideologies) began in the late 20th century, opposing classical liberalism and capitalism while advocating phenomena such as civil society. Not necessarily hostile to social liberalism, communitarianism rather has a different emphasis, shifting the focus of interest toward communities and societies and away from the individual. The question of priority, whether for the individual or community, must be determined in dealing with pressing ethical questions about a variety of social issues, such as health care, abortion, multiculturalism, and hate speech. Gad Barzilai has critically examined both liberalism and communitarianism and has developed the theory of critical communitarianism. Barzilai has explicated how non-ruling communities are constructing legal cultures while interacting with various facets of political power. Being venues of identity construction justifies collective protections of communities in law, while the boundaries with other communities, states, and global forces should be sensitive to preservation of various cultures. Gad Barzilai has accordingly offered how to protect human rights, individual rights, and multiculturalism in inter-communal context that allows to generating cultural relativism.

BUSINESS AND ORGANIZATIONAL COMMUNICATION

Effective communication practices in group and organizational settings are very important to the formation and maintenance of communities. The ways that ideas and values are communicated within communities are important to the induction of new members, the formulation of agendas, the selection of leaders and many other aspects. Organizational communication is the study of how people communicate within an organizational context and the influences and interactions within organizational structures. Group members depend on the flow of communication to establish their own identity within these structures and learn to function in the group setting. Although organizational communication, as a field of study, is usually geared toward companies and business groups, these may also be seen as communities. The principles of organizational communication can also be applied to other types of communities.

Ecology

In ecology, a community is an assemblage of populations of different species, interacting with one another. Community ecology is the branch of ecology that studies interactions between and among species. It considers how such interactions, along with interactions between species and the abiotic environment, affect community structure and species richness, diversity and patterns of abundance. Species interact in three ways:

competition, predation and mutualism. Competition typically results in a double negative—that is both species lose in the interaction. Predation is a win/lose situation with one species winning. Mutualism, on the other hand, involves both species cooperating in some way, with both winning.

INTERDISCIPLINARY PERSPECTIVES OF SOCIALIZATION

The process of learning to adopt the behavior patterns of the community is called socialization. The most fertile time of socialization is usually the early stages of life, during which individuals develop the skills and knowledge and learn the roles necessary to function within their culture and social environment. For some psychologists, especially those in the psychodynamic tradition, the most important period of socialization is between the ages of one and ten. But socialization also includes adults moving into a significantly different environment, where they must learn a new set of behaviors.

Socialization is influenced primarily by the family, through which children first learn community norms. Other important influences include school, peer groups, people, schools, mass media, the workplace, and government. The degree to which the norms of a particular society or community are adopted determines one's willingness to engage with others. The norms of tolerance, reciprocity, and trust are important "habits of the heart," as de Tocqueville put it, in an individual's involvement in community.

Community Development

Community development, often linked with Community Work or Community Planning, is often formally conducted by non-government organisations (NGOs), universities or government agencies to progress the social well-being of local, regional and, sometimes, national communities. Less formal efforts, called community building or community organizing, seek to empower individuals and groups of people by providing them with the skills they need to effect change in their own communities. These skills often assist in building political power through the formation of large social groups working for a common agenda. Community development practitioners must understand both how to work with individuals and how to affect communities' positions within the context of larger social institutions.

Formal programs conducted by universities are often used to build a knowledge base to drive curricula in sociology and community studies. The General Social Survey from the National Opinion Research Center at the University of Chicago and the Saguaro Seminar at the John F. Kennedy School of Government at Harvard University are examples of national community development in the United States. In The United Kingdom, Oxford University has led in providing extensive research in the field through its *Community Development Journal,* used worldwide by sociologists and community development practitioners.

At the intersection between community *development* and community *building* are a number of programs and organizations with community development tools. One example of this is the program of the Asset Based Community Development Institute of Northwestern University. The institute makes available downloadable tools to assess community assets and make connections between non-profit groups and other organizations that can help in community building. The Institute focuses on helping communities develop by "mobilizing neighborhood assets" — building from the inside out rather than the outside in.

Community Building and Organizing

In *The Different Drum: Community-Making and Peace,* Scott Peck argues that the almost accidental sense of community that exists at times of crisis can be consciously built. Peck believes that conscious community building is a process of deliberate design based on the knowledge and application of certain rules. He states that this process goes through four stages:

1. Pseudo-community: Where participants are "nice with each other", playing-safe, and presenting what they feel is the most favourable sides of their personalities.
2. Chaos: When people move beyond the inauthenticity of pseudo-community and feel safe enough to present their "shadow" selves. This stage places great demands upon

the facilitator for greater leadership and organization, but Peck believes that "organizations are not communities", and this pressure should be resisted.

3. Emptiness: This stage moves beyond the attempts to fix, heal and convert of the chaos stage, when all people become capable of acknowledging their own woundedness and brokenness, common to us all as human beings. Out of this emptiness comes
4. True community: the process of deep respect and true listening for the needs of the other people in this community. This stage Peck believes can only be described as "glory" and reflects a deep yearning in every human soul for compassionate understanding from one's fellows.

More recently Peck remarked that building a sense of community is easy but maintaining this sense of community is difficult in the modern world. Community building can use a wide variety of practices, ranging from simple events such as potlucks and small book clubs to larger–scale efforts such as mass festivals and construction projects that involve local participants rather than outside contractors.

Community building that is geared toward citizen action is usually termed "community organizing." In these cases, organized community groups seek accountability from elected officials and increased direct representation within decision-making bodies. Where good-faith negotiations fail, these constituency-led organizations seek to pressure the decision-makers through a variety of means, including picketing, boycotting, sit-ins, petitioning, and electoral politics. The ARISE Detroit! coalition and the Toronto Public Space Committee are examples of activist networks committed to shielding local communities from government and corporate domination and inordinate influence.

Community organizing is sometimes focused on more than just resolving specific issues. Organizing often means building a widely accessible power structure, often with the end goal of distributing power equally throughout the community. Community organizers generally seek to build groups that are open and democratic in governance. Such groups facilitate and encourage consensus decision-making with a focus on the general health of the community rather than a specific interest group. The three basic types of community organizing are grassroots organizing, coalition building, and "institution-based community organizing,".

If communities are developed based on something they share in common, whether that be location or values, then one challenge for developing communities is how to incorporate individuality and differences. Indeed, as Rebekah Nathan suggests in her book, My Freshman Year, we are actually drawn to developing communities totally based on sameness, despite stated commitments to diversity, such as those found on university websites.

Nathan states that certain commonalities allow college students to cohere: "What holds students together, really, is age, pop culture, a handful of (recent) historical events, and getting a degree". Universities may try to create community through all freshman reads, freshman seminars, and school pride; however, Nathan argues students will only form communities based on the attributes, such as age and pop culture, that they bring with them to college. Nathan's point, then, is that people come to college and don't expand their social horizons and cultural tolerance, which can prevent the development of your social community.

Community Currencies

Some communities have developed their own "Local Exchange Trading Systems" (LETS) and local currencies, such as the Ithaca Hours system, to encourage economic growth and an enhanced sense of community. Community Currencies have recently proven valuable in meeting the needs of people living in various South American nations, particularly Argentina, that recently suffered as a result of the collapse of the Argentinian national currency.

Community Service

Community service is usually performed in connection with a nonprofit organization, but it may also be undertaken under the auspices of government, one or more businesses, or by individuals. It is typically unpaid and voluntary. However, it can be part of alternative sentencing approaches in a justice system and it can be required by educational institutions.

TYPES OF COMMUNITY

A number of ways to categorize types of community have been proposed; one such breakdown is:

1. Geographic communities: range from the local neighbourhood, suburb, village, town or city, region, nation or even the planet as a whole. These refer to communities of *location*.
2. Communities of culture: range from the local clique, sub-culture, ethnic group, religious, multicultural or pluralistic civilisation, or the global community cultures of today. They may be included as *communities of need* or *identity*, such as disabled persons, or frail aged people.
3. Community organizations: range from informal family or kinship networks, to more formal incorporated associations, political decision making structures, economic enterprises, or professional associations at a small, national or international scale.

Communities are nested; one community can contain another—for example a geographic community may contain a number of ethnic communities.

Location

Possibly the most common usage of the word *"community"* indicates a large group living in close proximity. Examples of local community include:

- A municipality is an administrative local area generally composed of a clearly defined territory and commonly referring to a town or village.

Although large cities are also municipalities, they are often thought of as a collection of communities, due to their diversity.

- A neighborhood is a geographically localized community, often within a larger city or suburb.
- A planned community is one that was designed from scratch and grew up more or less following the plan. Several of the world's capital cities are planned cities, notably Washington, D.C., in the United States,

Canberra in Australia, and Brasília in Brazil. It was also common during the European colonization of the Americas to build according to a plan either on fresh ground or on the ruins of earlier Amerindian cities.

Identity

In some contexts, *"community"* indicates a group of people with a common identity other than location. Members often interact regularly. Common examples in everyday usage include:

- A "professional community" is a group of people with the same or related occupations. Some of those members may join a professional society, making a more defined and formalized group. These are also sometimes known as communities of practice.
- A virtual community is a group of people primarily or initially communicating or interacting with each other by means of information technologies, typically over the Internet, rather than in person. These may be either communities of interest, practice or communion. Research interest is evolving in the motivations for contributing to online communities.

Overlaps

Some communities share both location and other attributes. Members choose to live near each other because of one or more common interests.

- A retirement community is designated and at least usually designed for retirees and seniors—often restricted to those over a certain age, such as 56. It differs from a retirement home, which is a single building or small complex, by having a number of autonomous households.
- An intentional community is a deliberate residential community with a much higher degree of social communication than other communities. The members of an intentional community typically hold a common social, political or spiritual vision and share responsibilities and resources. Intentional communities include Amish villages, ashrams, cohousing, communes, ecovillages, housing cooperatives, kibbutzim, and land trusts.

Internet Communities

To a growing part of people the meaning of the word *"community"* indicates a smaller or larger group of internet users signing up to become members of a community page/ system on internet. Examples of internet communities include:

- A business community is often an administrative community with possibilities to add CV's and other business-related information.
- An interest community is a based on specialized areas such as art, golf or bird watching.
- A general community is wider in its range-opening for its users to create areas, pages and groups.

Special Nature of Human Community

Definitions of community as "organisms inhabiting a common environment and interacting with one another," while scientifically accurate, do not convey the richness, diversity and complexity of human communities. Their classification, likewise is almost never precise. Untidy as it may be, community is vital for humans. M. Scott Peck expresses this in the following way: "There can be no vulnerability without risk; there can be no community without vulnerability; there can be no peace, and ultimately no life, without community."

SENSE OF COMMUNITY

Sense of community (or psychological sense of community) is a concept in community psychology and social psychology, as well as in several other research disciplines, such as urban sociology, which focuses on the *experience* of community rather than its structure, formation, setting, or other features. Sociologists, social psychologists, anthropologists, and others have theorized about and carried out empirical research on community, but the psychological approach asks questions about the individual's perception, understanding, attitudes, feelings, etc. about community and his or her relationship to it and to others' participation—indeed to the complete, multifaceted community experience.

In his seminal 1974 book, psychologist Seymour B. Sarason proposed that psychological sense of community become the conceptual center for the psychology of community, asserting that it "is one of the major bases for self-definition." By 1986 it was regarded as a central overarching concept for community psychology.

Definitions

For Sarason, psychological sense of community is "the perception of similarity to others, an acknowledged interdependence with others, a willingness to maintain this interdependence by giving to or doing for others what one expects from them, and the feeling that one is part of a larger dependable and stable structure" (1974).

McMillan & Chavis (1986) define sense of community as "a feeling that members have of belonging, a feeling that members matter to one another and to the group, and a shared faith that members' needs will be met through their commitment to be together."

Gusfield (1975) identified two dimensions of community: territorial and relational. The relational dimension of community has to do with the nature and quality of relationships in that community, and some communities may even have no discernible territorial demarcation, as in the case of a community of scholars working in a particular specialty, who have some kind of contact and quality of relationship, but may live and work in disparate locations, perhaps even throughout the world. Other communities may seem to be defined primarily according to territory, as in the case of neighborhoods, but even in such cases, proximity or shared territory cannot by itself constitute a community; the relational dimension is also essential.

Factor analysis of their urban neighborhoods questionnaire yielded two distinct factors which Riger and Lavrakas (1981) characterized as "social bonding" and "physical rootedness", very similar to the two dimensions proposed by Gusfield.

Beneficial Antecedents Found in Early Work

Early work on psychological sense of community was based on neighborhoods as the referent, and found a relationship between psychological sense of community and greater participation, perceived safety, ability to function competently in the community (Glynn, 1981), social bonding, social fabric (strengths of interpersonal relationship), greater sense of purpose and perceived control, and greater civic contributions (charitable contributions and civic involvement). These initial studies lacked a clearly articulated conceptual framework, however, and none of the measures developed were based on a theoretical definition of psychological sense of community.

Primary Theoretical Foundation: McMillan and Chavis

McMillan & Chavis's (1986) theory (and instrument) are the most broadly validated and widely utilized in this area in the psychological literature. They prefer the abbreviated label "sense of community", and propose that sense of community is composed of four elements.

Four Elements of Sense of Community

There are four elements of "sense of community" according to the McMillan & Chavis theory:

Membership

Membership includes five attributes:

- boundaries
- emotional safety
- a sense of belonging and identification
- personal investment
- a common symbol system.

Influence

Influence works both ways: members need to feel that they have some influence in the group, and some influence by the group on its members is needed for group cohesion.

Integration and Fulfillment of Needs

Members feel rewarded in some way for their participation in the community.

Shared Emotional Connection

The "definitive element for true community" (1986), it includes shared history and shared participation (or at least identification with the history).

DYNAMICS WITHIN AND BETWEEN THE ELEMENTS

McMillan & Chavis (1986) give the following example to illustrate the dynamics within and between these four elements:

Someone puts an announcement on the dormitory bulletin board about the formation of an intramural dormitory basketball team. People attend the organizational meeting as strangers out of their individual needs (integration and fulfillment of needs). The team is bound by place of residence (membership boundaries are set) and spends time together in practice (the contact hypothesis). They play a game and win (successful shared valent event). While playing, members exert energy on behalf of the team (personal investment in the group). As the team continues to win, team members become recognized and congratulated (gaining honor and status for being members). Someone suggests that they all buy matching shirts and shoes (common symbols) and they do so (influence).

Empirical Assessment

Chavis et al.'s Sense of Community Index (SCI), originally designed primarily in reference to neighborhoods, can be adapted to study other communities as well, including the workplace, schools, religious communities, communities of interest, etc.

COMMUNITY SERVICE

Community service is donated service or activity that is performed by someone or a group of people for the benefit of the public or its institutions.

Volunteers may provide community service, however, not everyone who provides community service is seen as a volunteer, because some people who provide community service are not doing it of their own free will; they are compelled to do so by:

- their government as a part of citizenship requirements, in lieu of military service (such as the practice of Zivildienst in Germany);
- the courts, in lieu of, or in addition to, other criminal justice sanctions;
- their school, to meet the requirements of a class, such as in the case of service learning or to meet the requirements of graduation, or, in the case of parents,

required to provide a certain number of hours of service in order for their child to be enrolled in a school or sports team.

- The library
- Public transportation

There are also people providing community service who receive some form of compensation in return for their year of commitment to public service, such as AmeriCorps in the USA (who are called members rather than volunteers).

If one wants to volunteer and tutor kids at any elementary school, they must be a high school student or older to apply.

Youth Community Service

Community services performed by youth is also referred to as youth service. Youth service is intended to strengthen young peoples' senses of civic engagement and community, and to help them achieve their educational, developmental and social goals. Youth service hours and/or projects is often required for advancement, e.g. for a Scout to advance to the next rank or for a high school student to graduate.

Service learning is the deliberate connection of community service to stated learning goals. A common misconception among educators, youth workers, and young people is the notion that service learning can be assigned. Several experts attest to the necessity of engaging youth in deliberating, planning, implementing, and reflecting on their community service, thereby sustaining high-quality service learning. This is intended to make community service an effective learning tool. The Center for Information and Research on Civic Learning and Engagement (CIRCLE) at the University of Maryland, College Park researches young people and their community service. CIRCLE analyzes trends in community service/volunteering over time and by subgroups, such as sex, race and ethnicity.

Youth Organizations

Youth organizations actively involved in community service include Scouts, Camp Fire USA, 4-H, DeMolay, International Order of the Rainbow for Girls, Civil Air Patrol, Key Club,

Ashoka: Innovators for the Public,the Air Cadet League of Canada, the Army Cadet League of Canada, the Sea Cadet League of Canada, the Navy League Cadet Corps (Canada), the Royal Canadian Air Cadets, the Royal Canadian Army Cadets, Royal Canadian Navy Cadets, Royal Canadian Sea Cadets,and Interact Club

High School Graduation

Many educational jurisdictions in the United States require students to perform community service hours to graduate from high school. In some high schools in Washington State, for example, students must complete 60 hours of community service to receive a diploma.

Some Washington school districts, including Seattle Public Schools, differentiate between community service and "service learning," requiring students to demonstrate that their work has contributed to their education. If a student in high school is taking an AVID course, community service is required. The SFUSD (San Francisco Unified School District) made high school students complete 100 hours of community service (25 hours a year) in order to graduate high school.

Conditions of Participation

Contribution of service is a condition of enrollment in some programs. Most commonly, parents may be required to serve for their child to be enrolled in a school or sports team.

Colleges

Though technically not a requirement, many colleges make community service an unofficial requirement for acceptance. However, some colleges prefer work experience over community service, and some require that their students also continue community service for some specific number of hours to graduate. Certain academic honor societies such as Delta Epsilon Sigma have rejected 4.0 GPA students that lacked community service experiences on their applications, because they honor community service so much. Many community service projects are done by sororities and fraternities. For example, Alpha Phi Omega professes to be centered around the purpose of doing community service.

Alternative Sentencing

In this form of community service, convicted of crimes are required to perform community services or to work for agencies in the sentencing jurisdiction either entirely or partly in lieu of other judicial remedies and sanctions, such as incarceration or fines. For instance, a fine may be reduced in exchange for a prescribed number of hours of community service. The court may allow the convict to choose their community service, which then must be documented by credible agencies, or may mandate a specific service.

Sometimes the sentencing is specifically targeted to the convict's crime, for example, a litterer may have to clean a park or roadside, or a drunk driver might appear before school groups to explain why drunk driving is a crime. Also, a sentence allowing for a broader choice may nonetheless disallow certain services that the offender would reasonably be expected to perform anyway; for example, a convicted lawyer might be specifically prohibited from counting *pro bono* legal services. Most jurisdictions in the United States have programs by which the court may require minor offenders to perform work for city or county agencies under the supervision of the police or sheriff's department, often on weekends, as an alternative to confinement in jail. Jail and prison inmates are also typically used for labor either in the jail or at outside work that benefits society, such as in light manufacturing, repair work, office work, on labor camps or farms, on chain gangs or on land conservation projects. This is, however, more properly considered a form of penal labor than community service.

At least part of the philosophy behind this kind of sentencing is that providing a service to the community is more beneficial than punishment for its own sake. Through community service, the community sees a benefit while saving the costs associated with incarceration of the convict and having the work carried out by paid staff. It is also thought to be a way to educate convicts on what constitutes ethically acceptable behavior.

Corporate Social Responsibility

Some employers involve their staff in some kind of community service programming, such as with the United Way of America. This may be completely voluntary or a condition of employment, or anything in between.

Outside Canada

Community service in the United States is often similar to that in Canada. In Europe and Australia, community service is an option for many criminal sentences as an alternative to incarceration. In the United Kingdom, community service is now officially referred to by the Home Office as more straightforward "compulsory unpaid work". Compulsory unpaid work includes up to 300 hours of activities, such as conservation work, cleaning up graffiti, or working with a charity.

Starting in 2010, Danish High School students will receive a special diploma if they complete at least 20 hours of voluntary work. However, a number of the students fear that this will remove focus from their education, and representatives from the labor union fear that it will move tasks from paid job to voluntary work.

Exchange students are warned that use of the term community service on a transcript may damage future career possibilities as it could indicate a criminal record. The International Baccalaureate program requires 50 hours of community service, together with a written reflection on the service performed, to fulfill the requirement of 150 hours of CAS (Creativity, Action, Service) and receive an IB Diploma.

TYPES OF COMMUNITY EVENTS

Most communities sponsor events to celebrate holidays, raise funds for special projects or organizations, promote community networking, or for many other reasons. They can include crafts, music, children's activities, historic tours, demonstrations, rides, and food. They are social events that aim to provide the community's members a pleasant experience. Many are out of doors and can also include on-site buildings. Vendors are welcomed to sell all kinds of food and drink. The organizations that sponsor these events may benefit monetarily by charging vendors and attendees a fee for space or admission. These are also educational experiences for members of the community where firefighters, policemen, politicians and civic leaders are available to offer information of interest or benefit.

Significance

Community events can be major functions that bring people within a community together to spend a good part of the day enjoying themselves. Sometimes these events end late at night, such as a 4th of July celebration with fireworks as a finale. Attending these events can be inexpensive for families; many do not charge admission fees, parking can be free, the locale can be a short distance from home, and people can bring their own picnic baskets, lounge chairs or blankets. The purpose is to provide a convenient and pleasurable experience for all members of a family or group.

Types

Community events are often initiated on major holidays like Memorial Day, Labor Day, the 4th of July, and New Year's Day. Other events can include craft shows, concerts, county fairs, rodeos or just a day at the park where food vendors add to the enjoyment of the day. Another instance is Halloween. For example, Cypress Gardens, an historic park and former rice plantation in South Carolina, features an event called "Halloween in the Swamp." These are guided tours through the swamp on flat-bottom boats that include "ghosts" (scuba divers) who abruptly emerge from the black waters filled with alligators. It's all in fun and the lines are long with people wanting to take that "scary" ride every October.

Features

An array of food available for purchase at community events is one of the main ingredients for a successful function. This includes kettle corn, BBQ, funnel cakes, cotton candy, steak hoagies, hot dogs and hamburgers, to name just a few. Shady and comfortable areas, children's activities, restroom facilities and adequate parking are some of the features. There is a good amount of advance publicity to promote the event in local newspapers, websites and mailers. Successful events held year after year draw many people who plan to attend again and again.

Geography

Location for a community event may involve geography.

Stone Mountain Park in Georgia is an example of the influence geography can have on planning an event. Its location is a beautiful mountain setting and the 4th of July celebration there features an impressive laser light show against majestic rock carvings. Other geographic considerations can include beaches, lakes, rivers and national parks. Even city parks or areas that offer parking, spacious areas for picnicking, places where musicians can perform, or where carnival rides can be set up, are viable considerations as well. An annual boat race on the ocean will draw crowds of people that come to watch sleek, fast boats while relaxing in a chair on the beach with a cool drink in hand.

Benefits

Community events are often family affairs that bring people together. They are also opportunities for members of the community to reacquaint themselves with civic leaders and the other people who serve them—like those who put out fires or protect their homes. Policemen with K-9 dogs may give demonstrations of what the dogs can do—something many people rarely have an opportunity to see. Firemen may display their fire trucks for children to sit in and explore.

COMMUNITY ORGANIZING

Community organizing is a process where people who live in proximity to each other come together into an organization that acts in their shared self-interest. Unlike those who promote more-consensual "community building," community organizers generally assume that social change necessarily involves conflict and social struggle in order to generate collective power for the powerless. A core goal of community organizing is to generate *durable* power for an organization representing the community, allowing it to influence key decision-makers on a range of issues over time. In the ideal, for example, this can get community organizing groups a place at the table *before* important decisions are made. Community organizers work with and develop new local leaders, facilitating coalitions and assisting in the development of campaigns.

Common Aspects of Community

Organized community groups attempt to influence

government, corporations and institutions, seek to increase direct representation within decision-making bodies, and foster social reform more generally. Where negotiations fail, these organizations seek to inform others outside of the organization of the issues being addressed and expose or pressure the decision-makers through a variety of means, including picketing, boycotting, sit-ins, petitioning, and electoral politics. Organizing groups often seek out issues they know will generate controversy and conflict. This allows them to draw in and educate participants, build commitment, and establish a reputation for winning. Thus, community organizing is usually focused on more than just resolving specific issues. In fact, specific issues are often vehicles for other organizational goals as much as they are ends in themselves.

Community organizers generally seek to build groups that are democratic in governance, open and accessible to community members, and concerned with the general health of the community rather than a specific interest group. Organizing seeks to broadly empower community members, with the end goal of distributing power more equally throughout the community.

The three basic types of community organizing are grassroots or "door-knocking" organizing, faith-based community organizing (FBCO), and coalition building. Political campaigns often claim that their door-to-door operations are in fact an effort to organize the community, though often these operations are focused exclusively on voter identification and turnout.

FBCOs and many grassroots organizing models are built on the work of Saul Alinsky, discussed below, from the 1930s into the 1970s.

Grassroots and "Door-Knocking" Groups

Grassroots organizing builds community groups from scratch, developing new leadership where none existed and organizing the unorganized. It is a values based process where people are brought together to act in the interest of their communities and the common good. Networks of community organizations that employ this method and support local organizing groups include National People's Action and ACORN.

"Door knocking" grassroots organizations like ACORN organize poor and working-class members recruiting members one by one in the community. Because they go door-to-door, they are able to reach beyond established organizations and the "churched" to bring together a wide range of less privileged people. ACORN tended to stress the importance of constant action in order to maintain the commitment of a less rooted group of participants.

ACORN had a reputation of being more forceful than faith-based (FBCO) groups, and there are indications that their local groups were more staff (organizer) directed than leader (local volunteer) directed. (However, the same can be said for many forms of organizing, including FBCOs.) The "door-knocking" approach is more time-intensive than the "organization of organizations" approach of FBCOs and requires more organizers who, partly as a result, can be lower paid with more turnover.

Unlike existing FBCO national "umbrella" and other grassroots organizations, ACORN maintained a centralized national agenda, and exerted some centralized control over local organizations. Because ACORN was a 501(c)4 organization under the tax code, it was able to participate directly in election activities, but contributions to it were not tax exempt.

Faith-Based Community Organizing

Faith-based community organizing (FBCO), also known as Congregation-based Community Organizing, is a methodology for developing power and relationships throughout a community of institutions: today mostly congregations, but these can also include unions, neighborhood associations, and other groups. Progressive and centrist FBCO organizations join together around basic values derived from common aspects of their faith instead of around strict dogmas. There are now at least 180 FBCOs in the US as well as in South Africa, England, Germany, and other nations. Local FBCO organizations are often linked through organizing networks such as the Industrial Areas Foundation, Gamaliel Foundation, PICO National Network, and Direct Action and Research Training Center (DART). In the United States starting in 2001, the Bush Administration launched a department to promote community organizing that included faith-based organizing as well other community groups.

FBCOs tend to have mostly middle-class participants because the congregations involved are generally mainline Protestant and Catholic (although "middle-class" can mean different things in white communities and communities of color, which can lead to class tensions within these organizations). Holiness, Pentecostal, and other related denominations (often "storefront") churches with mostly poor and working-class members tend not to join FBCOs because of their focus on "faith" over "works," among other issues. FBCOs have increasingly expanded outside impoverished areas into churches where middle-class professionals predominate in an effort to expand their power to contest inequality.

Because of their "organization of organizations" approach, FBCOs can organize large numbers of members with a relatively small number of organizers that generally are better paid and more professionalized than those in "door-knocking" groups like ACORN.

FBCOs focus on the long-term development of a culture and common language of organizing and on the development of relational ties between members. They are more stable during fallow periods than grassroots groups because of the continuing existence of member churches.

FBCOs are 501(c)3 organizations. Contributions to them are tax exempt. As a result, while they can conduct campaigns over "issues" they cannot promote the election of specific individuals.

Power vs. Protest

While community organizing groups often engage in protest actions designed to force powerful groups to respond to their demands, protest is only one aspect of the activity of organizing groups. To the extent that groups' actions generate a sense in the larger community that they have "power," they are often able to engage with and influence powerful groups through dialogue, backed up by a history of successful protest-based campaigns. Similar to the way unions gain recognition as the representatives of workers for a particular business, community organizing groups can gain recognition as key representatives of particular communities. In this way, representatives of community organizing groups are often able to bring key government officials or corporate leaders to the table without engaging in "actions" because of their reputation. As Alinsky said, "the first rule of power tactics" is that "power is not only what you have but what the enemy thinks you have." The development of durable "power" and influence is a key aim of community organizing.

"Rights-based" community organizing, in which municipal governments are used to exercise community power, was first experimented with by the Community Environmental Legal Defence Fund (CELDF.org) in Pennsylvania, beginning in 2002. Community groups are organized to influence municipal governments to enact local ordinances. These ordinances challenge preemptive state and federal laws that forbid local governments from prohibiting corporate activities deemed harmful by community residents. The ordinances are drafted specifically to assert the rights of "human and natural communities," and include provisions that deny the legal concepts of "corporate personhood," and "corporate rights." Since 2006 they have been drafted to include the recognition of legally enforceable rights for "natural communities and ecosystems."

Although this type of community organizing focuses on the adoption of local laws, the intent is to demonstrate the use of governing authority to protect community rights and expose the misuse of governing authority to benefit corporations. As such, the adoption of rights-based municipal ordinances is not a legal strategy, but an organizing strategy. Courts predictably deny the legal authority of municipalities to legislate in defiance of state and federal law. Corporations and government agencies that initiate legal actions to overturn these ordinances have been forced to argue in opposition to the community's right to make governing decisions on issues with harmful and direct local impact.

The first rights-based municipal laws prohibited corporations from monopolizing agriculture (factory farming), and banned corporate waste dumping within municipal jurisdictions. More recent rights-based organizing, in Pennsylvania, New Hampshire, Maine, Virginia and California has prohibited corporate mining, large-scale water withdrawals and chemical trespass.

Political Orientations

Community organizing is not solely the domain of progressive politics, as dozens of fundamentalist organizations are in operation, such as the Christian Coalition. However, the term "community organizing" generally refers to more centrist or progressive organizations, as evidenced, for example, by the reaction against community organizing in the 2008 US presidential election by Republicans and conservatives on the web and elsewhere.

Fundraising

Organizing groups often struggle to find resources. They rarely receive funding from government since their activities often seek to contest government policies. Foundations and others who usually fund service activities generally don't understand what organizing groups do or how they do it, or shy away from their contentious approaches. The constituency of progressive and centrist organizing groups is largely low-or middle-income, so they are generally unable to support themselves through dues. In search of resources, some organizing groups have accepted funding for direct service activities in the past. As noted below, this has frequently led these groups to drop their conflictual organizing activities, in part because these threatened funding for their "service" arms.

Recent studies have shown, however, that funding for community organizing can produce large returns on investment ($512 in community benefits to $1 of Needmor funding, according to the Needmor Fund Study, $157 to 1 in New Mexico and $89 to 1 in North Carolina according to National Committee for Responsive Philanthropy studies) through legislation and agreements with corporations, among other sources, not including non-fiscal accomplishments.

COMMUNITY DEVELOPMENT

Community development (CD) is a broad term applied to the practices and academic disciplines of civic leaders, activists, involved citizens and professionals to improve various aspects of local communities. Community development seeks to empower individuals and groups of people by providing these groups with the skills they need to affect change in their own communities. These skills are often concentrated around building political power through the formation of large social groups working for a common agenda. Community developers must understand both how to work with individuals and how to affect communities' positions within the context of larger social institutions.

There are complementary definitions of community development. The Community Development Challenge report, which was produced by a working party comprising leading UK organisations in the field (including Community Development Foundation, Community Development Exchange and the Federation of Community Development Learning) defines community development as: "A set of values and practices which plays a special role in overcoming poverty and disadvantage, knitting society together at the grass roots and deepening democracy. There is a CD profession, defined by national occupational standards and a body of theory and experience going back the best part of a century. There are active citizens who use CD techniques on a voluntary basis, and there are also other professions and agencies which use a CD approach or some aspects of it."

Community Development Exchange defines community development as: "both an occupation (such as a community development worker in a local authority) and a way of working with communities. Its key purpose is to build communities based on justice, equality and mutual respect.

Community development involves changing the relationships between ordinary people and people in positions of power, so that everyone can take part in the issues that affect their lives. It starts from the principle that within any community there is a wealth of knowledge and experience which, if used in creative ways, can be channelled into collective action to achieve the communities' desired goals. Community development practitioners work alongside people in communities to help build relationships with key people and organisations and to identify common concerns. They create opportunities for the community to learn new skills and, by enabling people to act together, community development practitioners help to foster social inclusion and equality.

A number of different approaches to community development can be recognized, including: community economic development (CED); community capacity building; Social capital formation; political participatory development; nonviolent direct action; ecologically sustainable development; asset-based community development; faith-based community development; community practice social work; community-based participatory research (CBPR); Community Mobilization; community empowerment; community participation; participatory planning including community-based planning (CBP); community-driven development (CDD); and approaches to funding communities directly.

The History of Community Development

Community development has been a sometimes explicit, sometimes implicit goal of community people, aiming to achieve, through collective effort, a better life, and has occurred throughout history.

In the Global North

In the 19th century, the work of the early socialist thinker Robert Owen (1771–1851), sought to create a more perfect community. At New Lanark and at later communities such as Oneida in the USA and the New Australia Movement in Australia, groups of people came together to create utopian or intentional utopian communities, with mixed success.

In the United States in the 1960s, the term "community development" began to complement and generally replace the idea of urban renewal, which typically focused on physical development projects often at the expense of working-class communities. In the late 1960s, philanthropies such as the Ford Foundation and government officials such as Senator Robert F. Kennedy took an interest in local nonprofit organizations—a pioneer was the Bedford-Stuyvesant Restoration Corporation in Brooklyn—that attempted to apply business and management skills to the social mission of uplifting low-income residents and their neighborhoods. Eventually such groups became known as "Community Development Corporations" or CDCs. Federal laws beginning with the 1974 Housing and Community Development Act provided a way for state and municipal governments to channel funds to CDCs and other nonprofit organizations. National organizations such as the Neighborhood Reinvestment Corporation (founded in 1978 and now known as NeighborWorks America), the Local Initiatives Support Corporation (founded in 1980 and known as LISC), and the Enterprise Foundation (founded in 1981) have built extensive networks of affiliated local nonprofit organizations to which they help provide financing for countless physical and social development programs in urban and rural communities. The CDCs and similar organizations have been credited with starting the process that stabilized and revived seemingly hopeless inner city areas such as the South Bronx in New York City.

In the Global South

Community planning techniques drawing on the history of utopian movements became important in the 1920s and 1930s in East Africa, where Community Development proposals were seen as a way of helping local people improve their own lives with indirect assistance from colonial authorities.

Mohondas K. Gandhi adopted African community development ideals as a basis of his South African Ashram, and then introduced it as a part of the Indian Swaraj movement, aiming at establishing economic interdependence at village level throughout India. With Indian independence, despite the continuing work of Vinoba Bhave in encouraging grassroots land reform, India under its first Prime Minister Jawaharlal Nehru adopted a mixed-economy approach, mixing elements of socialism and capitalism.During the fifties and sixties, India ran a massive community development programme with focus on rural development activities through government support. This was later expanded in scope and was called integrated rural development scheme [IRDP]. A large number of initiatives that can come under the community development umbrella have come up in recent years.

Community Development became a part of the Ujamaa Villages established in Tanzania by Julius Nyerere, where it had some success in assisting with the delivery of education services throughout rural areas, but has elsewhere met with mixed success. In the 1970s and 1980s, Community

Development became a part of "Integrated Rural Development", a strategy promoted by United Nations Agencies and the World Bank. Central to these policies of community development were

- Adult Literacy Programs, drawing on the work of Brazilian educator Paulo Freire and the "Each One Teach One" adult literacy teaching method conceived by Frank Laubach.
- Youth and Women's Groups, following the work of the Serowe Brigades of Botswana, of Patrick van Rensburg.
- Development of Community Business Ventures and particularly cooperatives, in part drawn on the examples of José María Arizmendiarrieta and the Mondragon Cooperatives of the Basque Region of Spain
- Compensatory Education for those missing out in the formal education system, drawing on the work of Open Education as pioneered by Michael Young.
- Dissemination of Alternative Technologies, based upon the work of E. F. Schumacher as advocated in his book *Small is Beautiful: Economics as if people really mattered*
- Village Nutrition Programs and Permaculture Projects, based upon the work of Australians Bill Mollison and David Holmgren.
- Village Village Water Supply Programs.

Community development in Canada has roots in the development of co-operatives, credit unions and caisses populaires. The Antigonish Movement which started in the 1920s in Nova Scotia, through the work of Doctor Moses Coady and Father James Tompkins, has been particularly influential in the subsequent expansion of community economic development work across Canada.

In the 1990s, following critiques of the mixed success of "top down" government programs, and drawing on the work of Robert Putnam, in the rediscovery of Social Capital, community development internationally became concerned with social capital formation. In particular the outstanding success of the work of Muhammad Yunus in Bangladesh with the Grameen Bank, has led to the attempts to spread microenterprise credit schemes around the world. This work was honoured by the 2006 Nobel Peace Prize.

The "Human Scale Development" work of Right Livelihood Award winning Chilean economist Manfred Max Neef promotes the idea of development based upon fundamental human needs, which are considered to be limited, universal and invariant to all human beings (being a part of our human condition). He considers that poverty results from the failure to satisfy a particular human need, it is not just an absence of money. Whilst human needs are limited, Max Neef shows that the ways of satisfying human needs is potentially unlimited. Satisfiers also have different characteristics: they can be violators or destroyers, pseudosatisfiers, inhibiting satisfiers, singular satisfiers, or synergic satisfiers. Max-Neef shows that certain satisfiers, promoted as satisfying a particular need, in fact inhibit or destroy the possibility of satisfying other needs: e.g, the arms race, while ostensibly satisfying the need for protection, in fact then destroys subsistence, participation, affection and freedom; formal democracy, which is supposed to meet the need for participation often disempowers and alienates; commercial television, while used to satisfy the need for recreation, interferes with understanding, creativity and identity. Synergic satisfiers, on the other hand, not only satisfy one particular need, but also lead to satisfaction in other areas: some examples are breast-feeding; self-managed production; popular education; democratic community organizations; preventative medicine; meditation; educational games.

COMMUNITY MOBILIZATION

Community mobilization is an attempt to bring both human and non-human resources together to undertake developmental activities in order to achieve sustainable development.

Process

Community mobilization is a process through which action is stimulated by a community itself, or by others, that is planned, carried out, and evaluated by a community's individuals, groups, and organizations on a participatory and sustained basis to improve the health, hygiene and education levels so as to enhance the overall standard of living in the community. A group of people have transcended their differences to meet on equal terms in order to facilitate a participatory decision-making process. In other words it can be viewed as a process which begins a dialogue among members of the community to determine who, what, and how issues are decided, and also to provide an avenue for everyone to participate in decisions that affect their lives.

Requirements

Community mobilization needs many analytical and supportive resources which are internal (inside community) and external (outside Community) as well. Several of the resources are as following:

- Leadership
- Organizational capacity
- Communications channels
- Assessments
- Problem solving
- Resource mobilization
- Administrative and operational management.

Implications

Community mobilization is a frequently used term in developmental sector. Recently, community mobilization has been proved to be a valuable and effective concept which has various implications in dealing with basic problems like health and hygiene, population, pollution and gender bias.

3

Working with Communities, Society and Organizations

Individuals and families are embedded within social, political, and economic systems that shape behaviors and constrain access to resources necessary to maintain health.

The impact of social and environmental conditions is most visible in the growing gap between the health behaviors and health status of rich and poor, white and non-white. There is a need to better understand the role of organizational, community, and societal factors in determining health. This chapter continues to explore the ecologic framework, describing theoretical concepts and sample interventions at the organizational, community, and societal levels.

ORGANIZATIONS AND HEALTH

Formal and informal organizations constitute another framework for describing interactions between behavior and health. Organizations are important components of social and physical environments, and they exert considerable influence over the choices people make, the resources they have to aid them in those choices, and the factors in the workplace that could influence health status (e.g., work overload, exposure to toxic chemicals). As employees, consumers, customers, clients, and patients, people are influenced by the organizations to which they belong. Porras (1987) and Porras and Robertson (1992) suggest four major categories of work settings that are targets for change: organizing arrangements, social factors, technology, and physical settings.

Organizing arrangements include organizational goals and strategies for progressing toward them, organizational structure (e.g., formal division of labor, authority relationships, lines of communication), policies and procedures (the formal rules that govern the organization), and reward systems. Social factors include management style, informal social networks, and interaction processes (e.g., problem-solving, decision-making, conflict resolution). The technology category includes job design factors, work flow design, and technical systems. Physical settings include spatial configuration, interior design, and physical ambiance factors such as temperature, lighting, and noise. In their original typology, Porras and Robertson (1992) included individual attributes under the social factors umbrella. However, given the emphasis placed on individual beliefs, attitudes, and skills in health behavior research, those individual factors are suggested as a fifth category in the work setting for targeting change interventions.

Organizational Culture and Change

Organizational culture is the base upon which organizational and related individual behavior change occurs. The culture prescribes the "right way" to do things (Schein, 1990). An organizational culture that supports health is likely to adopt policies, procedures, and priorities that facilitate the healthy behaviors of employees; enhance employee health by reducing environmental risk factors; facilitate healthy behavior on the part of clients, customers, or members; and facilitate linkages to other organizations for health-enhancing purposes. The more health-enhancing policies an organization adopts, the more likely it is to be perceived as having a health-conscious culture.

Organizational development (OD) is a set of behavioral-science-based theories, values, strategies, and techniques aimed at planned change in the organizational work setting (Porras and Robertson, 1992). Three important foundations are briefly described here: *systems theory,* employee *participation* in change efforts, and *action research. Systems theory* (Katz and Kahn, 1978) says that a change in one part of the system will influence other parts, and so there is a need to vigilantly monitor unexpected (and often undesired) changes. Increased *involvement and participation* of organizational members in decision-making and problem-solving processes enhances the quality of decisions and solutions, increases members' commitment to following through on plans, reduces organizational stress, and enhances employee well-being. The *action research* involves outside change agents working with organization members in a cyclical process of diagnosing problems, planning, implementing plans, monitoring, and evaluating progress (Argyris and Schon, 1989).

Planned-Change Models

Lewin (1951) developed an early and influential model for conceptualizing the change process. He posited three stages: first is unfreezing the old behavior, second is moving to a new behavior, and third is refreezing or stabilizing the new behavior. Thus, change was conceptualized as moving from one equilibrium point to another. To begin the process, the balance between opposing forces (those that facilitate and those that hinder change) must change, Lewin's "force field analysis" was instrumental in the development of subsequent models of change. For example, organizational theorists such as Lippitt and co-workers (1958) and Schein (1987) built on Lewin's three stages and linked them to psychological mechanisms for change and to action steps that change agents should take to facilitate progress through the stages.

INTERVENTIONS TARGETED AT ORGANIZATIONS

Organizational change is an integral component of a comprehensive ecologic approach to health behavior change that emphasizes how individual decisions and behaviors are influenced by the multiple layers of systems within which individuals are embedded (Stokols, 1996). As important components of the social and physical environments, organizations exert considerable influence over the choices people make, the resources they have to aid them in those choices, and the factors in the workplace that could affect health status (e.g., work overload, exposure to toxic chemicals). People are influenced by organizations as employees, consumers, customers, clients, and patients.

Changing Employee Health Behaviors

National surveys of work organizations clearly document

a burgeoning interest in worksite health promotion programs. These programs focus either on a single behavioral risk factor (e.g., smoking) or on multiple risk factors (e.g., behavioral risk factors associated with cardiovascular disease). Because many of these interventions are aimed primarily at individual behaviors

In a review of 47 studies of health promotion programs that addressed multiple risk factors, Heaney and Goetzal (1997) found that almost all provided health education to employees. A smaller number of the programs (25%) incorporated modifications in organizational policy or the work environment to facilitate employee behavior changes. Such modifications included policies restricting or banning smoking on the premises, removing cigarette-vending machines, providing on-site exercise facilities, and providing healthier cafeteria food. A survey of health promotion programs funded by the Canadian Ministry of Health showed that more than half the programs reviewed reported modifications of health-compromising aspects of the organization (Richard et al., 1996). Most of the organization-level interventions addressed organizing arrangements. With the exception of providing on-site fitness facilities, few programs attempted to change physical settings, social factors, or technologies. Programs integrated into the culture of the organization were more likely to have multiple components and last longer than did those that had less support from top management and were less a part of the underlying fabric and culture of the organization. Heaney and Goetzal (1997) concluded that providing opportunities for individual risk reduction counseling was necessary but not sufficient for effective worksite health promotion programs.

Studies of programs aimed at individual risk factors also provide some support for the importance of changing the organizational context to support employee health behavior change. The example of smoking-control efforts at the workplace is illustrative. In their review, Eriksen and Gottlieb (1998) concluded that there is consistent evidence that smoking-control policies reduce cigarette consumption at work among smokers and reduce all employees' exposure to second-hand smoke. However, they found mixed evidence for policies aimed at prevalence of smoking and overall consumption of cigarettes (including during non-work hours). They also point out that many evaluation studies lacked the methodologic rigor necessary to permit confident causal inferences. And although several investigators have suggested the importance of looking at the degree of management support for smoking-control programs, the extent to which the organizational climate is consistent with control efforts, and the design and implementation of programs, few studies have done so.

Some worksite health promotion programs use organizational change theory to inform their strategies. More specifically, current standards of practice include employee participation in planning the efforts. This ranges from incorporating employee input into the assessment of employee health needs (e.g., through surveys or focus groups), to having employee advisory boards guide the planning process, to having employee groups take full responsibility for implementation. Although several large, randomized trials incorporated at least one strategy, a direct comparison of health promotion programs with and without planned employee involvement has not been made. In addition, results from randomized trials that incorporate employee involvement have been mixed.

Another strategy for incorporating organizational change into health promotion programming relies on training key figures in the organizations in methods for creating a supportive organizational culture and developing a comprehensive health promotion program. For example, Golaszewski and colleagues (1998) devised a seven-session curriculum for human resource managers who wanted to develop programs for employee heart health. The training addressed such issues as how to generate support among senior management; how to develop employee wellness committees; and how to conduct needs and resource assessments, diagnose organizational culture, and use employee benefits plans to support health promotion. Student interns were provided to the organizations, faculty from an academic medical center were available for consulting, and potential vendors for health promotion services were identified. Evaluated with a quasi-experimental design, the intervention organizations exhibited a significantly greater increase in organizational support for employee heart health than did the comparison organizations.

Reducing Environmental Risk Factors

Traditional worksite health promotion programs focus on individual change of personal risk factors. Occupational safety and health (OSH) programs address the influence of physical (e.g., noise, extreme temperatures), chemical, ergonomic, and psychosocial work hazards on employee health. According to Goldenhar and Schulte (1994), OSH programs can involve three strategies: engineering, administrative, and behavior change, used to address the different targets for organizational change presente. *Engineering strategies* modify technology or physical setting; *administrative strategies* modify the organizing arrangements or social factors; and *behavior change strategies* target beliefs, attitudes, and skills.

Examples of behavior change interventions in OSH include training to increase compliance with safety practices, use of personal protective equipment, and exercise to prevent occupationally related back injuries. Those interventions tend to focus almost exclusively on individual-level change (Goldenhar and Schulte, 1994). Strategies to enhance compliance with universal precautions among health care workers provide a case in point. Although descriptive research clearly indicates the influence of organizational safety climate and work task design on compliance rates, most interventions have targeted only individual employee knowledge, attitudes, and behaviors for change.

Few OSH interventions address more than a single type of environmental exposure or use more than a single intervention strategy. However, no matter the exposure or strategy used, organizational change principles are needed to initiate, implement, and maintain OSH programs. Programs oriented to reducing adverse psychosocial work exposures illustrate that point. A voluminous literature documents the consequences of occupational psychosocial stressors such as work overload, role conflict, job insecurity, unpredictability, ambiguity, responsibility for the work of others, and poor relationships with supervisors and co-workers. Much research supports the benefits of psychosocial resources, such as social support and control or decision latitude over how one's job is done. These psychosocial resources can directly affect employee well-being, and they can buffer employees from the negative effects of stress. Baker et al. (1996) give a comprehensive presentation of the stress process in occupational settings.

Strategies for reducing the harm caused by psychosocial stressors most often entail individual behavior change strategies or administrative change strategies. Those efforts focus either on developing personal strategies for alleviating stress-related symptoms (e.g., relaxation techniques, biofeedback, exercise) or on increasing employees' coping capacity (e.g., cognitive restructuring, problem-solving skill building, stressor recognition). Administrative strategies involve changing the way work is organized, distributed, supervised, and rewarded, for example by using clear job descriptions (to reduce uncertainty or unnecessary conflict), providing for flexible scheduling, and holding regular work team meetings so that employees can voice concerns and engage in group problem solving. Members of work teams that meet regularly or that have leaders trained in facilitating group problem solving report receiving more social support from their supervisors and experiencing less role ambiguity and higher job satisfaction.

In addition to these behavior change and administrative strategies, environmental psychologists suggest that changes in the physical setting can reduce occupational stressors and enhance psychosocial resources (Sundstrom and Altman, 1989). For example, the physical proximity of employee work stations and the presence of "gathering places," such as mailrooms or lunchrooms, have been associated with the quantity and quality of employee social interactions.

Behavior change strategies are usually "expert guided" (Karasek, 1992) in that they depend on health professionals or other outside consultants to counsel, train, or educate employees. The administrative strategies described here either were expert guided or were guided by the employees themselves. An example of the latter was the formation of an agency-wide labor/ management stress committee in a study of stress among social workers in a child protective services agency. Working with outside researchers, this committee developed goals to reduce sources of worksite stress, such as poor communication, and strengthen psychosocial resources, such as decision-making latitude over job tasks. Workers, management, and researchers then collaborated to develop, implement, and evaluate different interventions. For example, a computerized information system was introduced to reduce the workload and frustration associated with intake and tracking of clients. Economically correct computer workstations were provided. All employees were trained to use the new system and had easy access to technical assistance. Evaluation of the project suggested that the staff who were most involved in the intervention experienced gains in job decision latitude, productivity, and job satisfaction.

Karasek (1992) reviewed 19 case studies of occupational stress reduction programs gathered from countries around the world. He concluded that the programs that focused solely on individual-level coping enhancement—even when they involved substantial resources—were not effective. Programs that attempted to change work organization, task structure, or communication patterns in worksites were more likely to be effective. Karasek (1992) concluded that this was particularly true when participatory strategies (e.g., worker discussions in quality circles or "health circles" to identify stressors and develop plans to reduce them) were used.

Several intervention studies attempting to increase employee participation in and influence over work-related decisions have shown positive effects on employee stress and well-being. Participatory action research (PAR) has been proposed as a promising approach to occupational health interventions. PAR entails collaboration between researchers and members of an organization in a data-guided, problem-solving approach to enhance an organization's ability to provide a safe and healthy work environment. PAR builds on many of the tenets of organizational development and it has been used as a stress reduction intervention with some success, particularly in Scandinavia.

No direct empirical comparisons of individual behavior change approaches with organizational-level change approaches to stress reduction have been conducted. Indeed, an either/or approach is not likely to enhance understanding of the stress reduction process. The ecologic approach, models of the stress process, systems theory, and the organizational development literature suggest that stress reduction approaches that use several points of intervention are likely to be most effective. Thus, comprehensive programs that address both changing the organizational processes that are causing stress and strengthening employees' skills and resources for coping with stress could be most promoting of employee health. Some efforts along these lines are promising, but more research is needed to elucidate fully the potential of these interventions.

Organizational Change Interventions

In 1988, the observation was made that the "most striking feature" of studies examining the effects of organizational-level interventions to enhance worker control is "the sheer lack of them" (Murphy, 1988). This observation still applies today to the broader arena of organizational change strategies intended to enhance health. Although more studies are being done now, the scarcity of well-evaluated interventions is still apparent.

A few recurring themes emerge from the findings of existing studies. First, they address a relatively narrow set of organizational targets. Few interventions attempt to modify social factors, technology, or physical setting. The results of studies that do address these factors have been encouraging. Second, many studies did not consider the organizational culture of their participants. Given the potential importance of organizational culture to the success of change efforts (Schein, 1990), future studies should routinely assess and diagnose this factor. Several validated instruments for measuring organizational climate (the more superficial manifestation of organizational culture) and its receptivity to health innovations are available. Third, many studies found that when the external change agents terminated their involvement with the target organizations, intervention benefits quickly dissipated. Efforts to build capacity for sustaining organizational changes among organization members can address this problem.

The same critique applies to the areas of worksite health promotion and occupational health and safety programs. Over the past decade, it has become clear that generic programs are not likely to be optimally effective because they do not consider organizational culture or the beliefs, attitudes, needs, and resources of organization members. The prescription for this challenge is two-fold: strong formative research, and participation of all relevant stakeholders in the planning and conduct of health-promoting activities. Careful formative research is likely to illuminate important local issues and challenges, and stakeholders' participation is likely to enhance the program quality and increase commitment to follow through with the program activities.

COMMUNITIES AND HEALTH

Individual-level risk factors, families, and organizations influence health behavior and health status, and so do social and environmental conditions. This phenomenon is most visible in the growing gap between the health behaviors and health status of rich and poor, White and non-White. There is a need to better explain how the broader community and societal factors help determine the health status of individuals and groups. Some important conceptual constructs regarding the nature of communities as they relate to health outcomes are discussed below.

Communities of Identity

There are numerous definitions for and considerable confusion about what is meant by "community". Particularly important for this discussion of community-level change is the recognition that a "catchment area" or "population" is not a community but a geographic entity (e.g., city, county) that has a population aggregate with numerical but not a functional meaning (Steuart, 1993). Here, community means "unit of identity" created and recreated through social interactions. A community in this sense is characterized by the following elements (Israel et al., 1994):

- Its membership has a sense of identity and belonging.
- It has common symbol systems: similar language, rituals, and ceremonies.
- It has shared values and norms.
- It offers mutual influence—community members have influence and are influenced by one another.
- It has shared needs and a shared commitment to meeting them.

- It has a shared emotional connection—members share common history, experiences, and support.

Thus, a community of identity can exist within a defined geographic neighborhood or as a geographically dispersed group among whose members there is a sense of common identity. A city or catchment area might not be a community as defined here, or it might include numerous different and overlapping communities of identity (Israel et al., 1998).

Community-Level Constructs

Communities as units of identity are also indigenous "units of solution" that include members with the knowledge, skills, and expertise neeessary to solve problems at the community level (Steuart, 1993). Community-level change can reduce the numerous social, structural, and environmental stressors that affect health but that are beyond the ability of any one person to control or change (e.g., poverty, discrimination, income inequalities, crime, inadequate housing). Community-level change also can strengthen the situational factors (e.g., social support, community empowerment, community capacity, community cohesion) that protect against the effects of stress on health. Community-level change involves bringing together the skills and resources within a community to collectively identify stressors and protective factors and implement ways to promote good health. Although it often is possible to affect the stressors and protective factors within a given community of identity, it also is frequently necessary to bring together several communities of identity to extend the units of solution to address more complex issues (Steuart, 1993).

Geography versus Identity and Action

It is important to recognize the distinction between population-based, community-wide interventions (which have for the most part defined community as a geographic place within which to carry out interventions that usually are focused on individual behavior change) and community-level change interventions (in which the emphasis is on working with and strengthening communities of identity to foster social and structural changes that are associated with the health status of the community as a whole).

There are numerous community-level constructs to help inform the role of the community as a unit of identity and solution, such as "sense of community", "community competence", "community capacity" (Goodman et al., 1998), and "community empowerment".

Level Interventions

Interventions at the community level pose many challenges. Unlike clinical trials, it is usually impossible to have randomized control groups; even finding comparison communities is frequently unrealistic. Interventions at the community level are often dynamic and change with the interactions. The interventions can be complex, working toward change in social, economic, physical, and/or political factors among individuals, organizations, families, as well as the community itself. A number of useful conceptual constructs and typologies provide frameworks for thinking about community-level interventions.

Chin and Benne (1969) explicate three different theoretical assumptions regarding changes in human systems, each of which has different implications for conducting community-level interventions. First, the "rational-empirical" construct assumes that humans are rational and that they will follow their self-interest once it is made clear to them, and that a person or community will adopt a proposed change if it is rationally justified. Second, the "normative-re-educative" construct assumes that actions are supported by socio-cultural norms, values, attitudes, and significant relationships, and the commitments on the part of individuals and communities to these norms; and that change will occur only as those involved are brought to change their normative orientations. This is similar to Lewin's (1951) model, presented earlier, for conceptualizing change as a continuous process that involves an unfreezing, a changing, and a refreezing phase. Third, the "power-coercive" construct assumes that the change or influence process will either occur through compliance of those with less power to the ideas, direction and leadership of those with greater power (i.e., power over); or when that power is questioned or in conflict that there is collective power (i.e., power with) in which change occurs when those with less power come together to transform power relations from one group to another.

Warren (1975) conceptualizes purposive change in communities as being based on different configurations with respect to the agreement-disagreement dimensions of an issue, as well as other intervening variables. He posits three situations on a continuum that have different implications for community-level purposive change: (1) "issue consensus" —where there is basic agreement within the community on an issue and how it should be resolved; (2) "issue difference" —where no agreement yet exists on the issue, but there is the possibility that the community will reach issue consensus; and (3) "issue dissensus" —where members of the community either refuse to recognize the issue or are in strong disagreement with the change being proposed and there is little likelihood of achieving issue consensus.

Minkler and Wallerstein (1997), in their typology of community organization and community building, posit a two-by-two figure that is anchored on the horizontal axis by the constructs of "consensus" and "conflict," and on the vertical axis the constructs of "needs-based" and "strengths-based". Thus, different models or approaches to community change are based on different assumptions regarding the issues being addressed and the relationships that exist within the community (i.e., consensus or conflict), and the assessment of the community that drives the change process (i.e., needs-based or strengths-based).

Recently, Weiss (1995) proposed "theory-based evaluation," or the theory of change, challenging program planners to assess "how and why the program will work." In the theory of change approach, the first step is to articulate clearly the goals of the intervention and specific pathways to attain them (hypotheses). Consensus among the key participants about the goals is important. Agreement on the desired final outcome provides clarity on what to measure in the beginning and over the long term. Evidence from previous interventions is useful in identifying any weak assumptions in the hypotheses that might need rethinking. The pathways are likely to be a sequence of activities and their expected outcomes that lay out the key steps to the anticipated change. Specific interim outcomes provide options for measurements that can be used to see if the changes are occurring according to the original hypotheses.

In this way, theory of change can help to guide decisions about what to measure and when to expect the change. Multiple theories of change can be applied simultaneously within a program with multiple pathways leading to the goal of the intervention (Weiss, 1995). Effective implementation of the theory of change approach does not ensure that the goals will be attained, but does provide the framework for evaluating the success of the intervention. Furthermore, by tracking progress with interim goals, it can help to distinguish problems with the hypotheses from problems with the implementation of the intervention and thereby allow midcourse corrections in the interventions.

LEVEL INTERVENTIONS OF COMMUNITY

It is beyond the scope of this chapter to provide an exhaustive review of the various approaches to community change interventions. Within the community-organizing literature there is extensive discussion of change models, such as community development, social action, community building, and empowerment-oriented social action. There is also a long history of community organizing for health. However, as discussed throughout this report, within the field of public health per se, considerably less emphasis and fewer resources have been placed on conducting and evaluating community-level interventions in the United States. The very nature of these interventions— with their emphasis on the social, cultural, economic, and political context of communities of identity, and on the role of community involvement in and control of an evolving process for which full specification of goals and objectives is not possible at the beginning—and the necessary commitment to the long time frame required to bring about major community-level changes preclude application of traditional evaluation designs and methods to assess effectiveness. Therefore, for the purposes of this section, a brief description is provided of two key studies of community-level interventions.

Tenderloin Senior Organizing Project

Over a 16-year period, the Tenderloin Senior Organizing Project (TSOP) involved community members in the Tenderloin district of San Francisco, focusing on low-income elderly residents in single-room occupancy hotels. TSOP was established in 1979 by faculty and graduate students at the School of Public Health, University of California, Berkeley, with the initial goals of enhancing mental and physical health by reducing social isolation and providing health education, and of bringing together local residents to identify common problems and solutions for addressing those shared concerns (Minkler, 1992, 1997).

TSOP drew on four conceptual domains—social support, critical consciousness, social action, and democratic citizenship—to foster community empowerment and competence (Minkler, 1997). TSOP's intervention strategies evolved, including problem-posing discussions, support groups, leadership training, organizing tenants' associations, and the formation of interhotel groups and coalitions. Its accomplishments included establishment of hotel-based minimarkets, reduction of the neighborhood crime rate, improved pest control, upgrading of substandard plumbing and wiring, agreements for the removal of lead-based paint, cleanup of a va-cant lot used as an illegal dump, recognition by hotel management of the tenants' associations as the organized voice of residents in the buildings, and the successful diffusion and replication of the TSOP model in other cities (Minkler, 1997).

Minkler (1997) offers several lessons from the TSOP experience for those interested in community organizing in the health field:

- the importance of the community, rather than an outside organizer, in defining needs and priorities;
- the need for an initial and continuing community diagnosis and assessment to identify and build on community strengths and resources;
- the flexible implementation of theories and methodologies, tailoring them to a particular community context;
- the importance of using participatory and empowering approaches to evaluate community-level change interventions;
- the necessity of long-range planning and developing diversified bases of funding.

Village Health Worker Partnership

The East Side Village Health Worker Partnership (ESVHWP) is a project of the Detroit Community-Academic Urban Research Center, funded in 1995 through a cooperative agreement with the Centers for Disease Control and Prevention. The project is a partnership between the University of Michigan School of Public Health, the Detroit Health Department, seven community-based organizations, and the Henry Ford Health System. The partnership involves community-based participatory research with two broad goals: identifying and explaining the intrapersonal, interpersonal, organizational, community, and public policy factors in the stress model associated with poor health outcomes on Detroit's east side; and designing, implementing, and evaluating a collaborative lay health advisor intervention aimed at reducing stressors and strengthening protective factors associated with health, as identified by members of the community.

The objectives of this intervention incorporate change at several levels. Of particular importance is having lay health advisors (Village Health Workers [VHWs]) assist community residents in identifying and solving problems that affect the health of the community. More than 40 VHWs have completed an initial eight-session training program. They meet monthly to share experiences and skills and to participate in additional training in grant writing and community organizing, for example. The results of a random-sample community survey and in-depth interviews and focus group discussions with VHWs, steering committee members (representatives from each partner organization) and key community members identified four priority areas: parenting, support of women, crime and relationships with the police, and community organizing. VHWs participated in monthly meetings at the police precincts, assisted in arson prevention (Maciak et al., 1998), organized neighborhood block clubs, established a fresh fruit and vegetable minimarket for neighborhood residents, and developed support mechanisms for women who have child care responsibilities.

The ESVHWP is using quantitative and qualitative data collection methods for several purposes. For example, a group interview with the Steering Committee developed a local stress model and guided the design of items on a community survey. The survey is being used for basic research and evaluation purposes (e.g., to examine the effect of the intervention on reducing such stressors as crime and on strengthening such protective factors as social support and perceived control). One aim of the evaluation is to assess the extent to which the intervention has changed community-level factors, including the community's sense of competence, empowerment, and cohesion.

Community Change Interventions

Many social, economic, and environmental factors that affect health are disproportionately represented in minority communities and among women. Therefore, greater emphasis is needed on public health interventions that involve communities of identity with the goal of collectively identifying resources, needs, and solutions that can influence community-level variables. There are several challenges and barriers to this approach and several factors that facilitate intervention effectiveness. More resources are needed to support such community change efforts, as is an expanded set of methodologic tools to evaluate program success. The Theory of Change for communities may help in developing evaluation approaches. In addition, the limits of community change interventions and the need to engage in broader policy programs that can affect social and structural factors must be recognized.

SOCIETY AND HEALTH

Research consistently reveals an inverse relationship between social class and a variety of diseases. In addition, these differentials are also increasingly prominent in the prevalence of health behaviors. Studies have similarly reported that people with low incomes or minimal education levels are especially likely to exhibit multiple risk-related behaviors (Emmons et al., 1994). Interventions are needed to address the "pockets of prevalence" of risk-related behaviors to reduce the social inequalities of risk. The structure and function of society per se thus constitute the final framework within which interactions between behavior and health should be considered. Interventions designed for low-income populations also must consider the social context that influences health behaviors and health status. Socioeconomic class affects the availability of an array of social and material resources that ultimately have profound effects on health. For example, the Alameda County (California) Study (Berkman and Syme, 1979) identified multiple risk factors associated with low income, including smoking, obesity, unmet needs for food and medical care, unsafe neighborhoods, and lack of social supports (Kaplan, 1995). Graham (1994a,b) demonstrated the relevance of these socioeconomic factors for one risk-related behavior, smoking. Based on a qualitative study, she found that low-income women used smoking as a means of coping with economic pressure and the resulting demands placed on them to care for others. Indeed, spending on cigarettes appears to be protected because it is viewed as a necessary luxury. Using survey data, Graham (1994b) found that, compared with their nonsmoking counterparts, working-class mothers who smoke generally care for more children and for children in poorer health, and are more likely to be providing that care alone. A larger proportion of smokers had insufficient resources to meet the basic needs of their families, and they lived in less desirable neighborhoods than did women with higher incomes. She concluded that smoking among working-class women was linked to the caring responsibilities and material circumstances that shape their lives (Graham, 1994b). Similarly, Romano and colleagues (1991) found that African American individuals who reported experiencing high levels of stress associated with their socioeconomic circumstances—such as being out of work or not having enough money to meet basic needs—were more likely to smoke than were those reporting better circumstances.

Even beyond the stressors associated with low income, social structure clearly shapes people's daily lives. For example, there are many ways the effects of income extend beyond purchasing power to influence daily life. Middle-class neighborhoods have proportionally more pharmacies, restaurants, banks, and specialty stores; low-income areas have more fast food restaurants, check cashing stores, liquor stores, and laundromats. Typical food purchases cost approximately 15% more in poor neighborhoods, and fresh produce can cost as much as 22% more than in higher income areas. In addition, the quality of the food on average is poorer in low-income areas (Trout, 1993). Relatively higher food costs in low-income neighborhoods could be associated with their relatively fewer supermarkets and with greater reliance on small and medium-sized stores in which the quality, quantity, and variety of fresh fruits and vegetables and meats is limited. As a result, people living in low-income areas often are much less able to meet their needs for healthful foods.

The public health response to social class differences in health behaviors must extend to changes in social structure to improve the day-to-day realities of low-income populations—factors that clearly shape health behaviors and health status. Broad-based policy initiatives designed to reduce social inequalities are likely to contribute to improved health at the individual and community levels.

The constellation of factors operating at the society level constitutes an extremely complex system with multiple interactions and feedback mechanisms. It is beyond the scope of this report to address the full range of issues that function at this level or their ramifications for the health status of individuals and populations. Therefore, a brief description of several important factors is presented to illustrate the importance of considering them at the society level and of assessing some of their interactions with those that function elsewhere.

Government and Societal Constraints on Health

Many social, economic, political, and cultural factors are associated with health and disease for which changes in individual health behaviors alone are not likely to result in improved health and quality of life. Public health law has been defined as the legal powers and duties of government to assure the conditions for people to be healthy. Government uses a number of means to prevent injury and disease and to promote the population's health. Laws and regulations, like other prevention strategies, can intervene at each level discussed in this chapter in several ways to secure safer behavior among the population. Finally, public policy interventions undertaken by government are given particular emphasis, but an analogous role can be served by other large components of civil society:

employers, unions, health care organizations, citizens' groups, or public interest foundations. Similarly, the distinctions between levels of government (nation, state, county, etc.) are beyond the scope of this report. For the purposes of discussing behavior and health, government is treated as a single component.

LEVEL INTERVENTIONS OF SOCIETY

In 1979, the Surgeon General's report *Healthy People* (USDHHS, 1979) presented national goals for reducing premature deaths. Soon afterwards, *Objectives for the Nation* (USDHHS, 1980) provided health objectives for the following 10 years in the United States. These targets proved to be an effective approach to setting priorities and evaluating progress in health promotion and disease prevention. Subsequently, *Healthy People*2000 (USDHHS, 1990) and *Healthy People 2010* (USDHHS, 2000) cartied on the tradition with updated goals for the coming decade. Health targets have also become part of the strategies for health policy in the United Kingdom, Australia, and the World Health Organization. The advantages and drawbacks to this approach are reviewed by van Herten and Gunner-Schepers (2000). On the positive side, the process of formulating the targets provides insights, reveals gaps, and stimulates debate. By helping to establish realistic goals, it improves resource management and provides benchmarks for progress. The objections to this approach include the concerns that it oversimplifies the health issues and that some objectives that are more difficult to quantify will be ignored.

Health Communication Campaigns

Interventions can be aimed at individual behavior—providing education or incentives for healthier choices. Government health messages can be highly important in advancing the public's health by informing people about hidden risks and by providing guidance about safer alternatives. The effectiveness of national campaigns is extensively reviewed and analyzed in an IOM report (2001). One example, the National 5-A-Day Campaign, is described here to illustrate the scope of this type of intervention. This campaign was initiated by the National Cancer Institute in partnership with the Produce for Better Health Foundation, to increase the dietary intake of fruits and vegetables to the recommended five servings each day. The intervention has multiple components. Mass media marketing is used to increase public awareness through newsletters, websites, television, publications, special events, and promotional items. Consumers are targeted at time of purchase with brochures, recipes, advertising, coupons, etc. The food industry and retail stores are provided with training and promotional kits, and they agree to display materials and hold special events that advance the message. At the community level, programs are designed to meet the specific needs of the community members. Interventions are aimed at schools, worksites, clinics, religious centers, etc. Activities include such events as garden projects, wellness seminars, booths at state fairs, and local media events. The 5-A-Day Campaign also provides funding for evaluation to assess the impact of the various programs and the effectiveness of the advertising.

Regulatory Approaches

The government can exercise its legislative powers to deter risk behaviors by imposing civil and criminal penalties (e.g., seatbelt and motorcycle helmet laws). This kind of regulation prescribes specific behavior either for the entire population (e.g., speed limits) or for segments of it (e.g., age-restricted tobacco and alcoholic beverage sales). The government also can create incentives for individual behavior change. For example, it can exercise its taxation authority to discourage unhealthy activities, such as tobacco use or excessive consumption of alcohol, or encourage healthy ones, for example, by providing tax deductions for health care expenditures.

The law also can regulate the agents of behavior change, for example by requiring safer product design. Government can regulate unsafe products directly (e.g., passive restraints in cars, trigger locks on handguns, or childproof caps on medicines) or indirectly through the tort system (e.g., tobacco, automobile, or firearms litigation). Government also can help provide the means for safer behavior by removing legal impediments to behavior change (e.g., dismantling drug paraphernalia or needle prescription laws that impede access to sterile injection equipment).

Furthermore, the law can change the informational, physical, social, or economic environment to facilitate safer behavior. Government can demand accurate labelling and instructions (e.g., on foods, pharmaceutical products, nutritional supplements) or restrict commercial advertising of hazardous products and activities (e.g., tobacco, alcoholic beverages, gambling); enact housing and building codes to prevent injury and disease (e.g., sanitation, lead paint); and make environments safer (e.g., guards on upper-level apartment windows, median barriers on highways, regulations for safe disposal of toxic substances).

Addressing Socioeconomic Status and Health

The role of socioeconomic status in health is an issue that can only be handled at a societal level. The international scope of this issue is reflected in the concerns it has raised from the World Health Organization (WHO), the World Bank, and the European Community (Whitehead, 1998; Gwatkin, 2000). Many efforts have been implemented to review the evidence and to search for solutions to the problem. The concern goes beyond providing equitable access to health care to addressing the basic links between social inequality and health.

In 1992, WHO set the following target: "By the year 2000, the differences in health status between countries and between groups within countries should be reduced by at least 25%, by improving the level of health of disadvantaged nations and groups" (Dahlgren and Whitehead, 1992). Approaches were aimed at reducing poverty (e.g., compressed income scales or progressive tax systems), decreasing unhealthy living conditions (e.g., urban renewal programs), improving working conditions (e.g., legislation to eliminate physical health hazards at work or organizational reforms for less stressful working arrangements), decreasing unemployment (e.g., creation of new jobs or minimizing the impact through increased public awareness of available assistance), improving lifestyle (e.g., targeting the most disadvantaged groups for smoking or nutrition education or interventions), and providing access to health care (e.g., availability of insurance and culturally appropriate training for health care providers).

4

Community Power Structure and Social Worker's Perspective

INTRODUCTION AND MEANING OF POWER

Power implies the ability of an individual or a group to influence or change the behavior of other individuals or groups. Weber defines power as the chance of a man or a number of men to realize their own will in a communal action even against the resistance of others who are participating in the action. Power is an aspect of social relationships. An individual or a group does not hold power in isolation. They hold it in relation to others. To say that power is relational is also to imply it is behavioral.

For if power consists in an inter-relationship between two actors. Then that inter relationship can only be understood in terms of one actor's manifest behavior as affecting the manifest behavior of others. Further power is also situational. To know power one has necessarily to relate it to a specific situation or a specific role and an actor's power in one particular situation or role may vary from that in another. Weber's concept of power implies that those who hold power do so at the expense of others. It suggests that there is a fixed amount of power and therefore if some hold power others do not. This view is sometimes known as constant-sum concept of power. Talcott Parsons rejects this view and sees power as something possessed by society as a whole. According to him power is a generalized facility or resource in the society. In particular it is a capacity to mobilize the resources of the society for the attainment of goals for which a general public commitment has been made. In this sense the amount of power in society is measured by the degree to which collective goals are realized. Thus greater the efficiency of a social system for achieving the goals defined by its members more the power that exists in society. This view is sometimes known as variable-sum concept of power, since power in society is not seen as fixed or constant. Instead it is variable in the sense that it can increase or decrease. Alvin Gouldner has defined Power as among other things the ability to enforce one's moral claims. The powerful can thus conventionalize their moral defaults. According to David Lockwood power must not only refer to the capacity to realize one's ends in a conflict situation against the will of others, it must also include the capacity to prevent opposition arising in the first places.

Power Structure

Power structures are made up of decision makers who are largely responsible for the actions and non-actions in organizations at all levels. At the individual level, the ability to make decisions enables one to influence the behavior of another. At the community-system level, an organization or power group may be able to command the behavior of other individuals or organizations. System point of view, decisions involve every unit of human organization: the individual, the family, voluntary as opposed to involuntary organizations, the government, corporations, and the community (Hawley, 1971). Power is obtained by controlling that which is valued by people in society. Those who control economic institutions have power, influence decisions, and can implement decisions. Power structures are defined as the characteristic pattern within a community whereby resources are mobilized and sanctions employed in making decisions (Walton, 1967). Thus, a community is considered an organization of units held together through the use of power. Social science research indicates that influential community leaders usually control important economic and governmental positions, resources, and decisions.

Community Power Structure

Community power structure refers to the distribution of power at the local community level. There are numerous empirical studies to discover the nature of the distribution of power at community level. Among these community studies two categories can be clearly identified one supporting the major contention of the elite thesis and the other refuting the elitist argument and replacing it by what is known as the Pluralist Thesis. Lloyd Hunter's Community Power Structure based on the study of distribution of power in Atlantic is a prominent study in the elitist tradition.

Hunter's study was based on reputational approach. He made a preliminary list of 175 leaders who held formal important positions in politics, business and civic organizations and have reputation for leadership. Then he selected the panel of 14 judges representing religious, business and professional interest and asked them to select those who in their eyes are the top leaders. The result showed that half of these leaders were upper-class businessmen. The empirical study confirms the elitist thesis that a clear defined group of decision makers can be identified who are highly organized and who decisively dominate the public life of the organized and who decisively dominate the public life of the city.

Pluralists led by Robert Dahl have challenged the main elitist contention that a society is marked by the existence of a single centre of political power. They argued that in a society there are multiple centers of political power none of which are completely sovereign. The decision making maybe done by few but then this decision making cannot be understood except within the context of a continuous bargaining process among the elites and also of a general consensus established only through the mass approval which is hard to secure.

Further continuing his criticism of the elite model he argued that the elite theory confuses potential control with actual control. He agrees that it is quite possible that a group in the society has a very high potential for control. But that does not automatically make this group very powerful since the actual power of a group is established not only by a high potential for control but also by a high potential for nuclearity. Next according to Dahl the elite theories disregarded the fact that there may be different scopes of power and that a group having a high degree of influence over one scope may not necessarily have the same degree of influence over another scope within the same system.

Dahl selected three distinct decisions-areas covering urban development, public schools and political nominations. Within each area he studied a number of decisions thus he picks up three categories of political leaders which are political notables,social notables and economic notables and enquires whether each of these groups participate in decision-making only in one or in all of the three issue areas. He takes as the sign of power the ability to successfully initiate or veto the proposals for policies. After examining all the available data Dahl admits that the in The New Haven a tiny group the leaders exert great influence on individuals who are influential in one sector of public activity are found not to be influential in another sector and further leaders exerting influence in different issue areas do not come to be drawn from a single homogenous stratum of the community.

Dahl's pluralist model has been subjected to severe criticisms. Firstly the model wrongly locates power in concrete decisions or in activities having direct bearing on decision making. He ignores the fact that power is also exercised in creating and reinforcing social and political values and institutional practices that limit the scope of the political process to public consideration of only those issues that are comparatively harmless to the interest of the powerful. Thus the powerful groups may never let these issues which affect their vital interests come to the stage of public decision making. Thus Dahl's model fails to differentiate the unimportant issues arising in the political arena.

Elite Theory

Elite theory is a theory of the state which seeks to describe and explain the power relationships in modern society. It argues that a small minority, comprised of members of the economic elite and policy-planning networks, hold the most power no matter what happens in elections in a country. Through positions in corporations or on corporate boards, and influence over the policy-planning networks through financial support of foundations or positions with think tanks or policy-discussion groups, members of the "elite" are able to have significant power over policy decisions of corporations and governments. The theory stands in opposition to pluralism in suggesting that democracy is a utopian ideal. It also stands in opposition to state autonomy theory. Elite theory developed in part as a reaction to Marxism. It rejected the Marxian idea that a classless society having an egalitarian structure could be realized after class struggle in every society. It regards Marxism as an ideology rather than an objective analysis of social systems. According to Elite theory man can never be liberated from the subjugation of an elite structure. The term Elite refers to those who excel. The classical elite theorists identify the governing elite in terms of superior personal qualities of those who exercise power. However, later versions of elite theory place less emphasis on the personal qualities of the powerful and more on the institutional framework of the society. They argued that the hierarchical organization of social institutions allows a minority to monopolize power. Another criticism of the elite theories against the Marxian view of distribution of power is that the ruling class too large and amorphous a group to be able to effectively wield power. In their view power is always exercised by a small cohesive group of the elite. Elite theory argues that all societies are divided into two main groups a ruling minority and the ruled. This situation is inevitable. If the proletarian revolution occurs it will merely result in the replacement of one ruling elite by another. Classical elite theory was propounded by Pareto and Mosca.

The Classical Elite Theory

Pareto places particular emphasis on psychological characteristics as the basis of the elite rule. He argues that there are two main types of governing elite which he calls Lions and Foxes. Lion achieve power because of their ability to take direct and decisive action and as their name suggests they tend to rule by cunning and guile by diplomatic manipulation.Pareto believed that European democracies provide an example of this type of elite. Members of governing elite own their position primarily to their personal qualities either to their Lion like or Fox like characteristics. Major change in society occurs when one elite replaces another a process Pareto calls circulation of elites. All elites tend to become decadent. They may become soft and ineffective with the pleasures of easy living and the privilege of power or set in their ways and too flexible to respond to changing circumstances. In addition each type of the elite lacks the imagination and guile necessary to maintain its rule and will have to admit the foxes from the masses to make up for this deficiency. Gradually foxes infiltrate the entire elite and so transform its character. Foxes however lack the ability to take forceful and decisive action which is essential at various times to retain power. Thus an organized minority of Lions committed to the restoration of strong government develops overthrowing the elite of foxes.

Like Pareto, Mosca believed that rule by a minority of elite would be an inevitable feature of social life and societies in history were divided into two classes-A class that rules and a class that is ruled. The first class always the less numerous performs all political functions, monopolies power and enjoys the advantages that power brings whereas the second the more numerous class is directed and controlled by the first. Like Pareto, Mosca believed that the ruling minority is superior to the most of the population because they possess certain qualities that give them material, intellectual and moral superiority. The content of these qualities may vary from society to society in some society's courage and bravery in battle provided access to the elite. In others the skills and capacity needed to acquire wealth were valued. For both Pareto and Mosca democracies are merely another form of elite rule.

Pluralism

The political theory of pluralism holds that political power in society does not lie with the electorate but is distributed between a wide numbers of groups. These groups may be trade unions, interest groups, business organizations, and any of a multitude of formal and informal coalitions.

Power Elite

C Wright Mills has presented a new version of the elite theory. Mills limits his analysis to the American society only. He does not believe that elite rule is inevitable. In fact he sees it as fairly recent development. He rejects the view that the members of the elite have superior qualities or psychological characteristics which distinguish them from the rest of the population. Instead he argues that the structure of institutions is such that those at the top of the institutional hierarchy largely monopolized power. Certain institutions can be pivotal positions in societies and the elite comprise those who hold command posts in those institutions. Mills identifies three key institutions: The major corporations, the Military and the Federal government.

Those who occupy the command posts in those institutions form three elites. In practice however the interest and activities of the elite are sufficiently similar and inter connected to form a single ruling minority which Mills terms the Power Elite. The cohesiveness and unity of the power elite is strengthened by the similarity of the backgrounds of its members and another change and overlapping of personnel between the three elites. Members are largely drawn from the upper strata of the society.

They share similar educational backgrounds and mix socially in the high prestige clubs. Within the power elite there is frequent interchange of personnel between the elites. Mills has also rejected the Marxian view that political power automatically follows economic power. He has shown a preference for power elite rather than ruling class.

According to him class is an economic term and rule is a political one. The ruling class in its political connotations does not allow enough autonomy to the political order and its agents and it says nothing about the military. Thus power elite is a more suitable term than ruling class.R.K Merton has further supported Mills view that the power elite are recruited from the same social class and are educated in similar prestigious colleges and schools and have similar orientation.

POLITICAL PARTIES

A political party is essentially a social group having associative type of social relationship activity and inters personal relationship. Membership rests on formally free recruitment. It is a social group because firstly it embodies the system of interdependent activity and inter-personal relationships. Secondly it operates in terms of goal oriented coordinated actions. In so far it demands from its members of rational direction of their behavior towards commonly acknowledged goal. The goal of a political party is to secure political power and hold it either singly or in cooperation with the other political parties. A political party is very much a clientele-oriented organization that is a party has always been on gaining as much clientele as possible and hence it tries to remain as open as possible to its potential members. The party is a mutually exploitative relationship as it is joined by those who would use it. Gabriel Almond defined political party as the socialized aggregation structure of modern societies.

Functions of a Political Party

A political party performs a wide range of functions an important one among them is the aggregation of interests. A political party is multi-interested group that represent diverse interests of the society. It tries to harmonize these interests with each other; bridges antagonism between different groups of the society and thereby seeks to produce different groups of the society and thereby seeks to produce a consensus among as many groups as possible. Political parties act as very effective mediator in setting disagreements in society in a peaceful and institutionalized manner.

A political party ensures a two way communication process between the government and the people as it is mainly through the parties that the government is constantly kept informed about the general demands of the society about the interests and attitudes of the people in relation to the governing process. Similarly it is through the parties organize and articulate public opinion in order to bring this opinion to bear on governmental decisions. They educate and instruct the people on public issues.

These activities of the party are not confined to election time alone but they go on simultaneously. Political recruitment is another function of the political party. In a democracy political elite are recruited mainly through political parties. Leaders of governments are normally leaders of the political parties. The party plays a very significant role in the process of political socialization in a country. Party is a very important instrument for political participation of the people; it is in course of extending the opportunities of this political participation to the people that the party socializes them. The political socialization performed by political parties may however assumes two distinct forms the party may either reinforce the existing political culture or it may try to alter the established political cultural pattern by generating new attitudes and beliefs.

FRENCH AND RAVEN'S FIVE FORMS OF POWER

The most common description of power is French and Raven (1960). This divides power into five different forms.

Coercive Power

This is the power to force someone to do something against their will. It is often physical although other threats may be used. It is the power of dictators, despots and bullies. Coercion can result in physical harm, although its principal goal is compliance. Demonstrations of harm are often used to illustrate what will happen if compliance is not gained. Coercion is also the ultimate power of all governments. Although it is often seen as negative, it is also used to keep the peace. Parents coerce young children who know no better. A person holds back their friend who is about to step out in front of a car.

Other forms of power can also be used in coercive ways, such as when a reward or expertise is withheld or referent power is used to threaten social exclusion.

Reward Power

One of the main reasons we work is for the money we need to conduct our lives. There are many more forms of reward — in fact anything we find desirable can be a reward, from a million dollar yacht to a pat on the back. Reward power is thus the ability to give other people what they want, and hence ask them to do things for you in exchange. Rewards can also be used to punish, such as when they are withheld. The promise is essentially the same: do this and you will get that.

Legitimate Power

Legitimate power is that which is invested in a role. Kings, policemen and managers all have legitimate power. The legitimacy may come from a higher power, often one with coercive power. Legitimate power can often thus be the acceptable face of raw power. A common trap that people in such roles can fall into is to forget that people are obeying the position, not them. When they either fall from power or move onto other things, it can be a puzzling surprise that people who used to fawn at your feet no long do so.

Referent Power

This is the power from another person liking you or wanting to be like you. It is the power of charisma and fame and is wielded by all celebrities (by definition) as well as more local social leaders. In wanting to be like these people, we stand near them, hoping some of the charisma will rub off onto us.

Those with referent power can also use it for coercion. One of the things we fear most is social exclusion, and all it takes is a word from a social leader for us to be shunned by others in the group.

Information Power

While the difference between expert power and information power is subtle, people with this type of power are well-informed, up-to-date and also have the ability to persuade others. Another difference would be that people with Expert Power are perceived by his/her image of expertise to show credibility (i.e. a qualified doctor in a doctor uniform), while one with Information Power does not have a strict need to 'look the part of a professional', but they must keep up to date with new research, and have confidence in debating, or are persuasive.

BASICS OF SOCIAL POWER

Social power is the basic, common element in politics, economics, and all other social relationships. It is possessed by all individuals and social groups and arises out of their connections to each other. Robinson Crusoe, marooned on a desert island, didn't have to deal with it until he met Friday.

Social power has two aspects:

1) The ability to *influence* others so as to further our own interests or desires.
2) The ability to *resist* the activities of others.

In theory it is possible to be socially neutral-to further our own interests or desires in ways which do not affect other people. In practice, however, the vast majority of our activities have some social impact.

SOCIAL POWER IS TRANSMUTABLE AND FLUID

Physical energy can be easily changed from heat into light, motion or electricity by the engineer. Likewise, social power can be changed from one form into another by those who know how to use it. And just as electricity is more easily tranformed than most other forms of physical power, so there are differences in the various forms of social power.

Which form is most transmutable depends on the circumstances. For example, in a war, physical force is probably most transmutable. In highly industrialized, interdependent money economies, financial power is usually the most transmutable. Again like physical energy, social power may be either active or merely latent — like the power in a taut spring or a can of gasoline.

Not infrequently possessors of social power fail to realize what power they have (e.g., India's poor, prior to being organized by Gandhi; or industrial workers prior to being organized into unions; or citizens who don't vote). On the other hand, what *seems* like great social power is often based mainly on bluff, its effectiveness due to the ignorance or false beliefs of those over whom it is exercised. This is most obvious in games like poker, but it is a basic element in all power strategy, whether military, business, or political. This has been a chief reason for the lavish costumes, pageantry and ritual of authoritarian ruling groups throughout history. It's a major reason why *knowledge* is such an important form of power-to reveal the hidden weaknesses and bluffs of powerholders.

POWER DOESN'T COME IN SEPARATE PIECES

One of the commonest mistakes made by those attempting to analyse social power is thinking solely in terms of the *individual forms* of power. In the real social world these interlock and ramify in so many directions that it is almost impossible to isolate them. Social power usually occurs in big chunks, organized into systems or structures of power-family, community, religion, interest group, class, movement, political party, etc.

The individual forms of power are important chiefly as the *instruments of power* strategy, manipulated by competitors for social power as generals manipulate soliders, supplies and weapons.

No one form of power is "best." Forms of power-and strategies for using them-are best chosen in response to specific circumstances. A champion prize fighter wouldn't necessarily have much power in a chess tournament, nor a college president on a battlefield.

The social power possessed by any individual or group cannot be adequately evaluated by the mere sum of individual forms of power possessed-even where they can be added up. With social power, as with most other social phenomena, the whole is often greater (or less) than the sum of its parts, and is often different in kind. When one person becomes wealthy and another poor, there usually develops a greater difference between their relative social power than can be measured solely by their respective fortunes. This social truth underlies the Biblical saying, "To him who hath shall be given; from him who hath not, even that which he hath shall be taken away."

On the other hand, going to the other extreme and lumping all forms of social power together into a single concept such as *social class* also leads to errors of social analysis.

UNDERSTANDING POWER

At the core of the concept of empowerment is the idea of power. The possibility of empowerment depends on two things. First, empowerment requires that power can change. If power cannot change, if it is inherent in positions or people, then empowerment is not possible, nor is empowerment conceivable in any meaningful way. In other words, if power can change, then empowerment is possible. Second, the concept of empowerment depends upon the idea that power can expand. This second point reflects our common experiences of power rather than how we think about power. To clarify these points, we first discuss what we mean by power.

Power is often related to our ability to make others do what we want, regardless of their own wishes or interests (Weber, 1946). Traditional social science emphasizes power as influence and control, often treating power as a commodity or structure divorced from human action (Lips, 1991). Conceived in this way, power can be viewed as unchanging or unchangeable. Weber (1946) gives us a key word beyond this limitation by recognizing that power exists within the context of a relationship between people or things. Power does not exist in isolation nor is it inherent in individuals. By implication, since power is created in relationships, power and power relationships can change. Empowerment as a process of change, then, becomes a meaningful concept.

A brief exercise makes the importance of this discussion clear. Quickly, list three words that immediately come to mind when you hear the word power. For most people, words that come to mind when we think about power often revolve around control and domination. Focusing on these aspects of power limit our ability to understand and define empowerment.

The concept of empowerment also depends upon power that can expand, our second stated requirement. Understanding power as zero-sum, as something that you get at my expense, cuts most of us off from power. A zero-sum conception of power means that power will remain in the hands of the powerful unless they give it up. Although this is certainly one way that power can be experienced, it neglects the way power will remain in the hands of the powerful unless they give it up. Although this is certainly one way that power is experienced, it neglects the way power is experienced in most interactions. Another brief exercise highlights the importance of a definition of power that includes expansion. Answer the question; "Have you ever felt powerful?" Was it at someone's expense? Was it with someone else?

Grounded in an understanding that power will be seen and understood differently by people who inhabit various positions in power structures (Lukes, 199 4), contemporary research on power has opened new perspectives that reflect aspects of power that are not zero-sum, but are shared. Feminists, members of grassroots organizations, racial and ethnic groups, and even individuals in families bring into focus another aspect of power, one that is characterized by collaboration, sharing and mutuality.

Researchers and practitioners call this aspect of power "relational power", generative power (Korten, 1987), "integrative power," and "power with" (Kreisberg, 1992). This aspect means that gaining power actually strengthens the power of others rather than diminishing it such as occurs with domination/power. Kreisberg has suggested that power defined as "the capacity to implement" (Kreisberg, 1992:57) is broad enough to allow power to mean domination, authority, influence, and shared power or "power with." It is this definition of power, as a process that occurs in relationships, that gives us the possibility of empowerment.

Understanding Empowerment

Empowerment is a construct shared by many disciplines and arenas: community development, psychology, education, economics, and studies of social movements and organizations, among others. How empowerment is understood varies among these perspectives. In recent empowerment literature, the meaning of the term empowerment is often assumed rather than explained or defined. Rappoport (1984) has noted that it is easy to define empowerment by its absence but difficult to define in action as it takes on different forms in different people and contexts. Even defining the concept is subject to debate. Zimmerman (1984) has stated that asserting a single definition of empowerment may make attempts to achieve it formulaic or prescription-like, contradicting the very concept of empowerment.

A common understanding of empowerment is necessary, however, to allow us to know empowerment when we see it in people with whom we are working, and for program evaluation. According to Bailey (1992), how we precisely define empowerment within our projects and programs will depend upon the specific people and context involved.

As a general definition, however, we suggest that empowerment is a multi-dimensional social process that helps people gain control over their own lives. It is a process that fosters power (that is, the capacity to implement) in people, for use in their own lives, their communities, and in their society, by acting on issues that they define as important.

We suggest that three components of our definition are basic to any understanding of empowerment. Empowerment is multi-dimensional, social, and a process. It is multi-dimensional in that it occurs within sociological, psychological, economic, and other dimensions. Empowerment also occurs at various levels, such as individual, group, and community. Empowerment, by definition, is a social process, since it occurs in relationship to others. Empowerment is a process that is similar to a path or journey, one that develops as we work through it. Other aspects of empowerment may vary according to the specific context and people involved, but these remain constant. In addition, one important implication of this definition of empowerment is that the individual and community are fundamentally connected.

Interconnection of Individuals and Community

Wilson (1996) pointed out that recently, more researchers, organizers, politicians and employers recognize that individual change is a prerequisite for community and social change and empowerment. This does not mean that we can point the finger at those with less access to power, telling them that they must change to become more like "us" in order to be powerful/successful. Rather, individual change becomes a bridge to community connectedness and social change (Wilson, 1996).

To create change we must change individually to enable us to become partners in solving the complex issues facing us. In collaborations based on mutual respect, diverse perspectives, and a developing vision, people work toward creative and realistic solutions. This synthesis of individual and collective change is our understanding of an empowerment process. We see this inclusive individual and collective understanding of empowerment as crucial in programs with empowerment as a goal. It is in the critical transition, or interconnection, between the individual and the communal, or social, that programs such as ours, People Empowering People, can be invaluable for people and communities.

Empowerment and PEP

The People Empowering People (PEP) program uses the definition of empowerment to connect research, theory, and practice. The Connecticut PEP program builds on theory of critical adult education developed by Friere (1970), Horton (1989), and others. PEP focuses on the strengths of people, providing opportunities and resources for people to gain experiences and skills while they also gain control over their lives.

Underlying this process is mutual respect between participants, facilitators, advisory committee members, and others involved in the program. PEP opens to participants the recognition of their own values and beliefs, and encourages expression of their own issues as they define them. The focus is on the connection between individual action and community action, encouraging individual change through training sessions and discussions, and supporting community action through participants' efforts to change their communities. While we cannot give people power and we cannot make them "empowered," we can provide the opportunities, resources and support that they need to become involved themselves.

In conclusion, we see empowerment as a multi-dimensional social process that helps people gain control over their own lives. It is a process that fosters power in people for use in their own lives, their communities, and in their society by acting on issues that they define as important. In PEP as in Extension we strive to teach people skills and knowledge that will motivate them to take steps to improve their own lives — to be empowered.

5

Importance of Empowerment Process

Empowerment refers to increasing the spiritual, political, social, or economic strength of individuals and communities. It often involves the empowered developing confidence in their own capacities.

Definitions

The term empowerment covers a vast landscape of meanings, interpretations, definitions and disciplines ranging from psychology and philosophy to the highly commercialized self-help industry and motivational sciences. Sociological empowerment often addresses members of groups that social discrimination processes have excluded from decision-making processes through-for example-discrimination based on disability, race, ethnicity, religion, or gender. Empowerment as a methodology is often associated with feminism: see consciousness-raising.

Marginalization and Empowerment

"Marginalized" refers to the overt or covert trends within societies whereby those perceived as lacking desirable traits or deviating from the group norms tend to be excluded by wider society and ostracized as undesirables. Sometimes groups are marginalized by society at large, but governments are often unwitting or enthusiastic participants. For example, the U.S. government marginalized cultural minorities, particularly blacks, prior to the Civil Rights Act of 1964. This Act made it illegal to restrict access to schools and public places based on race. Equal opportunity laws which actively oppose such marginalization, allow increased empowerment to occur. They are also a symptom of minorities' and women's empowerment through lobbying. Marginalized people who have no opportunities for self-sufficiency become, at a minimum, dependent on charity, or welfare. They lose their self-confidence because they cannot be fully self-supporting. The opportunities denied them also deprive them of the pride of accomplishment which others, who have those opportunities, can develop for themselves. This in turn can lead to psychological, social and even mental health problems.

Empowerment is then the process of obtaining these basic opportunities for marginalized people, either directly by those people, or through the help of non-marginalized others who share their own access to these opportunities. It also includes actively thwarting attempts to deny those opportunities. Empowerment also includes encouraging, and developing the skills for, self-sufficiency, with a focus on eliminating the future need for charity or welfare in the individuals of the group. This process can be difficult to start and to implement effectively, but there are many examples of empowerment projects which have succeeded.

One empowerment strategy is to assist marginalized people to create their own nonprofit organization, using the rationale that only the marginalized people, themselves, can know what their own people need most, and that control of the organization by outsiders can actually help to further entrench marginalization. Charitable organizations lead from outside of the community, for example, can disempower the community by entrenching a dependence on charity or welfare. A nonprofit organization can target strategies that cause structural changes, reducing the need for ongoing dependence. Red Cross, for example, can focus on improving the health of indigenous people, but does not have authority in its charter to install water-delivery and purification systems, even though the lack of such a system profoundly, directly and negatively impacts health. A nonprofit composed of the indigenous people, however, could ensure their own organization does have such authority and could set their own agendas, make their own plans, seek the needed resources, do as much of the work as they can, and take responsibility-and credit-for the success of their projects (or the consequences, should they fail).

Numerous critical perspectives exist that propose that an empowerment paradigm is present, Clark (2008) showed that whilst there was a degree of autonomy provided by empowerment, it also made way for extended surveillance and control, hence the contradiction perspective (Fardini, 2001).

Women Empowerment

The empowerment of women, also called gender empowerment, has become a significant topic of discussion in regards to development and economics. Entire nations, businesses, communities, and groups can benefit from the implementation of programs and policies that adopt the notion of women empowerment. Empowerment is one of the main procedural concerns when addressing human rights and development. The Human Development and Capabilities Approach, The Millennium Development Goals, and other credible approaches/goals point to empowerment and participation as a necessary step if a country is to overcome the obstacles associated with poverty and development.

Measuring Gender Empowerment

Gender empowerment can be measured through the Gender Empowerment Measure, or the GEM. The GEM shows women's participation in a given nation, both politically and economically. Gem is calculated by tracking "the share of seats in parliament held by women; of female legislators, senior officials and managers; and of female profession and technical workers; and the gender disparity in earned income, reflecting economic independence." It then ranks countries given this information. Other measures that take into account the importance of female participation and equality include: the Gender Parity Index and the Gender-related Development Index (GDI),

Ways to Empower Women

One way to deploy the empowerment of women is through land rights. Land rights offer a key way to economically empower women, giving them the confidence they need to tackle gender inequalities. Often, women in developing nations are legally restricted from their land on the sole basis of gender. They encounter tremendous barriers to claim the land that should rightfully be theirs. Having a right to their land also gives women a sort of bargaining power that they wouldn't normally have, in turn; they gain the ability to assert themselves in various aspects of their life, both in and outside of the home. Another way to provide women empowerment is to allocate responsibilities to them that normally belong to men. When women have economic empowerment, it is a way for others to see them as equal members of society. Through this, they achieve more self-respect and confidence by their contributions to their communities.

Simply including women as a part of a community can have sweeping positive effects. In a study conducted by Bina Agarwal, women were given a place in a forest conservation group. Not only did this drive up the efficiency of the group, but the women gained incredible self-esteem while others, including men, viewed them with more respect.

Participation, which can be seen and gained in a variety of ways, has been argued to be the most beneficial form of gender empowerment. Political participation, be it the ability to vote and voice opinions, or the ability to run for office with a fair chance of being elected, plays a huge role in the empowerment of peoples. However, participation is not limited to the realm of politics. It can include participation in the household, in schools, and the ability to make choices for oneself. It can be said that these latter participations need to be achieved before one can move onto broader political participation. When women have the agency to do what she wants, a higher equality between men and women is established. It is argued that Microcredit also offers a way to provide empowerment for women. Governments, organizations, and individuals have caught hold of the lure of microfinance. They hope that lending money and credit allows women to function in business and society, which in turn empowers them to do more in their communities. One of the primary goals in the foundation of microfinance was women empowerment. Loans with low interest rates are given to women in developing communities in hopes that they can start a small business and provide for her family.

It should be said, however, that the success and efficiency of microcredit and microloans is controversial and constantly debated

Economic Benefits

Most women across the globe rely on the informal work sector for an income. If women were empowered to do more and be more, the possibility for economic growth becomes apparent. Eliminating half of a nation's work force on the sole basis of gender can have detrimental effects on the economy of that nation. In addition, female participation in counsels, groups, and businesses is seen to increase efficiency. For a general idea on how an empowered women can impact a situation monetarily, a study found that of fortune 500 companies, "those with more women board directors had significantly higher financial returns, including 53 percent higher returns on equity, 24 percent higher returns on sales and 67 percent higher returns on invested capital (OECD, 2008)." This study shows the impact women can have on the overall economic benefits of a company. If implemented on a global scale, the inclusion of women in the formal workforce (like a fortune 500 company) can increase the economic output of a nation.

Barriers

Many of the barriers to women empowerment and equity lie ingrained into the cultures of certain nations and societies. Many women feel these pressures, while others have become accustomed to being treated inferior to men. Even if men, legislators, NGOs, etc. are aware of the benefits women empowerment and participation can have, many are scared of disrupting the status quo and continue to let societal norms get in the way of development.

The Process of Empowerment

The process which enables individuals/groups to fully access personal/collective power, authority and influence, and to employ that strength when engaging with other people, institutions or society. In other words, "Empowerment is not giving people power, people already have plenty of power, in the wealth of their knowledge and motivation, to do their jobs magnificently. We define empowerment as letting this power out (Blanchard,

K)." It encourages people to gain the skills and knowledge that will allow them to overcome obstacles in life or work environment and ultimately, help them develop within themselves or in the society.

Empowerment includes the following, or similar, capabilities:-

- The ability to make decisions about personal/collective circumstances
- The ability to access information and resources for decision-making
- Ability to consider a range of options from which to choose (not just yes/no, either/or.)
- Ability to exercise assertiveness in collective decision making
- Having positive-thinking about the ability to make change
- Ability to learn and access skills for improving personal/ collective circumstance.
- Ability to inform others' perceptions though exchange, education and engagement.
- Involving in the growth process and changes that is never ending and self-initiated
- Increasing one's positive self-image and overcoming stigma
- Increasing one's ability in discreet thinking to sort out right and wrong.

Workplace Empowerment

One account of the history of workplace empowerment in the United States recalls the clash of management styles in railroad construction in the American West in the mid-19th century, where "traditional" hierarchical East-Coast models of control encountered individualistic pioneer workers, strongly supplemented by methods of efficiency-oriented "worker responsibility" brought to the scene by Chinese laborers. In this case, empowerment at the level of work teams or brigades achieved a notable (but short-lived) demonstrated superiority. Empowerment in the workplace is regarded by critics as more a pseudo-empowerment exercise, the idea of which is to change the attitudes of workers, so as to make them work harder rather than giving them any real power, and Wilkinson (1998) refers to this as "attitudinal shaping". However, recent research suggests that the opportunity to exercise personal discretion/ choice (and complete meaningful work) is an important element contributing to employee engagement and well-being. There is evidence that initiative and motivation are increased when people have a more positive attributional style. This influences self-belief, resilience when faced with setbacks, and the ability to visualize oneself overcoming problems. The implication is that 'empowerment' suits some more than others, and should be positioned in the broader and wider context of an 'enabling' work environment.

Empowerment to employees in the work place provides them with opportunities penda to make their own decisions with regards to their tasks. Now-a-days more and more bosses and managers are practicing the concept of empowerment among their subordinates to provide them with better opportunities.

In Management

In the book Empowerment Takes More Than a Minute, the authors, Ken Blanchard, John P. Carlos, and Alan Randolph, illustrate three simple keys that organizations can use to effectively open the knowledge, experience, and motivation power that people already have. The three keys are that managers must use to empower their employees are: share information with everyone, create autonomy through boundaries and replace the old hierarchy with self-managed teams.

Share information with everyone – this is the first key to empowering people within an organization. By sharing information with everyone, you are giving them a clear picture of the company and its current situation. Another strong point that this brings is trust; by allowing all of the employees to view the company information, it helps to build that trust between employer and employee. Create autonomy through boundaries – this is the second key to empowerment which also builds upon the previous one. By opening communication through sharing information, it opens up the feedback about what is holding them back from being empowered. Replace the old hierarchy with self-managed teams – this is the third and final key to empowerment which ties them all together. By replacing the old hierarchy with self-managed teams, more responsibility is placed upon unique and self-managed teams which create better communication and productivity.

DEFINITIONS AND USAGE OF EMPOWERMENT

The word.empowerment. is used in many different contexts and by many different organisations. For example, literature about.empowerment. is found in the fields of education, social work, psychology, in US radical politics in the 1960s and community development groups in the North and South, as well as in the work of feminist and development organisations.

There are a variety of understandings of the term empowerment due to its widespread usage. Although the term is often used in development work, it is rarely defined. The different ways empowerment has been described or qualified, with particular reference to women.s empowerment. The idea of.power. is at the root of the term empowerment. Power can be understood as operating in a number of different ways:

Power Over: This power involves an either/or relationship of domination/subordination. Ultimately, it is based on socially sanctioned threats of violence and intimidation, it requires constant vigilance to maintain, and it invites active and passive resistance;

- *power to*: This power relates to having decision-making authority, power to solve problems and can be creative and enabling;
- *power with:* This power involves people organising with a common purpose or common understanding to achieve collective goals;
- *power within:* This power refers to self confidence, self awareness and assertiveness. It relates to how can individuals can recognise through analysing their experience how power operates in their lives, and gain the confidence to act to influence and change this. (Williams *et al*, 1994).

Whilst understanding of power and empowerment have come from many different movements and traditions, the feminist movement has emphasised collective organisation (.power with.) and has been influential in developing ideas about.power within..

Power must be understood as working at different levels, including the institutional, the household and the individual. For some theorists power is a zero-sum: one group.s increase in power necessarily involves another.s loss of power. The idea of a redistribution of power is therefore seen as necessarily involving conflict. In this perspective, women.s empowerment would lead by implication to less power for men. Some feminist writers on power have challenged the idea that power must necessarily involve domination by some, and obedience or oppression of others. Men would also benefit from the results of women.s empowerment with the chance to live in a more equitable society and explore new roles. The kinds of power described above as power-to, power-with and power-within can be developed as alternatives to powerover. For example DAWN2 state:

The women.s movement...at its deepest it is not an effort to play "catch-up" with the competitive, aggressive "dog-eat-dog" spirit of the dominant system. It is rather, an attempt to convert men and the system to the sense of responsibility, nurturance, openness, and rejection of hierarchy that are part of our vision.

PERSPECTIVES ON EMPOWERMENT

The Human Development Report 1995, stresses that empowerment is about participation:

Empowerment. Development must be *by* people, not only *for* them. People must participate fully in the decisions and processes that shape their lives. (UN, 1995 b: 12) but at the same time promotes a rather instrumentalist view of empowerment; Investing in women.s capabilities and empowering them to exercise their choices is not only valuable in itself but is also the surest way to contribute to economic growth and overall development (UN, 1995b: iii) For Oxfam, empowerment is about challenging oppression and inequality: Empowerment involves challenging the forms of oppression which compel millions of people to play a part in their society on terms which are inequitable, or in ways which deny their human rights (Oxfam, 1995). Feminist activists stress that women.s empowerment is not about replacing one form of empowerment with another:

Women.s empowerment should lead to the liberation of men from false value systems and ideologies of oppression. It should lead to a situation where each one can become a whole being regardless of gender, and use their fullest potential to construct a more humane society for all.

Jo Rowlands points out that empowerment is a bottom-up process and cannot be bestowed from the top down: The outside professional cannot expect to control the outcomes of authentic of empowerment being given by one group to another hides an attempt to keep control.

From this multi-dimensional definition of power, it is evident that empowerment has several different and inter-related aspects. Empowerment is not only about opening up access to decision making, but also must include processes that lead people to perceive themselves as able and entitled to occupy that decision-making space (Rowlands, 1995). Empowerment is sometimes described as being about the ability to make choices, but it must also involve being able to shape what choices are on offer. Empowerment corresponds to women challenging existing power structures which subordinate women. As such, what is seen as empowering in one context may not be in another.

Empowerment in Gender Equality Discourse

The current popularity of the term empowerment in development coincides with recent questioning of the efficacy of central planning and the role of.the state., and moves by donor governments and multilateral funding agencies to embrace NGOs as partners in development. Political and institutional problems have gained prominence on the development agenda with a focus on human rights, good governance and participation.

Recent UN conferences have advocated that women.s empowerment is central to development. The United Nations Conference on Environment and Development (UNCED) Agenda 21 mentions women's advancement and empowerment in decision-making, including women's participation in national and international ecosystem management and control of environment degradation as a key area for sustainable development (quoted in Wee and Heyzer, 1995: 7). The International Conference on Population and Development (ICPD) in Cairo, discussed the population issue not just as a technical, demographic problem, but as a choice that women should be empowered to take within the context of their health and reproductive rights.

The Copenhagen Declaration of the World Summit on Social Development (WSSD), called for the recognition that empowering people, particularly women, to strengthen their own capacities is a main objective of development, and that empowerment requires the full participation of people in the formulation, implementation and evaluation of decisions determining the functioning and well-being of societies. The Report of the UN Fourth World Conference on Women called its Platform for Action an agenda for women's empowerment meaning that the principle of shared power and responsibility should be established between women and men at home, in the workplace and in the wider national and international communities..

The empowerment approach to women in development offers a number of attractions for development agencies over the other approaches. Because its origins are often stated as being from the South, it may appeal to Northern development institutions who wish to avoid charges of cultural imperialism, especially in relation to gender policies. The bottom-up characterisation of the empowerment approach can be regarded as more in tune with the growing interest in participatory forms of development. Current enthusiasm for NGOs, for bottom up development and for empowerment, from both advocates within development organisations and from outside activists, can also be understood as a reaction to the frustrating experience of attempts to institutionalise gender in mainstream development policies and programmes.

The empowerment approach which has its origins in feminist and third world organisations, emphasises the collective (.power with.) dimensions of empowerment.

FEMINIST VISION OF DEVELOPMENT

Development Alternatives for Women in New Era (DAWN) is a network of Southern activists, researchers and policymakers, which is closely associated with the development of ideas about women's empowerment. Founded in the mid-1980s, DAWN has questioned the impact of development on the poor, especially women, and advocated the need for alternative development processes that would give primary emphasis to the basic needs and survival of the majority of the worlds people. DAWN has sought to link micro-level activities from the experience of grassroots initiatives at community level, to a macro-level perspective. They challenge the assumption behind many projects and programmes targeting women, that the main problem for Third World women is insufficient participation in an otherwise benevolent process of growth and development. DAWN argue the need for a new vision of development based on the perspective of poor Third World women. This perspective focuses attention on the related problems of poverty and inequality and the critical dimensions of resource use and abuse.

DAWN stress the importance of women's organisations in demanding and promoting change towards their vision of society, and to create the political will for serious action by those in power. It is not just individuals but organisations which are the focus of empowerment processes. The core activities proposed necessary to help bring about change are political mobilisation, legal changes, consciousness raising and popular education. For DAWN, then, empowerment of poor women is central to their overall vision of development and has implications not just for the types of activity they promote but also for organisational structures and procedures: Empowerment of organisations, individuals and movements has certain requisites. These include resources (finance, knowledge, technology), skills training and leadership formation on the one side; and democratic processes, dialogue, participation in policy and decision making and techniques for conflict resolution on the other...Within organisations, open and democratic processes are essential in empowering women to withstand the social and family pressures that result from their participation. Thus the long-term viability of the organisation, and the growing autonomy and control by poor women over their lives, are linked through the organisations own internal processes of shared responsibility and decision-making.

However, the meaning of empowerment can be seen to have altered as it has gained currency in mainstream development discourse. In this context, empowerment is often envisaged as individual rather than as collective, and focused on entrepreneurship and individual self-reliance, rather than on co-operation to challenge power structures which subordinate women (or other marginalised groups). This individualistic approach to empowerment fits together with the belief in entrepreneurial capitalism and market forces as the main saviours of sickly or backward economies, and with the current trend for limiting state provision of welfare, services and employment (Young, 1993). It is also consonant with a liberal approach to democracy, emphasising individual rights and participation in decisionmaking, through the electoral process.

Empowerment as a Process

Empowerment is essentially a bottom-up process rather than something that can be formulated as a top-down strategy. Understanding empowerment in this way means that development agencies cannot claim to empower women.. Women must empower themselves. Devising coherent policies and programmes for women's empowerment requires careful attention, because external agencies/bodies tend to be positioned with power-over target populations. The training of development professionals, in government, NGOs or donor agencies does not always equip them to consult and involve others, which supporting empowerment requires.

Appropriate external support and intervention, however, can be important to foster and support the process of empowerment. Development organisations can, under some circumstances, play an enabling or facilitating role. They can ensure that their programmes work to support women's individual empowerment by encouraging women's participation, acquisition of skills, decision-making capacity, and control over resources. Agencies can support women's collective empowerment by funding women's organisations which work to address the causes of gender subordination, by promoting women's participation in political systems, and by fostering dialogue between those in positions of power and organisations with women's empowerment goals.

However, caution should be exercised against assuming that promoting a certain type of activity will necessary lead to empowerment., as will be illustrated in section 2. Empowerment cannot be defined in terms of specific activities or end results because it involves a process whereby women can freely analyse, develop and voice their needs and interests, without them being pre-defined, or imposed from above, by planners or other social actors. The assumption that planners can identify women's needs runs against empowerment objectives which imply that women themselves formulate and decide what these interests are. Planning suggests a top-down approach, and yet women may define their interests differently from planners (Wierenga, 1994).

Planners working towards an empowerment approach must therefore develop ways of enabling women themselves to critically assess their own situation and create and shape a transformation in society. To some extent this may run against the logic of planning., because the content of such a transformation cannot be determined by planners in advance, if it is to be truly empowering to women. Wierenga (*ibid.*) argues that this transformation should be seen as part of an ongoing process rather than as a fixed goal in the distant future.

This book examines the role of development agencies and organisations in processes of women's empowerment. Section two examines the empowerment approach in the policy and practice of gender equality initiatives in development organisations. Section three surveys different indicators that have been devised to assess women's empowerment. Section four draws out policy implications from the earlier discussion and proposes strategies for promoting women's empowerment.

EMPOWERMENT PROCESS

Empowerment is a process by which we increase the capacity of an individual or group in order to enable them to make choices and for them to transform their choices into the desired actions. These actions help build collective and individual assets and improve and as a result the efficiency of use of these assets is improved.

Rapport (1984) states that employee Empowerment is the process of unleashing an individuals potential and enhancing his abilities to nurture growth in the organisation, therefore empowerment involves a process by which an individual is provided with proper information regarding performance of the organisation. In an organisation empowerment is important in that it helps remove the feeling of powerlessness through enhancement of self efficiency of the individual. It therefore enables the individuals to coupe with problems that face them. Empowerment can be defined as the process, by which we can increase the capacity of an individual or a group in order for them to make their own choices which will lead to increased productivity in an organisation,

Empowerment enables or gives authority to an individual to take action and take control of his work by making decisions on his own. The organisation in which the individual works is therefore has a responsibility to enable the existence of an environment which helps the employee to undertake their tasks in an empowered manner. The organisation also has to remove any barriers that limit the process of empowerment.

Valuing Employees: This involves appreciating workers by managers or executive members in an organisation, this will aid in the process of showing that you appreciate and value them for the work they perform in the organisation and this helps in empowering workers. This is achieved through the words used in communicating with workers and also body language and fiscal expressions which should show appreciation to workers. (Thomas (1990))

Sharing Visions: According to Narayan (2002) Employees are also empowered by sharing information on the company's vision and objectives. This helps the employees to feel they are part of something big. Therefore the organisation should share the mission and the strategic plans of the organisation and this helps empowering workers, therefore communication of organisation goals and strategies plays an important part in employee empowerment process.

Direction and Goal Sharing with Workers: Sharing goals and directions according to Narayan (2002) is also a way to empower workers, This involves sharing information with workers on the goals and also the direction of the organisation, this involves sharing information on observable and measurable goals and this aids in empowering workers in accomplishing these goals.

Trust: The organisation should extend trust to their employees whereby they will allow workers to make their own decisions which may not be in line with the decided way of performing tasks. This is according to Rapport (1984) and it is a way in which trust is extended to workers which aids in empowering them.

Provision of decision making information: This involves the provision of information to employees that will help them make decisions on their own, this involves making sure that all workers have access to this information and this will help them to make sound decisions as they perform their tasks.

Involvement of workers in decision making: This involves including workers in decision making of the organisation, this helps in empowering workers because they will find a sense of power in the organisation future and they will have a felling of worth in the organisation. (Thomas (1990))

Feedbacks: It is important to frequently provide feedback to employees to show how they have performed in the organisation for a given period, this ensures that the employees feel a sense of recognition and also helps them develop their skills and knowledge. (Thomas (1990))

Solving problems: When problems occurs there is a need for the organisation to implement ways in which to deal with these problems, it is not right to blame the workers and instead of blaming them there is need to address the problem by asking the workers what problem is in the work system and not what is wrong with the workers. (Thomas (1990))

Communication: An organisation should ensure that it listens to its workers and at the same time provide guidelines to them. The organisation should avoid telling the workers what to do but should provide guidelines on how to undertake tasks and what should be done to accomplish organisational goals. (Rapport (1984))

Social reinforcements: This involves giving encouragement to workers for the purpose of boosting their self confidence in the work place, this involves giving praise and rewarding workers for their achievement and this aids in the empowerment process.(Rapport (1984))

Training: Training and the provision of information is a major way in which an organisation can empower its workers, this is because information itself is power, and this should also be accompanied by proper communication channels in the organisation. As workers receive more training they experience an increase in their skills and knowledge and this will increase their confidence when undertaking their tasks. (Kreisberg (1999))

Emotional support: An organisation should also provide emotional support to its workers as a form of empowerment. This process should be accomplished through clear role definition of employees and also providing assistance at work and encouraging team work in the work place to solve problems that face workers such anxiety and stress. (Rapport (1984))

IMPORTANCE OF EMPOWERMENT PROCESS

Employee plays a major role in the success of an organisation. Many organisations today have adopted these strategies that help them achieve growth and success in their business undertakings, the importance of employee importance include:

Positive Environment

Employee empowerment leads to the creation of a positive environment in the workplace; this will lead to increased productivity and boost employee morale, as a result the organisation gains due to increased productivity and efficiency in the workplace. Employee empowerment will increase employees learning, growth, improvement and enhancement of performance ability.

Creativity: Empowerment involves letting employees make decision on their own and also solve problems, this increases their creativity and also improve the working environment, and this encourages a positive working environment where employees are in a position to become more creative and productive to the organisation.

Productivity: Empowerment ensures that the employees perform their tasks in the most effective way that saves time and energy, as a result the employees become more productive than in an organisation does not empower its workers, as a result there is increased productivity of the workers which will benefit the organisation. (Rapport (1984))

Motivation: Employee empowerment will motivate workers which will in turn increase employee productivity, motivation as a result of empowerment will increase commitment by employees and As a result the employee will more satisfied with work.

Team Work : Empowerment will encourage team work and as a result there will increase motivation to undertake tasks

Conflicts: It will reduce conflicts between managers and workers; also there will be a decline in the demand for supervisors and administrators reducing the cost of production in the organisation resulting to increased competitive advantage of the organisation over its competitors. Also the involvement of workers in the decision making process will increase the possibility of workers agreeing to changes in the organisation. (Kreisberg (1999))

More skilled workers: Through empowerment the employees become more skilled through education and training offered by the organisation, this will lead to increased employee productivity, employees will also increase competence as a result of training offered.

Disadvantages

Empowerment in the organisation is important however there exist some disadvantages that arise as a result of employee empowerment and they include:

Increased costs: The organisation may experience a rise of costs as a result of training and educating workers, an organisation has to invest in the training and education of its workers and as a result there will be increased costs.

Abuse of power: Some of the organisation workers may abuse the power given to them, this include making decisions that may not be in line with the objectives of the organisation and may use the power to meet their own needs, also the responsibility that the employees are given may be too much a responsibility to some workers. (Kreisberg (1999)).

Time wastage: There may be time wastage in an organisation where time may be spent in groups and committees that are important in the process of empowerment and this will reduce the total time the employees spend undertaking their tasks.

Conflicts: Employees may tend to struggle for power among them as a result of group work, every worker may tend to acquire power on what should be done and how it should be done, for this reason therefore empowerment may result to conflicts among workers. (Kreisberg (1999))

Decisions: The employees may not have the ability to make appropriate decisions that are important in the organisation, therefore the decisions made by the employees may be biased, decisions may conflict where employees will make personal decisions rather than use logical reasoning to make decisions.

Empowerment unleashes an individuals potential and enhancing his abilities to nurture growth in the organisation, it gives authority to an individual to take action and take control of his work by making decisions on his own. The organisation should therefore make an enabling environment which helps the employee to undertake their tasks in an empowered manner by removing any barriers that limit the process of empowerment.

Empowerment involves Valuing employees, Sharing information and visions of the organisation, giving Direction and goal sharing with workers, enhancing Trust, Involvement of workers in decision making, training workers, provision of emotional support to workers and proper communication channels in the organisation.

Importance of empowerment include the creation of a positive environment at work, promotes Creativity, increased worker Productivity, increased motivation of workers, encouragement of team work, reduced conflicts and more skilled workers as a result of training.

Despite the many advantages of empowerment there exist disadvantages which include increased costs in the organisation due to training, there may occur Abuse of power by workers, time wastage in groups and committees, increased Conflicts among workers and the inability of workers to make right decisions at work.

However empowerment should be encouraged in an organisation through adoption of changes in decision making in order to increase the organisations productivity. There are many advantages associated with empowerment and this will aid in the achievement of organisation goals and objectives. The organisation however needs to implement ways in which the disadvantages that occur due to empowerment are avoided in order to achieve smooth running of the organisation that empowers workers.

IMPLICATIONS FOR THEORY AND PRACTICE OF EMPOWERMENT

The concept of empowerment is of increasing interest to researchers, practitioners and citizens concerned about mental health issues. In some respects, empowerment is a new buzzword. As Edelman (1977) has noted in relation to language and the politics of human services, sometimes new language is used to describe the same old practices. Others believe that empowerment language can actually lead to raised awareness (Rappaport, 1986). Regardless, a growing number of people are searching to understand the meaning of empowerment and ways it can be used to change their settings and lives.

Empowerment can begin to be understood by examining the concepts of power and powerlessness (Moscovitch and Drover, 1981). Power is defined by the Cornell Empowerment Group as the "capacity of some persons and organizations to produce intended, foreseen and unforeseen effects on others". There are many sources of power. Personality, property/wealth, and influential organizations have been identified by Galbraith (1983) as critical sources of power in the last part of this century. Others have pointed out that the class-dominated nature of our society means that a small number of people have vast economic or political power, while the majority have little or none.

At the individual level, powerlessness can be seen as the expectation of the person that his/her own actions will be ineffective in influencing the outcome of life events (Keiffer, 1984). Lerner (1986) makes a distinction between real and surplus powerlessness. Real powerlessness results from economic inequities and oppressive control exercised by systems and other people. Surplus powerlessness, on the other hand, is an internalized belief that change cannot occur, a belief which results in apathy and an unwillingness of the person to struggle for more control and influence. Powerlessness has, over the years, come to be viewed as an objective phenomenon, where people with little or no political and economic power lack the means to gain greater control and resources in their lives (Albee, 1981). As an illustration of powerlessness, Asch (1986) has noted that generally people with disabilities;... have so internalized the general negative attitudes towards them because of their disabilities that they cannot believe that collective action can improve their lives. They have seen the problems as inherent in their medical conditions and have not been urged to join others to demand structural changes that would render the environment useful for them.

Most of the literature also associates empowerment with personal control. Rappaport (1987) points out that "by empowerment I mean our aim should be to enhance the possibilities for people to control their own lives". Cochran (1986) believes that people understand their own needs far better than anyone else and as a result should have the power both to define and act upon them. The Ottawa Charter for Health Promotion notes that "people cannot achieve their fullest health potential unless they are able take control of those things which determine their health".

Increasingly, empowerment is being understood as a process of change. McClelland (1975) has suggested that in order for people to take power, they need to gain information about themselves and their environment and be willing to identify and work with others for change. In a similar vein, Whitmore (1988) defines empowerment as: an interactive process through which people experience personal and social change, enabling them to take action to achieve influence over the organizations and institutions which affect their lives and the communities in which they live.

Keiffer's (1984) work on personal empowerment is one of the only major empirical studies which examines personal empowerment as a process. He labels empowerment as a developmental process which includes four stages: entry, advancement, incorporation, and commitment. The entry stage appears to be motivated by the participant's experience of some event or condition threatening to the self or family, what Keiffer refers to as an act of 'provocation'. In the advancement stage, there are three major aspects which are important to continuing the empowerment process: a mentoring relationship; supportive peer relationships with a collective organization; and the development of a more critical understanding of social and political relations. The central focus of the third stage appears to be the development of a growing political consciousness. Commitment is the final stage-one in which the participants apply the new participatory competence to ever expanding areas of their lives. According to Wallerstein (1992), empowerment is a social-action process that promotes participation of people, organizations, and communities towards the goals of increased individual and community control, political efficacy, improved quality of community life, and social justice. While Whitmore (1988) feels the concept of empowerment needs to be more clearly defined, she states that there are some common underlying assumptions:

a) individuals are assumed to understand their own needs better than anyone else and therefore should have the power both to define and act upon them.
b) all people possess strengths upon which they can build.
c) empowerment is a lifelong endeavour.
d) personal knowledge and experience are valid and useful in coping effectively.

For the purpose of this study, empowerment was defined as *processes whereby* individuals achieve increasing control of various aspects of their lives and participate in the community with dignity.

Rappaport's (1987) concept of empowerment, "conveys both a psychological sense of personal control or influence and a concern with actual social influence, political power and legal rights". In this sense, empowerment can exist at three levels: at the personal level, where empowerment is the experience of gaining increasing control and influence in daily life and community participation (Keiffer, 1984); at the small group level, where empowerment involves the shared experience, analysis, and influence of groups on their own efforts; and at the community level, where empowerment revolves around the utilization of resources and strategies to enhance community control (Labonte, 1989).

While this current study was focused primarily on the personal level, it is important to note that it is difficult to clearly separate the three levels of empowerment; indeed, the three levels are highly interactive. Understanding individual change and empowerment informs community empowerment strategies and policy and vice versa. As a result, it is important that research on empowerment begin with an understanding of individuals, not in a clinical sense, but in an experiential sense (Lord, 1991). This means that understanding empowerment is complex and ecological. This study on empowerment looked at the "person in the environment" by trying to understand the lived experience of citizens in relation to family, groups, and other aspects of community life.

Purpose of the Research

The purpose of the research was to understand the process of personal empowerment as experienced by individuals who were currently involved in the struggle to become empowered. Specifically, the goals of the study were to:

1. document the participants' early and current experiences of devaluation and powerlessness in their personal, social, and community lives.
2. explore the transition from powerlessness to empowerment, including personal qualities, experiences, and elements which people indicated were helpful to them as they gained more control and increased participation in their lives.

3. analyse the meaning of people's life experiences, both of powerlessness and the empowerment process.

METHODS

Forty-one men and women who had experienced extensive powerlessness in their lives were selected as the research participants. Using qualitative interviews, this study was designed to understand participants' lived experience "from their own point of view", as they struggled to reduce personal powerlessness and dependency. This qualitative approach has provided an in-depth examination of the process of people's transition toward increased control in their lives.

The research team used four main approaches to study the process of personal empowerment: an extensive literature review; interviews with a number of key informants; in-depth biographical interviews with people who had experienced extensive powerlessness in their lives; and focused group interviews in order to gain further reflections on the initial findings from the biographical interviews.

Participants

Key informants. Eight key informants, four women and four men, came from several different areas such as the disability movement, the health promotion field, and human services. All the key informants were people with a vast array of experience and leadership who were assumed to have a strong sense of the meaning of personal empowerment. The ideas expressed by these individuals were used to assist the researchers in sorting out issues and concepts related to empowerment. Key informants also helped to identify the research participants for the biographical interviews.

People experiencing powerlessness. The researchers conducted in-depth biographical interviews with 24 women and 17 men. Participants were selected from five main groups: individuals with developmental handicaps from three communities (n=12); individuals with physical disabilities from birth from four communities (n=10); individuals with physical disabilities acquired later in life from two communities (n=5); individuals from two communities who were consumers/survivors of mental health services (n=6); and women from three communities who were identified as having been poor and disempowered, but are now involved in a process of empowerment (n=8). In the disability groups, men and women were divided equally and ranged in age from 21 to 67, with the average age being 42. Most of the individuals in the disability groups had lived in an institutional setting for part of their lives. At the time of the study, everyone with a disability was living in the community, either in small group homes, on their own, or with a friend or partner and more than half were employed. None of the participants were members of visible minorities.

Focus groups. Four small focus group interviews were conducted with fourteen (eight women and six men) additional people with disabilities, all of whom were chosen in the same way as the original group. They were interviewed to gain their reflections on the preliminary research patterns and themes from the biographical interviews. This group process verified and strengthened our initial findings.

Data Collection

The frameworks of qualitative research and biographical analysis were used to guide the research process. Most interviews were done in people's homes. All interviews were taped and transcribed verbatim and supplemented by field notes (Patton, 1990). Following the initial data analysis of the individual interviews, researchers returned to the field and conducted the focus group interviews. The data was analyzed in the tradition of qualitative research. A five step qualitative analysis process was designed to ensure that patterns and themes which might emerge from the data could be carefully verified. These included: *transcribing* the notes from the interviews; *coding* the data with key words as a way of identifying commonalities and variations; *identifying* common and variable patterns within each group as well as across groups; and *identifying themes* which link or explain the data.

RESULTS AND DISCUSSION

In this section, the process of personal empowerment as described by the research participants is outlined. Common themes which emerged from the four groups of individuals will be discussed. In addition, themes which illustrate differences amongst the groups will be reported. As the themes are presented, the findings will be linked to the literature. This integrated approach to research reporting is considered more meaningful when working with qualitative data. The five main themes that emerged during the analysis stage were:

1. Powerlessness
2. Impetus to the Empowerment Process
3. Support from People
4. Access to Valued Resources
5. The Role of Participation in Community Life.

Powerlessness

The research participants described in great detail the anguish of feeling powerless. No single factor or experience created a sense of powerlessness; rather, it was a build-up of factors and experiences that developed into a dis-empowering situation. The data showed that all four research groups experienced extended periods of powerlessness in their lives as a result of social isolation, unresponsive services and systems, poverty, and abuse.

Social isolation. For most of the people with disabilities, their social isolation began early in life. It was experienced at home, school, and in the community. As one young woman noted, she never went to school, "cause the school wasn't accessible, so we had a teacher come in a couple days a week to teach us."

As Foucault (1984) has pointed out, many groups in western culture are "maneuvered by myths" (p.8); one of the cruelest myths experienced by people with disabilities is that they do not have the same social needs as other citizens. For the group of low-income women, their experience of social isolation was somewhat different. Most of the women experienced very difficult childhood and/or adulthood years, and they talked extensively about the lack of support in their lives. They used terms such as neglect, isolation, and abandonment to describe their experiences. As people's lives unfolded, escaping social isolation was one of the major tasks to be undertaken on the road to empowerment.

Unresponsive services and systems. Almost all participants described the impact of service systems on their experience of powerlessness. Although many social critics have noted the problems with service systems, the perspectives of the participants in this study helped the researchers to understand that the failure of systems is twofold: first, failure through neglect, and second, failure through inappropriate interventions. Failure through neglect was personified by the number of individuals and families who simply got "worn down" by the constant demands of dealing with poverty or disability. Failure through inappropriate interventions was often characterized by efforts that addressed the effects of problems, not the problem itself. Thus, psychiatric patients were often mis-diagnosed and over-medicated, sent to more clinics, more physicians and more institutions. No one in the system recommended that these individuals seek alternative non-medical support or self-help that might address their real problems, issues of loneliness and powerlessness. The failure of existing services and systems to creatively address people's real problems had enormous consequences; people remained in states of prolonged dependency and the transition to empowerment was fraught with barriers.

Poverty. Poverty was a dis-empowering experience for all of the low-income women and for several of the participants with disabilities. Many of the women had lived on welfare for extended periods, and were forced to live in housing projects with other people who were poor. Women talked about many of their concerns: a loss of control and a perpetuation of dependency on the system; invasion of privacy; being robbed of their self-esteem; being seen as not trustworthy; being blamed for their own misfortune; and feeling oppressed. The literature on poverty and empowerment both point to the extensive and devasting effects that poverty can have on people's lives.

Abuse. Abuse was an important contributor to dis-empowerment, especially for the group of low income women. Most of the women reported some type of abuse during childhood and/or adulthood, whether it was physical, emotional, or sexual. The abuse was inflicted on the women by a variety of people, including fathers, mothers, siblings, teachers, relatives, and foster parents. Besides physical abuse, the women talked about a general lack of support in their lives. Several of the women were actually left by parents or siblings as adolescents to cope on their own or find other arrangements. As a result of these situations, most of the women were forced to work at a very early age, one as young as twelve, and in some cases, this included being forced to quit school. Almost all of the women married at a very young age. The scars of the abuse remained with the women and impacted on the way they saw themselves, the way they related to men, and the way they parented their children.

The few women who had stable, loving childhoods found their early positive experiences to be a sustaining factor for them during difficult times as adults. They knew life *could* be better and they aspired for it. For the women who were abused as children, overcoming the prolonged sense of powerlessness was continually a struggle. As one woman said: "You think scars heal. They don't... they hurt." In summary, powerlessness for the research participants was both a "global" experience and a "situational" experience. As a global concept, some people experienced a sense of total powerlessness, and became, for a period, unable to see themselves as being capable of having control or being able to influence others.

For these participants, this was a period in their lives of "surviving, not living." The consequences of prolonged dependency for these individuals included low self-esteem, few options, and limited experience with decision-making, not dissimilar to other research and literature. Most participants at this stage had very small, uninvolved social networks. The combination of social isolation and low self-esteem limited people's capacity to dream. It also affected their ability to believe in themselves and to take control of their lives. The conditions of global powerlessness experienced by these participants are similar to Goldenberg's (1978) conditions of oppression, which include containment, expendability, and compartmentalization. As a situational concept, a minority of participants experienced powerlessness only in some areas of life. These individuals were able to maintain control and self-esteem in other areas. This sense of self-efficacy became paramount for many of them later in the empowerment process.

Impetus to Empowerment

The transition towards personal empowerment was a uniquely individual and ongoing process. Charting the process required that attention be paid to each person's story, as well as to common themes across all participants. It was difficult to pinpoint exactly when the process started. Similarly, the transition to empowerment did not produce a fixed end point; few people "became empowered" and never looked back. For most of the vulnerable people who were part of this research, the process of personal empowerment was a constant struggle.

For most of the participants, their impetus to empowerment was not a conscious decision. Instead, it was motivated by some concrete factors that participants, in reflecting back, were able to identify. These factors or situations acted like catalysts for the empowerment process and led to two vital changes in participants. Individuals became aware of their own capacities and of alternatives to the experience of powerlessness. Second, individuals began to develop new directions for themselves. As shall be seen, these are critical elements of personal empowerment. The main factors which participants identified as providing the impetus for change were:

- being involved in a crisis or "life transition."
- acting on anger or frustration.
- responding to new information.
- building on inherent strengths and capabilities.

Being involved in a Crisis or Life Transition. Keiffer (1984), in his research with community activists, found that a provocation or crisis often prompted people to become critically aware of their own situations. How the research participants in this research dealt with crisis or life transitions varied widely. During rehabilitation, for example, people who had become disabled later in life had to come to terms with their changing life situation. The beginning of awareness was often related to questions people began to explore such as "what do I do now?" Interestingly, some people resolved this personal dilemma before they left the hospital, while others took months or years to begin to come to terms with the issue. As people gained awareness through this time, they began to realize they could still be human and still have control, despite their disability. Crisis in our culture often has negative connotations. Yet, for many of the participants, these unsettling situations were turned into new awareness and opportunities. People who responded most favorably to crisis or life transitions were those who believed in themselves and their own abilities (self-efficacy) and people who received support from others to expand their awareness and actions (social support).

Acting on anger or frustration. As already noted, most participants had experienced extensive frustration with their life situations. Many people talked about how frustrations built up until they finally decided that they could no longer accept what was happening. For several of the participants, it appeared that the drive to gain control over their lives was fueled by a combination of frustration and hope. For example, several women spoke about fighting back or standing up to someone in authority. For others, frustration which became anger led to action. Several people who became disabled later in life talked about feeling angry and frustrated with their new disability, and how these feelings motivated them to change their situation. Anger has been defined as a strong emotion that is part of everyday life. Anger can be immobilizing or be a major force behind an individual's desire to accomplish (Lerner, 1985). Several participants had experienced years of frustration and needed outlets and opportunities in order to act on their concerns. Most of the participants did find outlets for their frustration; in fact, it appears as if the anger was a way of not giving in to fear and passivity. A minority of participants, however, explained how they became "stuck on anger" for years and was unable to move on to effective action.

Having and responding to new information. Several participants noted that new information was significant to their initial process of change. Information that was most useful included: information on rights and choices; insights into participants' own strengths; information about the people who had abused them; taking a course about women's issues; knowledge about appropriate resources; and learning gained from getting a formal education. This new information allowed participants to get on with their lives and begin to make a contribution to their communities, their families, and themselves.

Building on inherent strengths and capabilities. Most men and women talked about personal characteristics and qualities which contributed to their personal empowerment. Some of these included: strong values, being resourceful, determination, taking responsibility, internal strength, growing self-confidence, strong desire to improve, and hope for a better future. Interestingly, it was in retrospect that participants realized that these inherent strengths and capabilities were significant in carrying them through many difficult years. At the same time, these strengths became part of the impetus for their involvement in an empowerment process.

Consistent with other research, the empowerment process identified by these participants involved both internal characteristics and external elements. As an example of the internal, most of the research participants attributed a high degree of their own empowerment to themselves. The basis of this insight seemed to be that people understood, or perhaps learned, that they had some responsibility for their own lives.

In essence, it seems that self-motivation was an essential part of empowerment, not in any egotistical sense, but rather in terms of self-control and self-participation. Self-efficacy is defined as people's evaluation of their capabilities to organize and carry out activities required to attain personal goals (Bandura, 1986).

In this sense, positive self-efficacy is seen as fostering confidence in ways that enhance participation and taking initiative. Personal characteristics helped people in this study to ease into the transition from powerlessness to a sense of personal control. For example, some people talked about having a drive within themselves that helped them to push for change even though life seemed desolate at times.

Developing self-efficacy was not an easy, straight forward task. Most of the participants struggled for years without resources and often by avoiding responsibility. It was not possible to identify exactly how people came to increase their self-efficacy, but it seemed that that those who believed in themselves early in the process were able to expand their empowerment quite considerably when appropriate supports and resources were made available.

Support from People

Personal supports were vital in expanding personal empowerment. Sometimes support from people was the catalyst that enabled participants to begin the journey towards more personal control. For most participants, however, the support provided by others was more useful when they had already started to become aware of alternatives. Every one of the research participants identified at least one significant person as being important to his or her personal empowerment. Participants noted that people who were most helpful played a variety of supportive roles. Three main types of support were identified as being particularly significant.

Practical support. Many participants identified practical, tangible help that other people provided during their struggle to become more empowered. Sometimes the practical support involved providing information that enhanced the person's ability to make decisions. Typically, the practical support enabled people to solve problems. For example, one woman who had been struggling with her family while searching for a place to live, noted how her service worker helped clear up a disagreement between herself and her sister and "she also helped me find a place to live." It was interesting to speculate whether this kind of helping contributed to empowerment by doing things for the person. It seemed clear from some of the participants that many of their lives were so troubling and so lacking resources that this kind of practical help was often one of the first steps toward the person regaining a sense of control. Other times, the practical support included help in finding a job, being visited regularly during a long period of depression, and being supported to get out of an institution.

Moral Support. Many participants found a person who provided important moral support. An ability to listen was the quality that was most often identified as the basis of moral support. One woman noted that she had found "people who I can now talk to who have said to me *go for it, you can do it...* I found a tremendous amount of encouragement." Sometimes the moral support came from fellow participants in a selfhelp group, other times from family or friends, and occasionally from a service worker. Participants often alluded to the influence of others in helping them to capture or recapture their dreams. As the experience of several participants attested, the development of a vision or sense of direction may require the support of others, but also requires that the person make use of that support to develop an internal commitment to the personal vision (Glouberman, 1989). Moral support seemed to provide people with an opportunity to confirm their own intuition, increase their belief in themselves, and recognize their own strengths and potential capacities.

Mentoring. Most of the low-income women and about one third of the participants with disabilities described a person in their lives who they perceived as a significant role model or mentor. For example, one woman talked about a social worker who encouraged and affirmed her strengths. "She wouldn't spend time focusing on my behavior; she focused on the gifts I have and the contributions that I could make." For the most part, participants identified mentors who were of the same sex and who had been through similar experiences to themselves.

Research and analysis has suggested that "building on people's strengths" is one of the key ways to facilitate personal empowerment. In this way, mentoring may be a significant aspect of the empowerment process. Mentors played several roles with participants including: believing in the person; providing appropriate information at the right time; demonstrating initiative so that the person could envision new possibilities for him or herself; and finally, challenging the person to change and participate. This research was consistent with the findings of Keiffer (1984), who found that mentors were important for individuals who were gaining a sense of empowerment through political action.

Access to Valued Resources

An important aspect of the empowerment process was having access to valued resources. When they experienced powerlessness, most of the participants had access only to resources which they perceived as being different or specifically for "rehabilitation" or "welfare." Beginning to have access to the same valued resources and opportunities as other community members was important for people's empowerment process. For some participants, gaining employment was a pivotal point in their lives as a way of expanding their economic power. Interestingly, a job was also perceived as a way to expand other people's respect for the person. Other examples of valued resources included independent housing, technical resources such as a motorized wheelchair, and money. Parenti (1978) describes power as the ability to control powerful resources in order to get what you want, despite resistance. In a society where powerful people have wealth, property, control of jobs, prestige, and access to goods and services, people who are experiencing powerlessness have little access to these valued resources. Interestingly, while some people spoke of services and service systems as useful, most were highly critical. When services were helpful, participants tended to mention an individual health or social service worker who was involved with them on a one-to-one basis. Participants were critical of systems which were bureaucratic, congregating, and controlling. Pinderhughes (1983) points out that too often service workers and systems see people as victims and keep people in inferior, powerless positions. These findings are consistent with social critics who have emphasized the limitations of service systems in terms of their contributions to community participation and empowerment (McKnight, 1987). Services that were of value had some common qualities, including being personalized, responsive, interactive, and providing a degree of self reliance and consumer control. It is significant to note that the health and social service workers who were seen as helpful were characterized as "a good listener", "an equal", "a guide", and a person "who really cares".

THE REALITY OF EMPOWERMENT

- Empowerment is viewed as authority that managers grant employees
- The reality is that many front line employees already have a lot of power.
- Recognize their power and motivate them to channel it productively.
- Employees who serve customers have the power to make or break a business.
- Empowering them means acknowledging how powerful they already are.

- The same applies to knowledge workers whose innovations can build your business.
- In the old days when most employees did only routine jobs, they had no power other than what managers condescended to grant them-this was called job enrichment!
- Now, employees are doing the critical jobs and managers are increasingly facilitators or coaches who need to get out of the way and let powerful employees do the business.
- This is a profound shift in organizational power.
- Nevertheless, it is hard for employees to fully utilize their power because the other reality is that managers still have the power to promote or fire them.
- So, both sides have their own sort of power and today the balance is more even than it used to be.
- An even balance of power implies partnership, not empowerment.
- The catch is that partners expect an even balance of reward distribution as well
- The key is not so much to empower employees who are already powerful but to motivate them to channel their power to maximize business results.

THE ELEMENTS OF EMPOWERMENT

Returning to the definition, let us now look at each of the elements:

Having Decision-making Power

Clients of mental health programs are often assumed by professionals to lack the ability to make decisions, or to make "correct" decisions. Therefore, many programs assume the paternalistic stance of limiting the number or quality of decisions their clients may make. Clients may be able to decide on the dinner menu, for example, but not on the overall course of their treatment. Yet, without practice in making decisions, clients are maintained in long-term dependency relationships. No one can become independent unless he or she is given the opportunity to make important decisions about his or her life.

Having Access to Information and Resources

Decision making shouldn't happen in a vacuum. Decisions are best made when the individual has sufficient information to weigh the possible consequences of various choices. Again, out of paternalism, many mental health professionals restrict such information, believing restriction to be in the client's "best interest." This can become a self-fulfilling prophecy, since, lacking adequate information, clients may make impulsive choices that confirm professionals' beliefs in their inadequacy.

Having a range of options from which to make choices. Meaningful choice is not merely a matter of "hamburgers of hot dogs" or "bowling or swimming." If you prefer salad, or the library, you're out of luck!

Assertiveness

Non-diagnosed people are rewarded for this quality; in mental health clients, on the other hand, it is often labeled "manipulativeness." This is an example of how a psychiatric label results in positive qualities being redefined negatively. Assertiveness-being able to clearly state one's wishes and to stand up for oneself-helps an individual to get what he or she wants.

A feeling that the individual can make a difference. Hope is an essential element in our definition. A person who is hopeful believes in the possibility of future change and improvement; without hope, it can seem pointless to make an effort. Yet mental health professionals who label their clients "incurable" or "chronic" seem at the same time to expect them to be motivated to take action and make changes in their lives, despite the overall hopelessness such labels convey.

Learning to think critically; unlearning the conditioning; seeing things differently. This part of the definition created the most discussion within our group, and we were unable to come up with a single phrase that encapsulated it. We believed that as part of the process of psychiatric diagnosis and treatment, clients have had their lives, their personal stories, transformed into "case histories." Therefore, part of the empowerment process is a reclaiming process for these life stories. Similarly, the empowerment process includes a reclaiming of one's sense of competence, and a recognition of the often-hidden power relationships inherent in the treatment situation. In the early stages of participation in self-help groups, for example, it is very common for members to tell one another their stories; both the act of telling and that of being listened to are important events for group members.

Learning about and expressing anger. Clients who express anger are often considered by professionals to be "decompensating" or "out of control." This is true even when the anger is legitimate and would be considered so when expressed by a "normal" person, and is yet another example of the way in which a positive quality becomes a negative once a person is diagnosed. Because the expression of anger has often been so restricted, it is common for clients to fear their own anger and overestimate its destructive power. Clients need opportunities to learn about anger, to express it safely, and to recognize its limits.

Not feeling alone; feeling part of a group. An important element in our definition is its group dimension. We believe that it is necessary to recognized that empowerment does not occur to the individual alone, but has to do with experiencing a sense of connectedness with other people. As was brought up numerous times during our discussion, we did not want to leave the impression that we considered the image of "John Wayne coming into town, fixing everything, and riding off into the sunset" to be synonymous with our definition!

Understanding that people have rights. The self-help movement among psychiatric survivors is part of a broader movement to establish basic legal rights. We see powerful parallels between our movement and other movements of oppressed and disadvantaged people, including racial and ethnic minorities, women, gays and lesbians, and people with disabilities. Part of all of these liberation movements has been the struggle for equal rights. Through understanding our rights, we increase our sense of strength and self-confidence.

Effecting change in one's life and one's community. Empowerment is about more than a "feeling" or a "sense," we see such feelings as precursors to action. When a person brings about actual change, he or she increases feelings of mastery and control. This, in turn, leads to further and more effective change. Again, we emphasized that this is not merely personal change, but has a group dimension.

Learning skills that the individual defines as important. Mental health professionals often complain that their clients have poor skills and cannot seem to learn new ones. At the same time, the skills that professionals define as important are often not the ones that clients themselves find interesting or important (e.g., daily bed making). When clients are given the opportunity to learn things that they want to learn, they often surprise professionals (and sometimes themselves) by being able to learn them well.

Changing others' perceptions of one's competency and capacity to act. If anything defines the public (and professional) perception of "mental patients," it is incompetency. People with psychiatric diagnoses are widely assumed to be unable to know their own needs or to act on them. As one becomes better able to take control of one's life, demonstrating one's essential similarity to so called "normal" people, this perception should begin to change. And the client who recognizes that he or she is earning the respect of others increases in self-confidence, thus further changing outsiders' perceptions.

Coming out of the closet. This is a term we have taken from the gay/lesbian movement. People with devalued social statuses who can hide that fact often (quite wisely) choose to do so. However, this decision takes its toll in the form of decreased self-esteem and fear of discovery. Individuals who reach the point where they can reveal their identity are displaying self-confidence.

Growth and change that is never ending and self-initiated. We wanted to emphasize in this element that empowerment is not a destination, but a journey; that no one reached a final stage in which further growth and change is unnecessary.

Increasing one's positive self-image and overcoming stigma. As a person becomes more empowered, he or she begins to feel more confident and capable. This, in turn, leads to increased ability to manage one's life, resulting in a still more improved self-image. The negative identity of "mental patient" that has been internalized also begins to change; the individual may discard the label entirely, or may redefine it to convey positive qualities.

THE GENDER EMPOWERMENT MEASURE

The Gender Empowerment Measure (GEM) is a measure of inequalities between men's and women's opportunities in a country. It combines inequalities in three areas: political participation and decision making, economic participation and decision making, and power over economic resources. It is one of the five indicators used by the United Nations Development Programme in its annual Human Development Report.

Methodology

Calculating the GEM involves several steps. First percentages for females and males are calculated in each area. The first area is the number of parliamentary seats held. The second area is measured by two sub-components: a) legislators, senior officials, and managers, and b) professional and technical positions. The third area is measured by the estimated earned income (at purchasing power parity US$).

Second, for each area, the pair of gender percentages, are combined into an Equally Distributed Equivalent Percentage (EDEP) that rewards gender equality and penalizes inequality. It is calculated as the harmonic mean of the two components. The EDEP for economic participation is the unweighted average of the EDEP for each of its sub-components. The EDEP for income is computed from gender sub-values that are indexed to a scale from 100 to 40,000 (PPP US$). Finally, the GEM is the unweighted average of the three Equally Distributed Equivalent Percentages.

EMPOWERING WOMEN

Despite many international agreements affirming their human rights, women are still much more likely than men to be poor and illiterate. They usually have less access than men to medical care, property ownership, credit, training and employment. They are far less likely than men to be politically active and far more likely to be victims of domestic violence. The ability of women to control their own fertility is absolutely fundamental to women's empowerment and equality. When a woman can plan her family, she can plan the rest of her life. When she is healthy, she can be more productive. And when her reproductive rights—including the right to decide the number, timing and spacing of her children, and to make decisions regarding reproduction free of discrimination, coercion and violence—are promoted and protected, she has freedom to participate more fully and equally in society.

Understanding Gender Equality and Women's Empowerment

Gender equality implies a society in which women and men enjoy the same opportunities, outcomes, rights and obligations in all spheres of life. Equality between men and women exists when both sexes are able to share equally in the distribution of power and influence; have equal opportunities for financial independence through work or through setting up businesses; enjoy equal access to education and the opportunity to develop personal ambitions.

A critical aspect of promoting gender equality is the empowerment of women, with a focus on identifying and redressing power imbalances and giving women more autonomy to manage their own lives. Women's empowerment is vital to sustainable development and the realization of human rights for all.

Where women's status is low, family size tends to be large, which makes it more difficult for families to thrive. Population and development and reproductive health programmes are more effective when they address the educational opportunities, status and empowerment of women. When women are empowered, whole families benefit, and these benefits often have ripple effects to future generations.

The roles that men and women play in society are not biologically determined — they are socially determined, changing and changeable. Although they may be justified as being required by culture or religion, these roles vary widely by locality and change over time. UNFPA has found that applying culturally sensitive approaches can be key to advancing women's rights while respecting different forms of social organization. Addressing women's issues also requires recognizing that women are a diverse group, in the roles they play as well as in characteristics such as age, social status, urban or rural orientation and educational attainment. Although women may have many interests in common, the fabric of their lives and the choices available to them may vary widely. UNFPA seeks to identify groups of women who are most marginalized and vulnerable (women refugees, for example, or those who are heads of households or living in extreme poverty), so that interventions address their specific needs and concerns. This task is related to the critical need for sex-disaggregated data, and UNFPA helps countries build capacity in this area.

Key issues and linkages:

- Reproductive health: Women, for both physiological and social reasons, are more vulnerable than men to reproductive health problems. Reproductive health problems, including maternal mortality and morbidity, represent a major – but preventable — cause of death and disability for women in developing countries. Failure to provide information, services and conditions to help women protect their reproduction health therefore constitutes gender-based discrimination and a violation of women's rights to health and life.
- Stewardship of natural resources: Women in developing nations are usually in charge of securing water, food and fuel and of overseeing family health and diet. Therefore, they tend to put into immediate practice whatever they learn about nutrition and preserving the environment and natural resources.
- Economic empowerment: More women than men live in poverty. Economic disparities persist partly because much of the unpaid work within families and communities falls on the shoulders of women and because they face discrimination in the economic sphere.
- Educational empowerment: About two thirds of the illiterate adults in the world are female. Higher levels of women's education are strongly associated with both lower infant mortality and lower fertility, as well as with higher levels of education and economic opportunity for their children.

- Political empowerment: Social and legal institutions still do not guarantee women equality in basic legal and human rights, in access to or control of land or other resources, in employment and earning, and social and political participation. Laws against domestic violence are often not enforced on behalf of women.
- Empowerment throughout the life cycle: Reproductive health is a lifetime concern for both women and men, from infancy to old age. UNFPA supports programming tailored to the different challenges they face at different times in life.

Experience has shown that addressing gender equality and women's empowerment requires strategic interventions at all levels of programming and policy-making.

WOMEN'S WORK AND ECONOMIC EMPOWERMENT

In nearly every country, women work longer hours than men, but are usually paid less and are more likely to live in poverty. In subsistence economies, women spend much of the day performing tasks to maintain the household, such as carrying water and collecting fuel wood. In many countries women are also responsible for agricultural production and selling. Often they take on paid work or entrepreneurial enterprises as well.

Unpaid domestic work – from food preparation to caregiving – directly affects the health and overall well being and quality of life of children and other household members. The need for women's unpaid labour often increases with economic shocks, such as those associated with the AIDS pandemic or economic restructuring. Yet women's voices and lived experiences – whether as workers (paid and unpaid), citizens, or consumers – are still largely missing from debates on finance and development. Poor women do more unpaid work, work longer hours and may accept degrading working conditions during times of crisis, just to ensure that their families survive.

Intergenerational Gender Gaps

The differences in the work patterns of men and women, and the 'invisibility' of work that is not included in national accounts, lead to lower entitlements to women than to men.

Women's lower access to resources and the lack of attention to gender in macroeconomic policy adds to the inequity, which, in turn, perpetuates gender gaps. For example, when girls reach adolescence they are typically expected to spend more time in household activities, while boys spend more time on farming or wage work. By the time girls and boys become adults, females generally work longer hours than males, have less experience in the labour force, earn less income and have less leisure, recreation or rest time.

This has implications for investments in the next generation. If parents view daughters as less likely to take paid work or earn market wages, they may be less inclined to invest in their education, women's fastest route out of poverty.

UNFPA in Action

UNFPA is committed to actions to attack poverty and powerlessness, especially among women. About half of the UNFPA programme countries have developed strategies to provide women with economic opportunities. The Fund has supported economic empowerment and micro-credit initiatives in Bangladesh, Chad, Kenya, Morocco, Palestinian women's centres, Tajikistan and elsewhere. As part of its Campaign to End Fistula, UNFPA also supports skills training for who have been marginalized by this debilitating injury of childbirth. UNFPA strongly supports addressing the feminization of poverty through the integration of gender concerns in macro economic policy and in poverty reduction strategies.

In Chad, a two-pronged programme unites microcredit and reproductive health education: while young women receive support that can lead to economic independence, they also learn to protect themselves against HIV and other reproductive health problems. In the Lao People's Democratic Republic, a seed fund is helping women gain respect – as economic partners, as well as mothers and wives. Women are learning about reproductive health issues through the programme as well.

In Bangladesh, a UNFPA-supported microcredit project provides skills training and small business loans to women, and also supports reproductive health and family planning services. In Viet Nam, UNFPA and partners support national efforts that link economic empowerment, environmental management and reproductive health services. Participation involves 500 Women's Savings Groups in nine provinces with a membership of over 12,000 women.

COMMUNITY EMPOWERMENT

When we use words, we often convey meanings that we do not intend, or meanings that we do not know we convey. There are emotions and assumptions associated with the words we use. Take the word "poverty" for example. In the assistance industry (helpers of development), we often see ourselves as soldiers in the so-called war against poverty. Poverty is what we want to defeat. But what is the opposite of poverty? Wealth. Somehow we do not like to admit we are "soldiers in the war in favour of wealth." Why?

Because while poverty and wealth are technically opposite, there are many assumptions, emotions and hidden values that are attached to both those words, and those are conveyed along with their overt meanings. Somehow it is morally OK to help poor people, but we do not always like to keep in our conscious thoughts that we are helping them to obtain wealth. The module on income generation is more acceptable when it is named as "income generation" than as "wealth generation" even though "wealth" is a more accurate economic term. (Where the objective is to generate wealth rather than merely transfer money). The term "wealth" comes with hidden emotional baggage that implies it means huge richness.

Poverty is a problem because there are disparities in wealth; some have more than others. If genuine equality were possible (and it is not, you may be happy to learn), then poverty would not be a problem.

Closely associated with "wealth" are "power" and "capacity." Communities (and individuals) that have lots of one, usually have lots of all three, and vice versa (those with low wealth usually have low power and low capacity). So when we want to improve the conditions of people in low income communities, poor communities, marginalized communities, we want them to have more wealth, power, and capacity.

But not too much. It is nice (we think) to help the poor, but (in our hidden desires) we do not want them to become rich, or at least we do not want them to become as rich as us. We do not want to admit that. Another of the emotionally laden words we use today is "democracy." We are all in favour of it, apparently.

But are we? When we look carefully at the meaning of democracy, it turns out that we are not always in favour of it, especially if it means having to give up some of our own relative power (or wealth, or capacity).

Many who say they are in favour of democracy are really in favour of a set of institutions that allow people to vote for candidates, putting into power those with the most votes, allowing them to represent the people. This is "representational democracy." That is almost a contradiction in terms. The meaning of "democracy" is "Power to the people" (demo = people, cracy = power). The process of voting for representatives takes power away from people and gives it to the vote winners.

When we say we want to empower a community, we mean that we want to democratize it. That does not necessarily mean we want them to have votes to choose their representative (as in the British or American political model). It means we want the people (not just individuals) as a whole (collectively) to have power. We want to find ways for the community to have more power, wealth and capacity. The communities most deserving of our assistance, then, are those with the least amount of power, wealth and capacity.

And we must be aware of our hidden desires to keep them poor, powerless and incapable just so that we can keep giving them our charity. If we genuinely want to empower them, we must do it in such a way that they become independent of our charity, that they become self reliant, that they can sustain their own development without our help. Our own desires for wealth and power are normal and natural. We need not be ashamed of them. Ze must, however, keep in mind that in our desire to help people who are poor and powerless, that we do not do so in ways that, in the long run, keep them poor and powerless — and dependent upon us.

The training documents on this web site are aimed primarily at the community mobilizer, and emphasize methods and techniques rather than theory or ideology. To effectively use those methods, however, we must be aware of what reasoning lies behind them, what principles apply, and what long term effects they have. Importantly, we must also constantly examine our own motives and purpose behind what we do.

Getting Stronger through Exercise

Many times throughout this web site, you are advised to take approaches that can be seen as empowering, rather than those which promote dependency. We sometimes use the term "charity approach" to name dependency producing methods of giving help. Charity in itself is not bad, in so much as it is based upon generosity, a value that we strongly support.

What we mean by the "charity approach," however, is a way of helping poor and powerless people that does not help them to become self reliant. Gifts that make the receivers more dependent upon the givers, are not truly generous. They sustain poverty. They keep the givers in a position of giving. If you give something to a person or group in need, you temporarily alleviate their need. You can be quite sure that when they are in need again, they will come back to where they received their first assistance.

This is not bad; it is human nature, or the nature of survival for any organism. If you want that person or group to become self reliant, you need to be sure they want something in the first place. Then you must find ways for them to work or to struggle for it, so that when they need it again they will not come begging for it. If they get something for free, they will know that it was worth (to them) every penny they spent on it.

Several times on this web site, you will see a sports analogy to explain the empowerment method. A coach does not do push ups for the athlete, nor does a coach practice putting the basketball into the hoop for the basketball player. The person who is to get stronger and more competent has to do the work. Another analogy is found in physiotherapy. If you hurt yourself and lose the use of your arm, you go to a physiotherapist for help. The physiotherapist may move your arm in the manner you need to move it, but only to show you where it must be exercised. You need to practice moving it yourself, and that is a painful and uncomfortable process. You need to want to get better. The result is that you get your strength back, and no longer need the services of the physiotherapist.

If the coach does the push ups for the athlete, the athlete does not become stronger. If the physiotherapist does the exercises for the patient, the patient does not become stronger. If the community worker does the work for the community, the community remains dependent, and poverty is sustained. Weakness. The empowerment approach to community development is one where first you determine that the community wants something (as discovered in a brainstorming session) and then shows the community members how to get it. The process of their getting it is the exercise (struggle) that strengthens them.

Why Choose a Community to Empower?

If the purpose of community mobilization is to increase its power, wealth and capacity, why would you choose to mobilize one community and not another? The world is not a fair place. There is inequality. There is strife. There is inhumanity towards mankind, by humans. Life is not fair. We need some purpose in life. Trying to set right the wrongs of the world; trying to help poor people to become independent and escape from their poverty, are among such purposes. Simply trying to become rich ourselves is the main purpose of some people, but it is a very shallow and unfulfilling purpose (the richer that people get, the more wealth they want; there is no satisfaction). There is no evidence, or even hope, that the world will become fair, that poverty will be eliminated. Yet the striving for it is a purpose that has its own rewards.

So we could spend our energy in trying to mobilize and empower a rich or relatively wealthy community, but that has less purpose than trying to help a poor community become stronger. The methods that are explained in this web site can be applied to rich or poor communities. Choosing to work with a poor community can be a way of putting more purpose in your life. Choosing a community simply because it is the one you were born in is perhaps equally valid, but less purposeful.

The documents on this web site are designed mainly to be applied to low income, poor capacity, poorly empowered communities. Writing them has purpose; no money is earned in putting them here on the internet. It is an element (regiment? ammunition?) in the war against poverty. Some people like to quote: "Charity should begin at home." They often say this to justify raising money to give out handouts to poor people in their home communities (which does not end their poverty, as we know). Unfortunately, such people often believe that it should not only start at home; it should also end there. What a short sighted and selfish notion.

The whole world has human beings in it. We are all related. We are one big human family. The people far way in isolated poor communities are our brothers and sisters. If we can help them, we have purpose in life. If we help them, we should concentrate on helping them to become independent of our charity, able to help themselves in the future. If we have a choice in which community to apply our skills as mobilizers, it is more meaningful (and has greater global effect) to choose the lowest income communities, those with less power and capacity.

Empowerment as a Social Process

In several places on this site, we point out that poverty is a social problem, and is contrasted with the individual problem of lack of cash or other resources. We must distinguish between the social level and the individual level, in our analysis, in our observations, and in our interventions. A community is a social organization, and is not an individual. It is far more than a mere collection of individuals. It is an entity, sometimes described as "*superorganic*," that transcends the individuals that compose it at any one time.

It is easy to see and interact with an individual. A "community," in contrast, is a scientific model, like an atom or a solar system, which can be seen at most only partly at any one time, but cannot be seen as a whole. (You know the story of the seven blind men and an elephant). A community does not behave like an individual. We sometimes anthropomorphise a community (think of it and talk about it as if it is a human being) but it is more like a social amoeba than like an individual human.

We can make individuals stronger (physically, psychologically) and we can make communities stronger (capacity, wealth, power); these are not the same. In our work as mobilizers, we must be careful to avoid making predictions and assumptions about communities as if a community is an individual, thinking, human being. It is easy, but wrong, for us to slip into that kind of thinking. While you, as a mobilizer, can see individuals, can work with individuals, your target is the community, a social organization, which you can not see in its totality, and with which you must work indirectly.

To be successful then, in empowering the community, it is necessary for you to understand the nature of social organizations, of the social level, of society. It is also necessary for you to know something about the relationship between an individual, or individuals, and community, and society.

While this web site tries to minimize theory and ideology, and tries to emphasize practical guidelines, methods and techniques, it encourages you to learn about the science of sociology, the nature of community as a social organization, and sociological perspectives, in order to do your work more effectively.

Remember, however, that sociology can not be very precise and very predictive as, say, is chemistry or astronomy, because the factors that affect social change are too many. It is made more difficult because as social organization, such as a community or an NGO, is a construct, a model, that you can not see directly.

Nevertheless, you need to set yourself a career goal of learning more about the social perspective, and to develop skills in understanding the social elements that are revealed by the indicators you can see, including the behaviour of individuals, social and economic statistics, some events, and demographic data. To help you in this, there are two modules which identify sixteen elements of empowerment. One is focused mainly on capacity development of an organization (such as an NGO or CBO), and the other is focused mainly on measuring increases (or decreases) in the capacity of a community. These sixteen elements, many of which also can not be seen except through characteristics of individuals, will help you to carefully and in detail look at the empowerment process as a social process.

Why Participation?

Empowering a community is not something that you can do to that community. Because the process of empowerment, or capacity development, is a social process, it is something that the community itself must undergo. Even members of a community, as individuals, can not develop their community, it is a growth process of the community as a whole, internally, as an organism (super organism or social organism).

Trying to force growth, trying to force social change, is called social engineering, and it does have its effects, but usually effects that are far from what you want. Our method is to stimulate the community to take action. We often refer to that action as a "project." By doing a project, the community will become more empowered, develop more capacity. The action it takes is its exercise to become stronger.

We noted above that the people must struggle in order to become stronger. The basic method of a community mobilizer is to first determine what the community as a whole wants, then guide it in struggling to achieve it.

An outsider can not decide what the community wants. The community members have to agree on what they all want most. That is the first of several reasons why they need to participate in decision making; that participation is needed first to determine what they want most. The brainstorm session is one of several techniques taught on this site that helps you to draw out of them their priorities. When done correctly it is a process that determines a communal choice, not the choice of a few people, or of a dominant faction.

After that is the decision of strategy, or what path to follow in order to reach the priority goal. Again, there are different ways to choose a strategy, but the more it represents the will of the community members as a whole, the more valid it is. Their participation is vital for success.

Whatever the project, it will have inputs and outputs. Inputs are the resources put into the project. An output is an objective when it is realized. While some of the inputs can come from outside donors, including the government, but the community itself, its members should make some sacrifices too. As well as participation in decision making, we suggest that they also make contributions of resources, as inputs. Monitoring is an essential, but often overlooked, element of any project. The community should also participate in monitoring the project. Members should not leave it only to the outsiders % donors or implementors % to see if it is going as planned.

In the course of carrying out the project, community members may identify some skills that they lack. These could be in accounting, in reporting, or in technical skills. If you are able to help them obtain training in such skills, we recommend that the training is participatory also. That people learn best by "doing" rather than listening to lectures or watching presentations. Participatory approaches are recommended throughout the empowerment process. Participation contributes to strength.

National Development

The nineteen fifties and sixties (and later) saw the end of colonial period for many new countries. Hope was high that it would also mean the end of poverty as countries became more self reliant and stronger. The reality was very different, and discouragement replaced optimism as poverty and the number of poor people grew. There are many historical causes for this, neo colonialism, multi national corporations each stronger and wealthier than whole countries, globalization of corporate culture, lack of sophistication and knowledge by leaders, and on and on. Everyone has her or his own favourite theories.

In Factors of Poverty, we distinguish between (1) historical causes and (2) factors that contribute to the problem remaining. This has a very practical purpose. We can not go back into history and change events. We can see current factors, and have some influence, however small, on them. The training on the web site is aimed primarily at the community mobilizer (and her or his manager, planner, programmer and administrator). In the gender module, we cite the slogan, "Think globally, act locally." This applies here, too. How can we contribute to a strong, self reliant, independent nation? If that country has strong, self reliant, capable communities, then it will become stronger.

You, as a mobilizer, can not (through your work) directly change the national characteristics of a country, but you can contribute to one or more community becoming stronger. Also, by teaching these methods and techniques to others, you can contribute indirectly to other communities becoming stronger. You may be able, too, to influence the legislature and ministry directives and regulations in ways that will contribute to an environment that promotes and supports strong self reliant communities. As more communities become stronger, the country benefits. Joseph Marie de Maistre wrote, "Toute nation a le gouvernement qu'elle merite" (Every country has the government it deserves) Lettres et Opuscules Inedits (vol. I, letter 53), sometimes incorrectly attributed to the second American president, Thomas Jefferson. If you work towards getting the society you want, you will contribute to getting the government you deserve.

National development will not come through wishful thinking or by bar room debate. It comes as a result of hundreds of thousands of small, steady, changes based upon hard work of many people with vision. You can be among them, and this web site gives you the tools with which to engage in that hard work.

Find the Best and Enhance It

A positive attitude with optimism and the willingness to keep trying are not mere luxuries in this work. They are necessities. No person, no community, no society, is perfect. We all make mistakes. If you spend any time and energy on criticizing, you will emphasize the fault you criticize, and hinder its correction. You will meet people who promise and fail, people who do not carry out their side of an agreement, people who lie and cheat, people who are inept, inefficient and inaccurate, people who are dishonest and misleading. From the time you were born, no one promised you that life would be fair. That is just the way it is.

To succeed at this kind of work, you need a positive attitude, and you need to accept that failures are inevitable, and be willing to, "Keep on keepin' on," even after failures. To get the best out of people, you need to see but not mention their weaknesses and failures, you need to recognize their strengths and achievements, and you need to let them know you expect their best. Build on strengths, not on weaknesses.

THE COMMUNITY EMPOWERMENT NETWORK

The Community Empowerment Network (CEN) is a US-based non-profit organization which empowers rural communities and individuals in developing countries to harness information and information technology to become more self-reliant and break out of poverty. CEN provides computers and computer skills along with mentoring individuals and communities to develop knowledge, skills, the mindset and networks necessary to successfully address (drive) their development priorities (improve their lives or, improve their living conditions, maintain a vibrant culture and preserve their environment). CEN promotes these activities and assists with entrepreneurial development and income-generation initiatives. It is currently applying its methodology to several small communities in the Brazilian Amazon, which has resulted in the communities' increased confidence and ability to drive and execute their development initiatives. CEN is helping to create more vibrant and independent communities.

History

CEN was founded by Robert Bortner in November 2004. Between 2002 and June 2004, Robert was managing the USAID-funded Rio Tapajós (Brazil) Telecenter Installation Project, which installed solar powered community operated telecenters in the communities of Suruacá and Maguari. After completion of this project, Bob continued to work with these communities and with the community of Xixuau, located approximately 500 km north of Manaus along the Rio Jauaperi, and he mentored key activists in the communities. Encouraged by their significant progress in addressing community challenges and becoming more independent, Bob launched CEN and continued this work as the Amazon Pilot Project. In April 2008 CEN began the implementation of the Creating a Culture of Learning and Empowerment i [...] he Amazon (cCLEAR) Project. Angela Viehmayer, Directo [...] zilian NGO (Link Social) and serving on the CEN b [...] e Field Manager for the project to add a sustaine [...] the communities.

The CEN Amazon P [...]

CEN is working o [...] consisting of three

communities in the Brazilian Amazon. In two communities located along the upper Tapajós River, it helped manage the installation of solar-powered, internet-connected telecenters, which was completed by mid-2004 The InfoCentro Comunitário contains information that is closely tailored to the specific health, education, civics and entrepreneurial needs and skills of the communities. The third community, located 500 km north of Manaus along the Roraima state border, already had computers and internet access. CEN is now working with the three communities to use this infrastructure to become more autonomous.

Several promising results have been seen within a relatively short period of time. For example, one of the communities in project, Suruacá, has made considerable progress on a project to provide adequate electricity throughout the community using a microhydroelectric dam. They have driven the process, identified partners, and prepared a project plan with only very modest assistance from CEN or any other outside organization. CEN is now working with them to help them secure funding; however they continue to drive the process. In another example, one of the communities in the pilot project, Xixuau, has been quite successful with eco-tourism, while many residents of Suruacá were very anxious to understand how eco-tourism — and the cash it would bring in-might impact their way of life. By discussing these concerns with Xixuau, Suruacá is more firmly united behind eco-tourism efforts.

The exchange of Xixuau's experience is also proving useful in helping Suruacá avoid some of the problems faced by other communities who have pursued eco-tourism. It is anticipated that such helpful exchange of ideas will continue through the Rede Amazônia, a network established by rural communities in the Brazilian Amazon.

During this project CEN achieved the following:

- Identified obstacles [illegible]hich prevent information technology and particula[illegible] information from achieving it's
- potential impact
- Identified a model for [illegible]ing these obstacles
- Stabilized the telecent[illegible]

- Developed islands (points) of expertise within the community
- Developed relationships with successful and innovative organization within the region and around Brazil
- Achieved palpable progress on our overall goal the program participants becoming more self-reliant.

cCLEAR Pilot Implementation Project

Today CEN is focusing its resources on communities in the Amazon, where its operating a pilot project in three communities. Although the tools and methodologies CEN has developed targets the specific needs of the communities where it is currently engaged, its approach addresses needs that are nearly universal among poor rural communities and is transferable to rural communities worldwide. This pilot implementation of first phase of the Creating a Culture of Learning and Empowerment in the Amazon Region (cCLEAR) Program is scheduled to run until April 2009.

30 learners will directly benefit from the pilot project. Half of the participants will come from the community of Suruacá and half will come from Maguary. All residents of both communities, each of which has approximately 5001, will indirectly benefit from the project, as participants will apply the knowledge and skills they gain from the program to carry out development initiatives that will benefit larger groups or, in some cases, the whole community. Thus, 1,000 individuals will benefit indirectly from the pilot of the cCLEAR program.

Future Plans

In 2009 CEN intends to replicate Phase 1 of the cCLEAR Program in a new set of communities in the region through another local partner, and to implement Phase 2 in the original Rio Tapajós communities as well as the community of Xixuau. Phase 2 includes an integrated entrepreneurship development program. CEN will work with the communities to leverage the skills they have learned in order to generate additional income. Although entrepreneurship development has been an important emphasis for CEN programs, CEN intends to enhance opportunities available to the communities by improving access to markets and capital through this integrated entrepreneurship development program. By 2010 CEN hopes to replicate to other regions, such as Mozambique or South Asia, where it has received a lot of interest and there are many potential synergies with its current work. CEN hopes to disengage from the original communities through Phase 3, while leaving behind a sustainable infrastructure.

The work CEN does will scale by partnering with select local organizations which have compatible values and have gained trust with communities in the region. CEN will work closely with the local partner on the first set of implementations, help them adapt CEN's methodologies to local realities, and build their capacity. After a defined period CEN will disengage this intensive level of interaction, but leave behind a set of infrastructure, including social networks, to ensure their success at replicating the methodology throughout the region they serve.

BARRIERS TO EMPOWERMENT

Policies and programmes alone cannot guarantee empowerment. Unless people's individual and social capabilities can enhance their position in competitive bargaining or to hold institutions accountable, they may not be able to take advantage of the opportunities created by reforms. Both policies and institutions must be examined to assess their relevance to the challenges faced by the poor – and the very causes of their poverty.

Socio-cultural Empowerment

Socio-cultural empowerment is the process through which people and groups become aware of the societal and cultural forces at work in their lives and learn how to influence their dynamics – particularly those of deep-rooted social inequality and exclusion. If we understand the term "culture" in the widely accepted sense of all the capabilities and habits acquired by human beings as members of societies, we can begin to appreciate the weight of Nepal's deeply hierarchical social structures with their interlocking systems of caste and ethnicity. Despite the country's 100 ethnicities, 92 languages and nine religions, its people can be broadly examined in five cultural categories: caste-origin Hindu groups; *Newars*; the ethnic/tribal groups (nationalities); Muslims; and "others". These categories have significantly impeded the pace of empowerment. Nepal has been described as a "Hindu kingdom and Hindu polity, though not necessarily a Hindu society" and as "cultural pluralism within a hierarchical caste system", certainly since the 18th century. The many communities subordinated by the unifying King Prithvi Narayan Shah and his followers "responded with accommodation and assimilation, but also with out-migration or resistance, sometimes violent".3

Nepalese culture is rooted in discriminations based on religion, which have perpetuated both practices of untouchability and the exploitation of women. It has also worked against the preservation of the cultures of various ethnic groups, including indigenous people of the country. Without eliminating these biases, the empowerment process cannot become sustainable. Despite the provisions in the Constitution of 1990, which clearly state the freedom to "profess and practice one's own religion", Hindu values have exerted vast influence over the nation's other religions and its general cultural practices. Although the National Country Code of 1963 abolished the caste system, it remains very much alive in practice. Indeed, the National Country Code amended in 1992 has upheld the preservation of"traditional practices".4 Even the Constitution contains some degree of ambiguity in this regard.

The low status of women, systems of patrilineal descent, patri-local residence and rules of inheritance interact to isolate and subordinate women throughout the country.

Gender issues are thus interwoven systematically into the basic social structure of Nepalese society, as are other traditional cultural values. Deeply embedded, they obstruct the empowerment of the poor and the disadvantaged groups throughout the country.

The Effectiveness of Educational Reforms

In 1951, Nepal could boast a literacy rate of only 2%; 321 primary schools and 11 high schools constituted the whole of its public educational establishment. By 2002, the literacy rate had mounted to 54%, the number of primary schools to 25,927, lower secondary schools to 7,289 and secondary schools to 4,350.5 Under the 1971 National Education System Plan, the government assumed the full cost of primary education and 75% of the costs of vocational school. However, the state-controlled education system discouraged people's participation in school management, undermined educational quality and also ignored the deep-rooted discriminatory practices of the school system.

The new Constitution of 1990 guaranteed the universal right to education and therefore encouraged the introduction of preferential policies for educating girls and other disadvantaged groups. Since 1992, the government has taken a number of additional steps to increase access to education and improve its quality, including the establishment of the National Education Commission to frame policy and oversee the implementation of a variety of programmes and projects aimed at enhancing basic and primary education. Since 1996, early childhood education (at the preprimary level) has been emphasized in conjunction with the slogan "Education for all" to meet the goal of universal education by 2015. School management also changed, with added emphasis on the community management of schools.

The Ninth Plan period (1997-2002) witnessed additional reforms, notably:

- Ensuring that within one decade, all children enrolled complete a five-year primary education;
- Developing an integrated cycle of secondary education linked to the labour market and widely accessible to girls and to poorer students;
- Improving the quality of university and other tertiary education;
- Introducing greater cost recovery and targeting public subsidies to students from poor households, thereby restructuring a system that subsidizes the upper classes, especially because of skewing towards the tertiary level;
- Developing a school management system; communities now manage their own primary schools, with a view to reducing costs, broadening access and improving quality through local supervision.
- Encouraging further private sector investment in education. In 2001, private schools constituted 8.7% of

all primary schools, 17.8% of all lower secondary schools and 21.3% of all secondary schools, percentages that are increasing.

The Tenth Plan/PRSP (2002-07) envisages the extension of education in the spirit of Education for All (EFA). Accordingly, EFA 2004-2009 was initiated at the beginning 2004. This programme is expected to cope with the country's low literacy and the low access of girls, *Dalits*, ethnic communities, disabled persons and people living below the poverty line – and to achieve the goal of "ec' ıcation for all by 2015". A number of innovations have therefore been undertaken in the education sector to ensure universal primary education and to attain equity. Nonetheless, despite all these initiatives and others, Nepal's education system has been unable to enhance the access of women, disadvantaged indigenous communities and *Dalits*. The shortfalls reinforce the impression that statesubsidized education benefits the privileged:

- Neither "backward" communities nor settlements in the mountain and remote hill regions have adequate access to education; the rural/urban gap persists;
- Less than half of all children complete the primary cycle and only 10% of those entering grade 1 reach grade 10, even after repeating several times; less than half of the secondary level students pass the School Leaving Certificate (SLC) examination; pass rates in higher secondary and at the University are comparable.

These inequities stem both from the supply side (limited physical access and poor quality of schooling) and the demand side (high perceived cost of education in relation to foregone benefits). They also suggest that unless primary education is made compulsory, the principle of universalization will not become operative. The high subsidies to tertiary education, the politicization of educational institutions and the rigidity of general education have all discouraged reforms of the present education system. In addition, most teachers receive little training; no provision exists for pre-service training, there is very limited in-service training, and teachers are poorly motivated because of inadequate incentives, coupled with few options for career growth.

Moreover, community participation in the education system has remained low, in large measure because the centralized system of teacher recruitment, resource allocation and monitoring school operations have excluded community members from decision-making processes. Local elites continue to dominate even the school management committees, silencing the voices of women, *Dalits* and disadvantaged/indigenous groups. However, there are some innovative community-managed schools, which have proved to be quite successful as demonstrated by the UNDP-supported Community Owned Primary Education (COPE) project in some districts of Nepal.

The Effectiveness of Health Reforms

In 1971, Nepal had only 58 hospitals, 277 medical doctors and 2,098 hospital beds. By 2001, these figures had increased, respectively, to 89, 5,415 and 5,310, plus 3,921 nurses. As in education, the democratic change of 1990 fostered many new policy and programme initiatives, including:

- The 1991 National Health Policy aimed at expanding primary healthcare facilities for the rural population and giving priority to preventive health services so as to reduce infant and child mortality rates.
- Emphasis on community participation at all levels of healthcare especially through the participation of female community health volunteers (FCHVs) and traditional birth attendants. And, indeed, the 45,000 FCHVs have contributed significantly to polio eradication, Vitamin A distribution and family planning practices.
- According priority to the supplies of drugs by increasing domestic production.
- The special focus of both the Second Long-term Health Plan (1997-2017) and the Nepal Health Sector Plan (2002-2007)9 on improving the health of the most vulnerable groups, notably by placing technically qualified health personnel in under-served areas.
- The formulation of Nepal Health Sector Reform Strategy to move the health sector towards strategic planning and sector wide approach. This strategy has three programme outputs – prioritized essential health care

services, decentralized management of health facilities and the expansion of public/private partnership.

The Nepal Health Sector Strategy Implementation Plan (2004-2009) provides operational guidelines to implement the activities of the Health Sector Reform Strategy during the first five years. The main focus of the Plan is to expand outreach and improve the quality of essential healthcare services with special emphasis on the poor and vulnerable groups.

Nonetheless, life expectancy in Nepal remains one of the lowest in South Asia, while its infant and maternal mortality rates rank among the highest with appalling statistics:

- Nepal's infant mortality rate (IMR) of 64 per 1,000 live births in 2001 compares ill with that of 17/1,000 in Sri Lanka. The female rate (96) is slightly lower than the male IMR (100) and rural babies are exposed 1.6 times more to risks of death than their urban counterparts.
- Maternal mortality, a key indicator of reproductive healthcare services, stands at 539 per 100,000 women aged 15-49 years, one of the highest in the world; 27% of all deaths of women aged 15-49 years are attributed to childbirth complications. This level of maternal mortality stems in large measure from the low level of access to antenatal, delivery and post-natal care; about 90% of births take place at home and without professional health assistance.
- Gradually, HIV/AIDS has emerged as a major problem; WHO estimates more than 50,000 cases and a prevalence rate of 0.29%.

Nepal's public sector per capita health allocation – US$ 2 per annum in 1999/00 – compares unfavourably with the average per capita annual cost of US$ 12 for essential healthcare alone in a developing country in the mid-range of the HDI. Even the fiscal year 2003/04 allocation still stood at US$ 2 per capita. Accessing public healthcare outlets and procuring the drugs they prescribe consumes 59% of household expenditure on health. The regional distribution of available facilities is also highly uneven, with the mid-western and far western development regions and mountain ecological belts lagging far behind the others. Life expectancy in the mountain trails that of Tarai by 7 years; rural people generally live 10 years less than their urban counterparts. For the most part, the country's health services are centrally managed – with little participation by local communities in either health policy decision-making or the monitoring of health service delivery. Procurements, staff recruitment and transfers, and supervision of local health institutions remain outside local purview, one factor in the shortfalls of local authorities in fostering a sense of stakeholding in the delivery of public health services. Moreover, the state has not set out clear roles and responsibilities for the central and district level health authorities regarding decentralization. Nor has it provided an effective system to ensure the quality and fair pricing of private sector health services. Although the involvement of the private sector in service delivery has expanded service availability, these services remain costly, effectively shutting out the poor. And in the absence of a universal healthcare system, the poor, women and disadvantaged groups remain deprived of the basic services necessary for a decent life in a competitive society. Although the rural health service infrastructure is both large and relatively equitable in its penetration of the countryside, the quality of its services remains extremely poor because of a number of administrative problems:

- Inadequate number of medical and paramedical staff positioned in Primary Healthcare Centers and Service Centers;
- Inadequate residential accommodation for health staff;
- Unsatisfactory supply and maintenance of equipment, medicines and vaccines. Unless these needs are met by the regular budget, the health infrastructure will remain an unproductive investment. Encouraging community participation in primary healthcare by their members' involvement in decision-making processes would give local units greater responsibility for planning and budgeting, collecting fees, and determining how collected funds and government transfers would be used. T his would
- improve incentives for fund collections;
- increase accountability;

- ensure appropriateness of services to the local service centre; and
- minimize administrative costs.

The effectiveness of local institutions for the promotion of primary healthcare requires empowering local bodies through the devolution of power and other necessary support. Universalizing primary health is even more urgent. Until it becomes the fundamental goal of health policy, all other goals and objectives matter very little.

Drinking Water

Drinking water facilities have strong implications for the domestic work burdens of women and girls, time-saving for more productive work, sanitation services and the health benefits that they promote. But access of the Nepalese people to drinking water services is low. Although drinking water coverage reached 71.6% of the population in 2002, the quality of water supply is very poor. Contaminations at source, at water collection points, in water collection jars and in storage within households, among other dangers, are common in Nepal, contributing significantly to high rates of water-borne diseases such as diarrhea, dysentery, jaundice, typhoid and cholera. In addition, arsenic contamination in tube-well water is now emerging as a major problem. Although drinking water from pipes, tubewells and boreholes is regarded as safe, its quality from different sources is poor, and does not meet either the former or recently defined national standards. In 2001, it is believed that only 4.4% of the total population had access to first-grade quality water and only 6.4% to the medium-quality standard.

Approximately 60% of the population falls into the third category supplied with a basic service level of drinking water facilities. Current plans call for providing 25% of the total population with high-quality drinking water, while almost the entire population now living with the basic service water supply will move into the second category, having access to medium quality water by 2015. Government budgetary allocations to the drinking water sector have declined in recent years, from approximately 4% in 1990 to 2% of the entire budget in 2002. Greater resources demanded by the Melamchi Water Project are likely to crowd out the resources available to small drinking water projects. The sustainability of water supply projects has also remained challenging. The process of urbanization has exerted strong pressures for faster extension of water supply services with greater resource demands.

Social Protection

The social protection system safeguards people who cannot find jobs, who cannot work because of sickness, disability, old age or maternity, who have lost breadwinners, or who suffer from natural disasters, armed conflict or forced displacement. Because poverty in Nepal is deep and widespread throughout a large population base, vulnerability is high because of the large number of people near the poverty line for whom even a marginal income fluctuation can have serious consequences. Limited government budgetary capacity constrains a broader provision of significant social assistance arrangements. Although a variety of formal safety net programmes (such as food for work, cash transfers and food subsidies) exist, their coverage is very limited; only a small fraction of the population has been benefited from these schemes.

Nepal recently initiated universal social security through the introduction of social assistance to the citizens above the age of 75, the disabled, and widows. No single institution in Nepal has the mandate for supervising social security affairs. Provident funds and pensions, the most popular social security arrangements, are confined to the government sector and some of the public enterprises that cover no more than 5% of the labour force.

Nepal has a predominantly informal economy; the formal sector can currently provide job opportunities to less than 10% of the employed labour force. This means that social protection schemes designed for the formal sector can cover a very small proportion of the population at this stage of development. While a number of social security schemes exist in the public enterprises, they are neither uniform nor justified in terms of the financial capabilities of these bodies – an issue that often provokes labour conflicts and strikes. Moreover, as most of such benefits remain unfunded, the sustainability of such schemes is questionable and constitutes another major policy challenge in this general area. Access to basic social services is one of the major protections against unemployment and other income risks. To reduce their financial vulnerability and to achieve a decent standard of living, people must have access to basic public goods, including basic and primary education, primary healthcare and nutrition, drinking water and sanitation. Progress in poverty reduction, empowerment and human development in Nepal is critically dependent on expanding the provision of basic social services.

The present economic reform programme risks marginalizing people who cannot compete in the marketplace or survive its vagaries. New labour market arrangements such as contracting, sub-contracting and outsourcing pose new threats to the social security of the labour force. Protecting people from income risks and actually empowering them economically require putting extensive social protection institutions and practices in place.

WOMEN'S PERSONAL DEVELOPMENT

When you face your fear, most of the time you will discover that it was not really such a big threat after all. We all need some form of deeply rooted, powerful motivation it empowers us to overcome obstacles so we can live our dreams." Les Brown

Empowerment is a choice is what I told a group of ladies at my Women's online Boot Camp. We can either choose to live our best empowered life by pursuing resources, tools and connecting with key individuals to support our empowering personal development plan, or just drag along day by day with a victim mentality. We may also at times sabotage our own empowerment by disempowering behaviors. I am going to give you a few barriers to empowerment. You must make a concerted effort to learn to eliminate these barriers at all costs or you will be working against your plan for empowerment.

Fear

Fear is the opposite of faith. Many people are overcome by fear when they focus more on their circumstances and the dictates of society. Look at fear this way: False, Evidence, Appearing, Real. Many of the fears that we are concerned with may never manifest in our lives.

Unforgiveness

This area could take up quite a bit of time because of the impact that it can have on your life if it is not identified and eliminated from your lifestyle. I've heard it said this way: Unforgiveness is the poison taken by an individual with the hope of the other dying. That's right! It's a misplaced hope because it is not the other individual that is dying or will die, however, It's slowly causing death to your "spirit, soul and body." You must learn to lead a lifestyle of forgiveness.

Procrastination

There is a psychological aspect to the activity of procrastinating. It is known that we can tend to develop a habit that is learned by our doing certain activities, which don't result in a satisfactory manner, and therefore it may cause us to feel discouraged. After continued episodes we don't desire or are not inspired to continue in that manner. When an opportunity does arise for another episode we withdraw because of our association with past feelings surrounding this area.

Lack of Focus

Losing focus can immobilize you, bind you and hinder your endeavours toward success in life. This is a clear barrier to empowerment. Learning how to focus is a huge step toward a better life for yourself and those around you. There you have it 4 barriers to empowerment. What can you use tonight before your head hits the pillow? Write down two areas you will begin eliminating and/or tweak this week for a realized life of empowerment.

6

Models of Community Organization

"Macro intervention involves methods of professional changing that target systems above the level of the individual, group, and family, i.e., organizations, communities, and regional and national entities. Macro practice deals with aspects of human service activity that are non-clinical in nature, but rather focus on broader social approaches to human betterment, emphasizing the effective delivery of services, strengthening community life, and preventing social ills. Macro practice, thus includes the areas of community organization, social policy and administration.". Rothman has developed three models of community organizing which are locality development, social planning, and social action. Locality development is the model that most closely subscribes to the values and outcomes of what is typically referred to as "community development."" In practice however, many community development workers employ a range of techniques and approaches from locality development, social planning and social action models in their work with communities.

LOCALITY DEVELOPMENT MODEL

This model of community practice is based on the belief that in order to effect change, a wide variety of community people should be involved in planning, implementation, and evaluation. Key themes include the use of democratic procedures, voluntary cooperation, self-help, the development of local leadership, and educational objectives.

Social Planning Model

A rational, deliberately planned, technical process of problem-solving with regard to substantive social problems, characterizes this model. The degree of community participation may vary. However, building community capacity or fostering radical or fundamental social change is not a major goal of this model of community practice.

Social Action Model

Practitioners practising this model assume that a disadvantaged segment of the population needs to be organized in order to make demands on the larger community for increased resources or improved treatment. Key themes in this model are social justice, democracy, and the redistribution of power, resources, and decision making.

PURPOSE IN CONSIDERING THE VARIOUS MODELS

To identify and make explicit the assumptions and conditions that influence the selection of a model (or mixing models) of organizing, as it effects the process and the outcomes of the community assessment. To integrate theory with the practice of community work. To facilitate discussion and reflection on the process of community work. To identify the types of skills and roles required by a community worker in different projects and the focus of how one spends his/her time.

To structure the tasks and techniques that will aid in achieving the process goals of community development. To assist community workers in understanding how their orientation towards a particular model has affected the kinds of community projects they have become involved in and how they have chosen to work within a community. To provide a framework for community workers to revisit those decisions and do future planning.

COMMUNITY (LOCALITY) DEVELOPMENT

Suppose the quality of life in your community is declining. The major employer has packed up and moved to a place where labor and utilities are cheaper. Without steady paychecks, a lot of people in town don't have the money to keep up their houses and yards, or to support charitable organizations. Many people have found other jobs, but have to commute long distances to get to them. In some of the worst situations, individuals and families have become homeless, and are living in shelters or in their cars. Violence has increased, partially because those long commuting times leave many youth unsupervised during off-school hours, partially because of increasing substance abuse brought on by people's difficult circumstances. The community has turned into a depressed and depressing place, and most citizens feel powerless to do anything about it. How can you change this situation so that people start to take action to improve their lives?

One answer is to convince people that they can make a difference and get them to work together in thinking out what they can do, and then doing it. But what if there are serious divisions in the community, or what if most people don't see themselves as able to change anything?

Perhaps some groups are shut out of the political process or discriminated against economically or socially. Perhaps the many diverse groups in the community have little contact with or knowledge of one another. Before you can get people working together, you have to help them make contact with and begin to trust one another.

This is a situation when locality development is desperately needed. If community members can learn to communicate across class, ethnic, and racial lines, and to set up organizations, systems, and policies to take advantage of their resources and address their problems, they can make life better for everyone. In this section (and the two that follow) we'll discuss three different but overlapping approaches to community organization and community change. In this section, we'll discuss how to lay the groundwork and create a foundation for such a community-wide cooperative effort.

What is Locality Development?

As we stated in the first section of this chapter, community or locality development is community building through improving the process by which things get done. This can be an end in itself, but it can also be seen as the beginning of a larger process.

Section 1 identifies four types of community organizing:

- *Locality development* creates an infrastructure for community activism and action.
- *Social planning and policy change* uses the political and other systems to create policies that work toward improving the quality of life for all citizens.
- *Social action and systems advocacy* engage citizens in understanding and building power, and using it to advocate and negotiate for the interests of the community.
- *Coalition building* constructs community-wide groups of organizations and individuals, either to work on specific issues or to address more general community needs.

These four aspects of community organization are usually viewed as separate, but it might be more useful to consider them as overlapping parts of a whole. If you do a good job at locality development, you'll have a secure base of people with the capacity to act in any of several ways. True community organization works to create a community that's ready for anything. Locality development is the building of an inclusive, community-based infrastructure that can then respond in whatever way is necessary to meet challenges, take advantage of resources, and create positive social change.

The terms "community development" and "locality development" are sometimes used interchangeably, but a community and a locality are not the same, and working with each may require its own approach. (For convenience, in this section we'll use the term locality development to refer to working in a particular way with both localities and self-defined communities.)

A locality is a place — a town, a city neighborhood, a housing project, a rural area — and locality development looks on that place as a community.

The word "community" is commonly used to refer to a locality where people live, as well as to all the people who live there. A community can also refer to a group of people that identifies itself as a community because of shared experiences, backgrounds, values, religion, or culture. The mayor of a city may call his town a community, but most cities have a number of self-defined communities within them — an Italian-American community, a gay community, a Jewish community, an African-American community, a business community, etc. While not all members of these communities share the same points of view or act in the same ways, they do see themselves as having something important in common with fellow community members.

The difference here comes in attempting to organize a locality that isn't a self-defined community, but merely a collection of people who happen to live in the same place. Members of a self-defined community start with some trust in one another, and with the assumption of at least one major shared idea or experience or value. Citizens of a locality may feel that they have very little in common with one another, or even that their interests conflict. Thus, development in a self-defined community may be able to start relatively easily once community members have accepted the fact that it's a good idea. In a locality, nothing may be able to happen until residents are able to make connections, identify common interests, and start to see themselves as a community... and that may take a long time.

So what does locality development actually consist of? What kind of infrastructure does it refer to? In brief — we'll go into more detail later when we discuss how to engage in locality development — it's a matter of creating inclusive and participatory systems and processes that bring everyone in the community together to work on a common problem or toward common goals. It also entails encouraging leadership from within the community, developing communication networks that span all sectors, and establishing the process as an accepted part of community life.

Locality development — often, but not always, in contrast to social action — emphasizes positive action on the part of a whole community, rather than assuming the necessity of conflict. The purpose might be to gain economic stability, to improve social and/or political conditions, to protect the community against a threat — the demolition of a neighborhood to make way for a highway or for expensive housing — or to preserve its historic, cultural, environmental character.

Whatever form it takes, the process is meant to build the community and make it stronger, to help its members see that they need to work together toward common purposes, and to motivate them to create ways to make that happen.

LOCALITY DEVELOPMENT AND COMMUNITY

Locality development can break down barriers within the community by encouraging and improving communication among diverse individuals and groups in the population. When citizens from many sectors of the community work together to assess assets and needs, they get to know one another as human beings, rather than as abstractions (e.g., "youth," "the poor," "business people"). This interaction not only makes it possible for people from different backgrounds and circumstances to work together, but also fosters mutual respect and empathy.

Locality development can bring together people who normally have no contact, and define the community as including all of them. Just as it breaks down barriers, locality development binds community members together, and allows them to see everyone as part of a unit that only functions well when all its parts have what they need.

Locality development can lay a solid foundation for community support of activism around issues of importance. When a community has a process by which to include everyone in the discussion of strategy about how to deal with issues, the resulting action plans belong to the community. When they feel that the plans are theirs, community members will work hard to see them carried out.

Locality development can help individuals and groups acquire new skills and knowledge. Some of these may include:

- Leadership and administrative skills.
- A better understanding of, and ability to communicate with, people from a variety of backgrounds.
- Interpersonal skills.
- Facilitation skills.

- Analytical skills.
- An overview of how systems interact to influence the life of the community.
- An understanding of how economics, on both the large and small scales, affects people's lives.

Locality development can bring forth the natural leaders from within the community. This happens both naturally, as the result of the locality development process, and through the encouragement of current leaders.

Locality development can encourage the community to identify its own resources and understand its own strengths. Once people have a clear sense of what they have available and what they themselves can do, they can use their resources to their best advantage.

Locality development can make the community self-sufficient and able to identify and solve its own problems. The advantages of being in this position include:

- An increase in community confidence and self-esteem, motivating citizens to tackle and solve tough problems.
- The reduction or elimination of the need for the community to be dependent on outside sources for help, and thus not having "experts" determine what is good for the community.
- An increase in the speed with which the community can respond to problems and mobilize resources.
- Assurance that the problems the community addresses are those that really concern it.

Locality development can give voice to everyone, and make participatory democracy the normal method of community decision-making. Building an inclusive, participatory infrastructure ensures that everyone's opinions and needs are heard, and leads to the establishment of community systems that involve all sectors.

Locality development can build a foundation for real community and equity, leading to a healthy community and long-term, positive social change. When people work together as a community, it's much harder to write off particular groups, or to ignore their needs, and much easier to envision and work toward a community in which all the necessary underpinnings of health are available to everyone.

When and where should you engage in locality development? In most sections of the Community Tool Box, the answer to the "when?" question begins with a sentence similar to "While this activity is almost always appropriate, there are certain times when it's especially useful." In this instance, however, we'll make an exception to that practice. While locality development usually starts because of a specific need or difficult conditions, it is, in fact, called for at virtually any time and in any place where there are inequities in the social system, where the quality of life for at least some members of the community is unacceptable, where systems or resources are inadequate to meet all the community's needs, or where the community is threatened from within or without. It's even appropriate when things are going well, since this may be a good time to make positive changes that would be harder in difficult times (improvements in environmental conditions, for instance, or a push for pedestrian-friendly areas). In other words, locality development is needed at almost any time in almost any community or locality.

In some communities, the need may be immediately obvious: major employers have left, housing stock is deteriorating, Main Street storefronts are empty and decaying, violence is on the rise or already at frightening levels, etc.. There may be racial or ethnic tensions, many homeless people on the streets, or major problems relating to the public schools, the environment, or corruption in local government. Whatever the situation, it will be apparent that the community needs to do something before things get even worse.

In many cases, however, problems are hidden, or are unacknowledged. There may be an unspoken agreement that widespread alcohol abuse and domestic violence are accepted parts of community life, for instance. Community members may turn their heads and fail to notice the hunger and poverty that exist in isolated pockets, or simply not realize that a large number of their fellow citizens have no access to health care. Until there's a crisis, many communities can't or won't see the problems they face. It may take a disaster — as in the case of the flooding and devastation of New Orleans in the wake of Hurricane Katrina in 2005 — for a community (or a nation) to face up to its realities.

An ongoing locality development process can not only lead to a healthier community, it can help a community weather bad times, and even prepare for calamity, and take advantage of good times to make things even better. For that reason, locality development is appropriate in any community at any time.

Who should be involved in locality development? To be most effective, a locality development process should be inclusive and participatory. That means it should include all sectors of the community (and give all an equal voice) and that their role should not be to act as advisors or consultants, but as full participants in all phases of addressing community issues and working toward their resolution and a better quality of life.

It's important not to think about self-identified communities as all of a piece. The "African-American community" in any U.S. city is not made up of people who all think alike, or who are all of the same income or education level. It may have leaders, but they don't necessarily speak for all members of that community, any more than any other individual does. It may have institutions or organizations that occupy important places in the community, but they don't represent everyone. Diversity refers to more than skin color or background: it encompasses opinions, political stances, income, attitudes, and a multitude of other factors, and as many of those as possible should be included when you're recruiting people to take part in locality development.

Some of the factors that a locality development effort might consider in putting together a grassroots group are:

- Interest in the effort.
- Race.
- Ethnicity.
- Gender.
- Sexual orientation.
- Geography. This may mean including people from a variety of neighborhoods, from several rural areas, or even from different city blocks. Geography is especially

important when people from different areas have different interests because of differences in outlook, income, culture, etc..

- Income. This is purely an economic measure.
- Class identification. Class identification may or may not be tied to income. Some industrial workers may have higher incomes than most middle managers, but still identify themselves as working class, rather than middle class. Those middle managers, as well as teachers and other professionals and "white collar" workers with similar incomes, on the other hand, may be more likely to think of themselves as middle class. A woman on welfare who's been to college may think of herself very differently from a woman in similar circumstances who's a high school dropout. Class identification is as much a matter of attitude, personal history, and other factors as it is of income.
- Age.
- Religion.
- Culture. This may be linked to ethnic or racial background (the factors that usually come to mind when culture is mentioned), age, religion, etc.. Teenagerss have their own language, norms, and styles, for instance, as do many immigrant groups and faith communities. Each is a culture unto itself, and needs to be considered when engaging in locality development.
- Language.
- Organizations and institutions. Service clubs, fraternal organizations, community-based organizations, hospitals, universities, libraries, and other bodies need to be involved. They can bring valuable resources and constituencies with them.
- Local government and government agencies. Not only elected and appointed officials, but police and firefighters, welfare workers, and others in similar positions should be drawn in. As policies and systems change, they'll bear much of the burden, and should share in ownership of the development process from the beginning.

LOCALITY DEVELOPMENT AND IRON RULE OF COMMUNITY

The "Iron Rule" of community organizing is to never do for people what they can do for themselves. Thus, the process is participatory by definition.

The participatory nature of organizing is crucial, regardless of the type of organizing it is. The inclusive process we've been describing may ultimately depend on direct action and the exercise of political power for success, but it may also depend on collaboration. Locality development can also be an exercise in bringing together all the sectors of a community — even those that normally wield the power — in an effort to improve conditions and the quality of life for everyone.

Get to know the community. The term "get to know" really means three things here:

- Learn about the history, relationships, issues, factions, and other aspects of the community or locality you're working with before you start.
- Get acquainted with the people in the community. Develop relationships, so that they know who you are, what you're doing there, and why they should talk to and trust you.
- Understand how people in the community view themselves and others.

We'll briefly examine what each of these means in practice.

Community History

Knowing some community history is absolutely necessary. If you don't understand the alliances, rivalries, conflicts, and successes of the community, particularly those of the recent past, you're apt to make huge blunders. The time spent cleaning up after yourself will be far greater than the time you spend making sure you don't make a mess in the first place.

To learn community history, you have to talk to those who've experienced it or heard about it directly from the source. Conversations with community elders or long-time residents can yield a great deal of information (of course, not all of it necessarily objective or accurate). If you make contact with a broad range of people, you can at least sort out where stories agree or disagree. Some research in newspaper archives or on the Web could also be helpful here.

Getting Acquainted and Building Trust

In many communities — whether defined by geography or by class, ethnicity, or some other criterion — it's difficult for an outsider to make any inroads. Especially if you're obviously different from community members, they may be reserved about spending time with you or listening to what you have to say. Even if you're already a member of the community, or come from a background or culture similar to that of the community with which you're working, you won't automatically gain their trust. You'll have to do that by proving your commitment and staying strong.

You have to spend time in the community and meet people where they live — in the streets, at community events, in stores and bars and restaurants, in people's houses. There's a reason that the Peace Corps and similar organizations insist that volunteers live in the communities in which they work. Familiarity breeds familiarity. If community members actually know and have a relationship with you — have had conversations with you about your family, your likes and dislikes, your values and ideals — they're far more likely to trust you and listen when you ask them to join in a development effort.

Understanding how community members view themselves and others: Understanding how community members view themselves and others both inside and outside the community will help you understand where you and the community need to start. Some of the factors you might explore:

- How much do community members interact with one another? How well do they know one another? Is there a sense of community solidarity, or are there deep divisions between natives and newcomers, or between people of different races or ethnicities? Are there existing mechanisms in the community that serve to bring people together or keep them apart?
- Do community members see themselves as a community? Do they see themselves as part of multiple communities? Do people identify with the community as you've defined

it, or with any community? Or is their world bounded instead by family or friendships or work?

- How do community members view change and their own ability to effect change? Do they want changes? Do they feel that change is possible? Are they angry? Afraid? Apathetic?
- Does the community have a sense of pride, or a sense of inferiority? Does it feel put upon by outside forces?
- What kinds of current or potential connections do community members have to policymakers or other influential people or groups? Do they see those connections as possible or useful?

Identify the reasons that the community is likely to be willing to organize. The reason that Saul Alinsky, commonly seen as the father of modern community organizing, was able, in 1930s Chicago, to bring together neighborhood groups that had been hostile to one another is that they all shared a common interest in improving working conditions in the stockyards, and a common resentment of the bosses who were exploiting them. If a community is to come together, it has to have good reasons for doing so, and those reasons have to be determined by the community itself, not by an authority or expert or outside organizer, no matter how well-intentioned.

Those reasons may be small specific issues (the deterioration of a neighborhood park, the need for more streetlights) or larger concerns (the fear that the community is dying economically or socially; feelings of resentment and powerlessness; a sense that opportunities are being missed; widespread discrimination and inequity; hostility from without; etc.). Furthermore, the reasons may not be understood or shared by everyone. It's crucial to find out what community members are concerned about, and to determine what might move them to unite and take action to address their concerns.

Determine who are the opinion leaders and trusted individuals and groups in the community. Opinion leaders are those whose opinions are valued and whose advice is followed by a majority of community members. They may be leaders because of their position (CEOs, clergy, college presidents, government officials), because of their assumed intelligence (doctors, professors), or simply because they have demonstrated level-headedness and fairness in the past. Often, they are average citizens who have gained their neighbors' respect through their exercise of common sense, compassion, and strong values.

Find those people and start with them. They'll know how to attract others, and who among those others can bring still others with them. Their support will lend credibility to a locality development effort. In addition, they're likely to be able to identify and help in negotiating the personality and group conflicts and other pitfalls of locality development.

Perhaps the most important thing you can do is to treat everyone with respect. If you can develop a reputation as someone who's straightforward and honest, and who respects everyone, people will be more than willing to hear what you have to say. If you're condescending, or present yourself as knowing more than community members, you might as well leave and find another use for your time.

Recruit community members to the effort. First and foremost, locality development relies on personal contact. Meetings in people's living rooms, door to door canvassing, outreach to organizations and institutions and agencies — all of these and other methods are the base of an organizing effort. It's difficult to convince anyone of anything without direct communication.

Recruitment is really inseparable from building trust and becoming part of the community. Many organizers believe that they have to actually live in the community to establish any credibility, and, in at least some communities, that may be true. Having the support of opinion leaders and other trusted community members and groups can sometimes serve the same purpose, but it's not a substitute for doing the core work of any organizing: making personal contact with as many people as possible, and maintaining contacts day in and day out.

Build a communication system. The first of the system improvements necessary to locality development is a communication network that makes it possible for anyone to reach anyone else. Not only can such a system make working together a great deal easier, but it also helps to squelch rumors and head off trouble before it happens. The ability to make direct contact with someone and to find out exactly what she meant in that newspaper quote, or whether she's actually planning what you've heard she is, can make all the difference. She may not have meant her remark to be offensive (or may not have made it at all); she may not have meant to release her plan until she'd discussed it with you and others first. On the other hand, if there's actually a problem, it's better to deal with it straightforwardly and resolve it than to complain and wait until it's too late before protesting.

A communication system, in this sense, doesn't refer to hardware — a complicated phone system, for instance, or a computer network — but, rather, to people knowing whom to call on for what, and making sure that everyone has access to everyone else. This may be as simple as circulating a list of names, mail and email addresses, and phone numbers, or as complicated as setting up communication trees (and allowing for the fact that many low-income people don't have their own computers or phones).

Encourage leadership from the community from the beginning. Identify, train, and mentor natural leaders, so that they can take on increasing responsibility and ultimately direct the effort. One of the key pieces of infrastructure that locality development is meant to create is local leadership, making it possible for the effort to be sustained indefinitely by the community.

Some community members may have very little experience in attending meetings, speaking in public, or even in sorting out their own opinions from what they've been told. They'll need support and training in learning those skills.

Create a structure to help the community accomplish its goals. In order to solidify and coordinate the development effort, it is generally necessary to create an organization of some sort, or even more than one, to provide structure for and coordinate your action. The exception to this rule is a situation in which an organization already exists that has credibility and can take on the work of locality development.

There are a number of reasons for establishing an organization or other structure:

- *It makes the work easier.* An organization gives the effort an identity that can then be used to seek out resources, devise and carry out actions, gain official status, and state positions. It makes it easier to operate in the world of government regulations and fundraising, it's easier to explain than a still-formless locality development process, and it can attract members more easily as well.
- *It makes the work more efficient and more effective.* A structure makes it easier to divide and delegate tasks efficiently, to contact people when things need to be done, and to keep track of everything.
- *It gives the effort standing in the community.* An organization legitimizes the development effort, and shows that it's serious and well-supported.
- *It lends form to the development effort.* An organization is something community members can point to as a result of their coming together. It has substance and purpose, rather than simply being a group of people talking about doing something. It has a name, and people are associated with it. It's real.
- *It creates a focus for community work.* An organization can act as a coordinating body for whatever comes next. It provides both a physical focus — an office, a phone, a computer, even if they're in someone's kitchen — and a social and political one. People belong to it, or work with it or for it. They care about what it stands for, because it stands for them.
- *It unites those involved in locality development.* An organization gives community members something formal to belong to and participate in. It both brings people together physically — for meetings and other activities — and identifies them with the organization, and with other members of or participants in the organization.
- *It gives the community an entity that it created and owns.* If the development effort has been conducted well, the organization will grow out of the participation and ideas of the community. Because they own it, they'll work hard to make it successful.

Define the most important issues that relate to the community's overall concerns. Just as when your group came together, the issues to be worked on must come from the community itself and reflect community members' concerns and needs. Some of these issues may be the same reasons you cited for coming together; others may be stepping stones to a larger goal. In either case, people won't find them compelling unless they generate them themselves.

Develop a strategic plan. Once you've determined where you're going — i.e., the issues or problems to be addressed — the next step is to figure out how to get there. The way to do that is by developing a strategic plan — a step-by-step blueprint for accomplishing your goals. This means embarking on a participatory process to establish a vision for the community, a mission for your effort, objectives to be reached, a strategy by which to reach them, and actions that will carry out the strategy (VMOSA).

An important part of planning is considering what's possible and what will help to keep the development process going. It's wise, for instance, not to try to reach your ultimate goals all at once, but to work in stages. Aim first for something that's achievable, so that the effort will have an initial success to build on. When that goal is met, strategize again and set your next, somewhat more difficult, goal. With each stage of the effort, people will become more confident and more committed to reaching the ambitious goals set out in the strategic plan.

Implement your plan. Here's where all your organizing and hard work pay off. The community takes action to achieve the results it wants, based on the plan that's been developed.

Continually monitor and evaluate your work. The Community Tool Box considers these functions so important to any effort that it devotes four chapters (36-39) to evaluating community organizations and initiatives. Monitoring and regularly evaluating your work gives you the opportunity to change what's not working and to respond to changes in the community. It also tells you what you're doing well, and may give you ideas about how to build on your successes.

You should be looking at both the process and the results of what you're doing. How successfully have you brought in all sectors of the community? How invested are they in making or causing changes that will improve people's lives? How well is your organization running, and does it meet the community's needs? Is the action you're involved in effective at keeping you moving toward your goals? Are you achieving the outcomes you're aiming for?

Make the locality development effort self-sustaining and community-run, so that it's established as a permanent fixture. The Back of the Yards Neighborhood Council (BYNC) that Saul Alinsky helped establish in 1939 still exists as an organization, even though most of those originally involved are long dead, and the neighborhood has gone from being virtually all white and Eastern European to mostly Hispanic and African-American. You may not be interested in that level of longevity, but locality development is an ongoing process. Individuals and groups move, and others that know nothing of your effort take their places. If you build a strong community and a strong organization that belongs to and is run by community members, it will continue as long as it's needed.

COMMUNITY MOBILIZATION AND ORGANIZATION

We have defined community mobilization as a process whereby a group of people have transcended their differences to meet on equal terms in order to facilitate a participatory decision-making process. In other words it can be viewed as a process which begins a dialogue among members of the community to determine who, what, and how issues are decided, and also to provide an avenue for everyone to participate in decisions that affect their lives. In the favela of Cachoeira it is evident that there are a number of obstacles which are serving to prevent a mobilization process from occurring.

On the one hand there is quite a strong network in the favela in terms of interdependence or cooperation amongst friends, families, and neighbours. Unfortunately there is little formal organization and strategizing around community organizations which could potentially serve as a means to address their needs. This sense of immobility arises from a number of factors: (1) the misperception that politicians and bureaucrats will alleviate their problems for them (yet the problems of corruption and poor administration are evident),

(2) a lack of expertise amongst the community to facilitate such organization, (3) the unwillingness of the community as a whole to give up individual interests to form a broader cooperative, and (4) an extreme shortage of available resources to facilitate the mobilization process.

The solutions to Cachoeira's problems are rooted within the resource capacities of the favela. The organizing structure presented here is based on the concept of self-help, encompassing various distinguishing features of community development theory, practice, and ideology. While it is not assumed that all of the problems of the favela can be resolved by community's efforts alone, it is seen as a means of achieving broad community participation and effort. Through this means it is suggested that the living conditions, facilities and services of the community will improve, along with the empowerment of the community.

In the context of Cachoeira there are a number of pre-existing community groups such as the Mother's Club, the SABE, and church groups which can potentially serve as a the basis for such a mobilization strategy. Based on the articulated goals of the community as indicated in the survey there is potential for new groups to be established to formulate strategies to address pressing problems in the community. In this regard our report looks at four central areas to be addressed: (1) Education and Health, (2) Employment (3) Physical Infrastructure, and (4) Land Tenure.

COMMUNITY ORGANIZATION

Empowering and educating people to participate as citizens in an evolving social and political order is one of the most important and challenging of tasks in human development today.

In developing countries, EDC helps organize communities whose voices have previously been excluded from their education and governance systems. We convene teachers, school and government officials, parents, businesspeople, and other leaders to assess educational needs and mobilize available resources, human and otherwise. The action-oriented process results in school improvements such as better teaching, enhanced learning environments and/or materials, more effective management, and increased accountability in the education system. EDC also helps individuals and communities rebuild from political, economic and even geographic instability. Working with local residents and their community leaders, EDC initiatives support basic literacy and numeracy education, peace and reconciliation skill-building, civic participation and life skills education.

COMMUNITY ASSOCIATION LITIGATION

The Firm's Community Association Litigation Practice is dedicated to providing strategic, innovative, and aggressive representation for our Community Association clients in all litigation matters. Becker & Poliakoff status as a pioneer in Community Association law is well known throughout the litigation community. Judges, arbitrators, and attorneys are aware that Becker & Poliakoff is the leading firm when representing Community Associations. The Firm's reputation leads to superior outcomes for our clients. Community Association litigation is specialized and the attorneys practicing Community Association litigation must be familiar with the nuances of this area of law. With over 4,000 Community Association clients, no firm has more experience and knowledge in this area of law than Becker & Poliakoff.

Condominiums, Cooperatives, and Homeowner Associations are each governed by a separate section of the Florida Statutes. Therefore, each Community Association dispute requires a distinct analysis of the governing substantive and procedural law. It is the Firm's job to efficiently and successfully guide our clients through the entire litigation process, from the beginning of the dispute, until the final disposition of the matter.

In addition, the firm is very active in representing community associations in multi-million dollar casualty claims against their insurance carriers, such as hurricane damage claims. Our representation has included giving general insurance advice, representing associations in casualty insurance policy defence issues, representing association in the claims adjustments and appraisal process as well as representation in litigation, both in the state and federal courts through out Florida. The attorneys who practice in this area are highly-skilled and experienced attorneys who are able to guide and counsel our association clients from the inception of the disaster to the final resolution of the insurance claim. The Firm's Community Association Litigation Practice routinely provides our clients with the following services: Initial analysis of the dispute, including a thorough investigation of the facts;

- Determination of the proper causes of action or defenses, and Anticipation of possible defenses or counterclaims.
- Determination of the appropriate jurisdiction and venue (i.e. Mandatory, Non-binding Arbitration; County or Circuit Court; or Mediation).
- Determination and opinion on the likelihood of success in consideration of the remedies sought.
- Fact finding through the discovery process specified to the forum that the action lies.
- Thorough representation in hearings, arbitrations, mediations, non-jury and jury trials.
- Aggressive pursuit of the recovery of attorney fees for our clients, if provided by law.
- Representation of our clients throughout any appellate actions.

COMMUNITY EVALUATION

CME is more of an approach rather than a specific technique to involve citizens in gathering evidence of government performance and may include specific activities such as budget tracking or community scorecards which are described elsewhere in this toolkit.

The CME approach evolved from other techniques to involve communities in monitoring and evaluating the effectiveness of specific development projects. Such approaches have been used by many development agencies which has generated extensive literature on the subject. Much of this focuses on conducting monitoring and evaluation in a way that does not merely use the communities for data but also encourages them to voice and express their concerns, realities and the extent to which a given project has impacted and improved their lives.

The emergence of CME can be linked to two separate trends that emphasize the central role of government in development. First, the rights-based approach increasingly adopted by civil society organisations holds the government squarely responsible for service provision meant to secure people's rights. Therefore, many CSOs have shifted their role from being service providers towards advocacy, civic engagement and public participation. Second, over the last decade or so, the donor discourse on development has increasingly emphasised the role of the state in development. The donors would like to ensure that the aid being channelling through governments is reaching the intended beneficiaries (poor communities), and whether it is leading to desired impact. So, as donor aid is increasingly supporting governments for provision of public services, NGOs have increasingly supported communities to appreciate the role of the state in the provision of public services and to enhance their capacity to participate in monitoring those services.

It is important to note that CME tools being developed and applied by CSOs are not merely limited to monitoring the access to and quality of services but also to monitor government's response to human rights violations, tracking environmental degradation, monitoring and evaluating government contracts with private sector; and to track implementation of any public policy.

In general, the aims of Community Monitoring and Evaluation are:

- Ensuring communities are aware of their entitlements and strengthening their capacity to hold governments accountable to secure their entitlements.
- Strengthening the relationship between governments and citizens which in turn influences government to play a proactive role in the interests of citizens and respond to their needs.
- Ensuring governments are working towards fulfilling their promises
- Ensure that the actions of the governments are reducing poverty and making a real difference to the lives of poor communities.

STRATEGY IN COMMUNITY ORGANIZATION

As globalization and privatization visibly impact various spheres of people's lives, it is evident that for the upper classes there are more choices and lifestyle changes as consumers. However, for the poorer and disadvantaged sections, life gets more difficult since struggles for livelihood increase.

In the early decades of the twenty-first century, the economic, political, and social risks seem high indeed for vulnerable populations such as refugees and immigrants, those sold into wage or sexual slavery and the poor, lower middle-class, and economically marginalized workers throughout the world. In short, globalization offers possibilities both for global human advancement and for increasing disparity of income and opportunity throughout the world. In order to understand this increasing gulf between different sections of society, an examination of the shifts in employment patterns and relationships with regard to specific occupations is as imperative as is a macro level overview.

In India, 92 percent of total employment is informal in nature and a large percentage of those in the informal economy are the poor. In January 2005, the total employment in the Indian economy was 458 million of which the unorganized sector accounted for 395 million. This direct estimation shows that the unorganized sector constituted 86 percent of total workers in 2004– 05. Informal employment which is the mainstay of the majority of the jobs is in fact likely to grow further in developing countries as forces of globalization and privatization make their impact felt. As Bhowmik explicates, 'there is an attempt to scale down permanent employment by replacing permanent workers by temporary, contract or casual labour.... Employers find that casual or contract labour is cheaper and easier to control. Second, sub-contracting through the putting-out system adopted by most of the large industries has reduced the need for permanent labour... ' The growing ranks of unprotected contract and casual labour within the organized sector and in the unorganized sector are a result of the high level of unemployment in the wider society. The employers have, no doubt, taken advantage of the large pools of cheap labour available. Nonetheless, they could not have adopted the strategy of cutting labour costs had these sections of the working class been unionized.

Unorganized informal workers, whose ranks are swelling, are most vulnerable to exploitation whether as wage earners or self-employed/own account workers. Unionizing as a strategy can help them to bargain for their entitlements. However, unionizing such groups is not without its challenges, since they are often geographically scattered, with work patterns and employment relationships established over a period of time to their disadvantage. Wherever such initiatives meet with some measure of success, or demonstrate the significance of struggles for the rights of the marginalized, they are of immense value for other disadvantaged groups as they hold out a ray of hope. For disciplines such as Social Work, such social movements are an important training ground for students, while challenging curricular perspectives and content.

UNION AND ACADEMIC INSTITUTION IN COMMUNITY ORGANIZATION

Community organization (CO) practice in India has had a strong thread of social action as seen through various social movements and social advocacy initiatives backed by mass mobilization. Effective CO in India is necessarily a political process as it is concerned with power, equity and justice. Social movements and other organized social actors – political parties, mass organizations, labour unions and small non-profit organizations and collectives reflect the rich organizing tradition in India. They have played a significant role in mobilizing specific constituencies. Yet these important processes of mobilization and subsequent assertion of the constituencies are still struggling to find an appropriate space within the knowledge system of social work curriculum as traditional social work teaching in most universities has not consciously aligned itself to these processes.

The experience of teaching Community Organization at TISS2 for more than a decade has required confronting one of the criticisms levelled at academia from social activists about Social Work being non-political, both in terms of its largely perceived status quo orientation as well as its steering clear of any political party processes.

As Community Practice Educators, there is no denying the role of structural factors in the marginalization of entire communities and sections of society. Class, caste, gender, and ethnicity inform the analysis of social development. Field education too is a critical component of the Social Work curriculum and facilitates the strengthening of field-theory linkages. One of the challenges as educators is to identify and work with partners in the field who can provide role modelling for the students both through their work in the field and as ideologues whose world view shapes their practice. From the early 1990s onwards, there was a conscious shift towards aligning with certain types of organizations and social action groups through fieldwork placement of students from the Department of Urban and Rural Community Development (called Centre for Community Organization and Development Practice (CODP) since 2006).3

The fieldwork agencies were consciously expanded to include trade unions, women's organizations, people's movements and advocacy groups. These organizations reflect the process of CO, provide political education and enhance political consciousness of students. The CO perspective is refined in exploring the ideology, orientation, and approach of these organizations where use of democratic processes and an awareness of rights are considered a significant strategy. Many of these organizations do not employ trained social workers; do not have offices or conventional staff hierarchies. Many are small, localized initiatives.

In 1997, an association between TISS and a union of contractual workers, Kachra Vahatuk Shramik Sangh (KVSS), meaning 'Waste Collectors' and 'Transporters' Union' began through field placement of Master's level students in Social Work. The union aimed at collectivizing the unorganized garbage collection and transportation workers, employed by private contractors, who were hired by the Municipal Corporation of Greater Mumbai. They hoped that students working along with them would contribute to the work, while learning in the field. This association of the Centre for CODP and KVSS continues till date. The range of struggles of different sections of workers in solid waste management (SWM) in Mumbai that have been taken up by the Union have provided an excellent learning ground for students in social action and mobilization. Faculty involvement has contributed to advocacy initiatives of the union on a number of issues.

Elements of this unionization process in Mumbai through the lens of interface between the Centre for CODP at TISS and the Union in the broader and rapidly transforming context of SWM practices in the country are highlighted in the ensuing sections.

SWM and the Context of Conservancy Work

In India, more than 70 percent of the population lives in 550,000 villages (2001 Census). However, there has been a rapid growth of urban centres since the decade of the 1990s in terms of the size and expanse of the cities as well as the rise in population. At the dawn of the new millennium, 300 million Indians lived in its nearly 3700 towns and cities, in sharp contrast to only 60 million in 1947 when the country became independent. During the last 50 years, the population of India has grown two and a half times, but the urban population has grown nearly five times (Dhar Chakrabarti, 2001).

One of the concomitants of the growth of urban centres has been a rise in solid waste generation. About 39 million tonnes of solid waste is generated in the urban areas everyday. Of this not more than 60 percent is collected daily (Dhar Chakrabarti, 2001). The per capita quantum of solid waste generated daily ranges from 100 g in small towns to 500 g in large towns. The population of Mumbai grew from 8.2 million in 1981 to 12.3 million in 1991, registering a growth of 49 percent. On the other hand, municipal solid waste (MSW) generated in the city, in the same period registered a growth of 67 percent (Central Pollution Control Board, 2000). This clearly indicates that the growth in MSW in (our) urban centres has outpaced the population growth in recent years (Singhal and Pandey, 2001).

SWM has been a key function of the urban local bodies (ULBs) with workers specifically employed to perform these jobs. These are the 'permanent' workers who are on the regular payroll of the municipal authorities. Permanency of employment brings with it job and wage security, regular working hours, entitlement to paid holidays and social security for the workers. Each ULB has hundreds or thousands of workers on its rolls engaged in the tasks of garbage collection and transportation to landfill sites, roadside sweeping and cleaning; cleaning of underground sewers through the manholes and related tasks.

The number of employees depends on the size of the city area, population and also the quantum of solid waste generated.

Since the late 1990s, a period which coincides with the liberalization of India's economy, there have been moves to privatize this function of SWM. The Committee Constituted by the Supreme Court of India regarding SWM in Class I Cities in India, in its report (March, 1999), while making a strong case for efficiency and effective handling of urban waste, recommended that private sector participation be encouraged in this activity through suitable amendments in the Contract Labour (Regulation and Abolition) Act, 1970.5 Among its other recommendations was to keep conservancy work out of the purview of the Scheduled Caste/Scheduled Tribe (Prevention of Atrocities) Act, 1984 (The Report, 1999).

Further, regarding incentives to the private sector it states: 'SWM, processing and disposal are an area where the private sector has still not shown much interest. The private sector has, therefore, to be given some incentives by way of long-term contracts, assured supply of garbage at the plant site, lease of land at nominal rates for entering this field.'

The report argues that, 'NGO6 as well as private sector participation may be encouraged in such a way that it does not affect the interests of the existing labour, it does not violate the provisions of the above law, does not exploit the private labour and yet reduces the burden of the ULB. This will substantially help in improving the quality of service of the ULBs, effect economy in expenditure and also give scope to the private sector to enter the waste management market'.

A case is therefore made for effective and efficient management of solid waste with the stated concern that newer practices should not be an additional burden for the ULB or exploit private labour (M. Vyas, unpublished work).

In recent years, urban India has witnessed a shift towards privatization of SWM. In certain cities, entire zones (as administrative units) are given on contract to private firms or contractors; in others, there could be a division of various tasks given to contractors. Hence, roadside sweeping and cleaning of specific stretches of city roads; garbage collection and transportation; manhole cleaning are all parcelled out as jobs to different contractors. A study (Srinivasan, 2006) in Chennai examined the SWM practices of three types of organizations viz. public (the municipal corporation), private (a business firm with the contract of SWM in three of ten zones in the city) and a voluntary organization providing neighbourhood-based SWM services to the residents through collectives of volunteer-workers. Hence, there is a multiplicity of tasks, of contractors as well as of agencies engaged in SWM in various urban centres.

This emerging pattern of SWM in cities across the country has implications for the nature of employment, employer–employee relationship, and hence, the conditions of workers in the ULBs, the private firms, contractors and voluntary organizations. The public-private partnership in SWM has in fact led to a situation where the contractual workers are engaged alongside the 'permanent' or regular workers at the same or related tasks, but with none of the wage and social security benefits of the latter. With most of these workers doing this job for as long as fifteen or twenty years, the need for a permanent workforce of this strength is well established.

Organizing workers in this sector is perhaps the only pathway to better work conditions or permanency. In order to capture the dynamism and challenges of such an initiative, the social and legal context needs discussion.

Informal Wage Earners in SWM

There are several categories of workers who work with waste in India, either as wage earners or self-employed workers. They are part of the burgeoning informal economy in the country. The contractually employed wage earners mentioned above work for a contractor or private firm at garbage collection and transportation, or to sweep the streets. On the other hand, the earnings of those who are waste pickers collecting and selling dry waste from neighbourhoods, streets and landfill sites depend on the amount that they collect and the price that they get for the paper, glass, plastic and metal from daily sales to the retail buyer who is the next person in the waste recycling chain.

Workers with waste are at the lower rungs of the informal sector as the job is considered unclean and difficult. This group faces social ostracism by not being allowed into buses, restaurants... public places due to their appearance and foul odour emanating from them due to their working conditions and absence of washing facility. Most of them live in unauthorized hutments that are demolished frequently. Those who live in rented tenements, pay Rs. 500–700 for a room that does not have water, electricity or drainage... only about 8–10 percent of these workers are literate. Lack of protective clothing adds to the health hazards and absence of social security enhances their vulnerability. Almost all these workers in cities like Mumbai are Dalits[9] and first generation migrants into the city from other districts of Maharashtra or South India. Economic and social marginalization is an evident basis for choice of waste related work.

Government policies such as the MSW Rules, 2000, have impacted either the pattern of work or the very access to waste (and hence source of livelihood) of these informal workers. While basic concerns of better work conditions and income are common to all informal workers in the sector, there are some differences among the wage earning contractual workers and the self-employed, due to the nature of employment. Here we focus on the process of unionization of wage earners who are employed by individual contractors to collect and transport garbage to landfill sites and sweep the roadsides.

The vulnerability and voicelessness of this category of workers is high as daily wagers can be fired at will and replaced easily. However, the Contract Labour (Regulation and Abolition) Act, 1970, contains certain provisions that are critical when arguing for betterment of the conditions of the contractual workers, chief among which is Section 10, which declares that work that is perennial in nature cannot be given on contract. There are grounds, therefore, for these workers to be made permanent.

In addition, the Act contains provisions regarding payment of wages and the responsibility of the contractor and the Principal Employer. These are significant in protecting the interests of contractual employees. The Minimum Wages Act, 1948, provides for a minimum wage that workers doing different kinds of jobs need to be paid. This wage is determined by each state, though a floor level minimum wage is prescribed by the Centre. Such laws define the goals of unionization efforts.

Unionizing the Contractual Workers

The sight of a truck loaded with garbage and two workers sitting atop it, eating their lunch, was what moved Milind Ranade into finding out about where they were headed and more about their situation. Trucks and workers would congregate either at roadsides across the city while loading the trucks with garbage or at the landfill sites when unloading them. Talking to them about the importance of coming together to form a union was one of the first steps of what later came to be known as KVSS. These workers spent a large part of their day working in the midst of garbage, since they were paid on the basis of the number of trips that they made from a designated part of the city to the landfill site. Certain municipal wards being more than 20 km from the dumping site, the pressure was on the workers to hurriedly load the truck and complete a trip. In the midst of this, it was by no means easy to stop to listen to what someone was trying to tell them about the union. Milind Ranade spent almost ten months travelling in the driver's cabin of rickety trucks and at the dumping site, talking tc whichever workers he met about the importance of union formation. This was the phase when students of Social Work joined him for two days each week. Their first lesson in community practice being that of bringing together a community of workers that was scattered across the vast city. In order to build the union, it was important that they reached the workers since the workers were not likely to come to them.

There were insights into how the workers perceived their work, how they dealt with it, as well as how the others that they encountered during their day treated them and spoke to them. Consumption of alcohol was common (and later explained as a way of dealing with the job). When the students accompanied Milind on the rounds, they observed that the 'regular' long sentences of explanation that camemore easily to them,were of no use in explaining to the workers why they should unionize. Sentences needed to be crisp and clear, as did the rationale for collectivizing. Watching Milind and subsequently, his other team members communicate in this manner, taught them that no matter how important a logic one may have arrived at, if one is not able to get across to those concerned, it does not mean much. In fact, asking the worker to repeat what had been told to him was a sure check of whether one had got across to him or not, and the extent to which one had. In the first few months of mobilization, a one-day hunger strike called by the group under the banner of KVSS was successful in obtaining water for drinking and washing at the dumping ground. This was the first victory for them, and an acknowledgement by the municipal authorities that they were in someway responsible for the welfare of the workers.

A few principles guide social mobilization strategies. First, because people are mostly aware of problems that cause them concern, mobilization is about showing it is possible to do something about those problems. Next, successful mobilization requires a personal touch – people are more likely to become active if an organizer or their friends and neighbours approach them individually. Third, for mobilization to last, people must gain the emotional satisfaction that comes from successful actions. Avisible victory... strengthens people's willingness to participate by showing success is possible. Membership meetings help expand the commitment to the group as people share the stories of progress and past successes and see the potentialpower of the group through the large numberof people attending. Other rewards for participation include the satisfaction of battling an injustice and the personal growth that comes from such involvement.'

As the union membership grew to include workers in the western suburbs of the city, so did the team of activists across the city that increased contact with workers. Interestingly, most of the workers in this part of the city spoke Tamil and were migrants from Tamil Nadu, a state of South India. Like the others, they had engaged in this work for more than a decade. Tamil speaking activists were pressed into their mobilization with others attempting to learn key sentences for basic communication. Students with this language skill were handpicked for fieldwork placement.

In 1999, with a strong membership base, the Union filed a case in the Bombay High Court arguing for permanency of almost 1500 workers engaged in waste collection and transportation, on the basis of the Contract Labour (Regulation and Abolition) Act, 1970. The cultural dimension in grassroots organizing was visible as the non-Tamil speaking activists struggled with the preparation and verification of union member lists. Utter confusion prevailed with the names of Tamilian workers! Students who worked with the union assisted with this task. Given the neo-liberal policy context, many observers commented that when the state departments were trying to reduce their employment liabilities, the chances of this new Union winning the case were very slim. However, with the High Court ruling in favour of the workers, the outcome was very heartening for the labour movement in general and the union in particular. Each victory, no matter how large or small needs to be celebrated. Workers congregated through a procession shouting slogans, this victory was celebrated with distribution of sweets to the gathering, speeches and discussions among members at all levels in the union. The Municipal Corporation appealed to the Apex Court of the country, challenging this judgment. In the meanwhile, the decision of the High Court on the employment of the 782 workers was to be upheld with a daily wage of Rs. 100 to be paid to each worker through the period till the Supreme Court pronounced its judgment.

The case in the Supreme Court went on for almost four years. This was the period in which one of the key tasks for students was to update the workers in different parts of the city about its progress. By this time, most contractual workers in the western and central suburbs of the city (where they lived with their families in low income settlements) had joined the union. Meetings began to be held in the areas where they lived. Around this time, the importance of reaching the families/ neighbourhoods of the workers and start addressing issues of indebtedness, substance abuse, as well as access to basic amenities, came to the fore.

This phase of intervention in the community was fraught with its own challenges. For instance, problematizing alcoholism was not simple as there was a strong rationalization given by the workers; women took some time to open up and get into discussions; it also became evident that this was not a household level problem, but one that was rampant in the entire neighbourhood. Secondly, many of the families found it difficult to access healthcare, education and other services due to the costs involved or the experience of public systems that were not approachable. These were the issues that students with the union now got involved with for some years through fieldwork. In such situations, community practitioners play an important role through advocacy and making the State agencies respond. As the case at the Apex Court dragged on, keeping up the morale of the almost 1200 workers whose future depended on it became part of the students' task. Intermittent meetings, providing updates, handling other issues of the workers and the corporation officials, formed the mainstay of the worker-union link. In the early years of the new millennium, the moves towards privatization of SWM for stated reasons of efficiency were being made in the country, leading to a shift in the role of the State with regard to essential functions. Through uncertain and changing times, through changes in political leadership in the state, the activists continued the negotiations and advocacy at the Centre and the state levels. Various statutory bodies/Commissions, people's representatives and other institutions were involved through advocacy initiatives.

Finally in February 2003, as a consequence of several years of advocacy, the Government of Maharashtra announced that it would make permanent the 1100 workers who were on the lists of the union and the Corporation and had been working on a contractual basis. 'And then the trumpets blew!' With this, a milestone had been reached after eight long years of struggle.

LEARNING THROUGH THE INTERFACE IN SOCIAL WORK EDUCATION

Aligning with groups/organizations is a political choice that a faculty/academic institution makes. Placing students for fieldwork with the union has been significant for the teaching of community practice. Interesting insights through this collaboration between the union and the Centre for CODP have emerged on a number of aspects. First, the trajectory of the struggles waged by the union demonstrated the increasing marginalization of contractual conservancy workers across the country. Hence contest and conflict as strategies of organizing increase in significance, even as the very context of mobilization becomes more challenging. Secondly, simultaneous facilitation to access basic services is imperative. For the workers, while the struggle for job security entailed a high degree of confrontation and negotiation with the state machinery, the processes of intervention at the family and neighbourhood level needed to continue in order to enhance quality of life. Without these parallel processes, increase in wages and eventual job security would not make the desired difference in their lives. The ability to see these inter-linkages contributed to students' education in community practice.

More thansixty students haveworked with theunion over the last ten years. However, not all of themadapted alike to the work, the perspective and ethos of the organization. One of the earliest students to be placed there for fieldwork requested within two days that his placement be changed – he was unable to eat after visiting the dumping ground and could not comprehend how he would learn social work here. Eventually, he did settle into the work of the union. Apart from a couple of students who resisted the work and action that the union offered, most of the others took to it and responded with passion, commitment and good work, demonstrating excitement and eager questioning. The activists that they worked and interacted with welcomed the critical interrogation, channelled it and nurtured the students. The students who work with the union come from different regions in the country and belong to different social and economic backgrounds from the workers. Learning to communicate, ridding themselves of inhibitions in conversing with 'new' people, and grasping the significance of the issues in the lives of workers – these are starting points for their connecting to the union. As interactions become frequent and informal, there is considerable mutuality among students and workers in terms of sharing about their lives, their families and so on. In terms of adopting the strategies of the union, there is a need to build convictions in most of the students. Their middle and upper class upbringing would have been largely characterized by affordability and access to quality services. For some of them, therefore, negotiation with officials on behalf of workers came after considerable struggle. Their identification with workers' situations needs to be built over a period of time and through creative pedagogy such as role plays, so that a sense of injustice and anger can build the conviction to argue. The faculty member (also the fieldwork supervisor) needs to make an enormous effort towards this student preparation.

In the mass mobilization by the union are experiences for young practitioners at addressing large gatherings. The space that this union gives to the students to get fully involved in issues, to follow-up and to take forward the questions that they feel strongly about, is edged with faith and confidence. The union being a membership-based organization, draws clear lines in demarcating where its responsibility ends and that of the workers begins. This is a facet that often sets it apart from other voluntary organizations that receive funds to work on particular issues and define their relationship with communities on a different keel. Field placement of students has strengthened the praxis in the CO curriculum. In reworking the curriculum, the Centre for CODP has introduced courses and modules on the informal economy and on strategies of organizing (one among them being that of unionizing). Student participation in some of these challenges of intervention through their fieldwork has enabled them to understand that unionizing in the informal economy is clearly an arena where trained community practitioners can and need play a role in a rapidly liberalizing state.

At the broader level, the tendency for schools of social work to remain beginner could prevent social work from realizing its full-potential, especially in the post-liberalization era where the 'merit' discourse creates fragmentation and individualization of 'troubles' and prevents mobilization, and where the very language of social transformation and right are subsumed or usurped by market forces and the Corporate Sector.

Challenges in the Urban Context

Through this experience of collectivizing contractual workers, there are some issues that must be highlighted. First, the sheer expanse of the city and distances that have to be travelled to reach points of congregation of workers is immense necessitating a decentralized organizational structure and the possibility of limited participation from members in some events. Workers speak different languages and relate to each other in linguistic/neighbourhood/ward-wise clusters. Transcending this fragmented sense of community to build and sustain a class consciousness is an important aspect in large city-based organizing. Hence, within the same union, for the now regularized (garbage collection and transportation) workers to come forward to support the struggle for the contractual roadside sweeping workers is not a given; this solidarity has to be built.

The union is now fighting the contract system for the latter category of workers viz. those employed by contractors to carry out the work of roadside sweeping for the ULBs these concerns, whether with wages or with laying off the workers when the contract period is over (and employing fresh recruits so that they cannot bargain for better conditions), span the length and breadth of the country. The contours of these struggles have perhaps changed with the thrust not so much on permanency, but security of work through assurance that the worker would not be replaced when the contract ends after three months or a year or whatever its duration.

7

Strategy and Roles of Community and Society

COMMUNITY STRATEGY

The preparation of the Commission's new programme concerning health and safety at work must bring this programme within the framework of the general employment strategy, as defined in Luxembourg, Lisbon, Nice and Stockholm, for more and better jobs, with the emphasis on the quality of employment and the modernisation of the organisation of work. In this integrated strategy the responsibilities of the different actors and levels of actions must be clearly established; this means emphasising the central role of the public authorities in the area of standardisation and co-ordination and the need for the social partners to more closely involved in the management of the changes.

The ETUC supports a strong European programme for health and safety at work focused on efficient legislation implemented at the work place and progress through evaluation and control, the use of open co-ordination based on benchmarks, indicators and objectives to be achieved, the strengthening of the role of the social partners, the attainment by the public authorities of the highest health and security standards for their own employees, the improvement of worker representation, the development of the information, consultation and participation of workers and their representatives concerning decisions in the area of health and safety and the organisation of work. The workers group of the Luxembourg Consultative

Committee has worked with the TUTB and the ETUC Secretariat to finalise a document on Community strategy in the field of health and safety. This resolution summarises the key points of that document, the ETUC commitment to ensuring the successful implementation of that strategy and the priorities in terms of action.

The Context

The realities: The statistics concerning accidents at work show over a long period a clear improvement in the situation, but at the same time there is a worrying trend in certain sectors and forms of employment and there has been a deterioration in working conditions and an increase in occupational ill-health (including devastating increases in death resulting from exposure to asbestos). This apparent contradiction demonstrates the inappropriateness of the evaluation instruments. The risks and categories concerned have changed and are not or only partly reflected in the studies and statistics established. The deterioration in working conditions is focused on certain categories of workers, companies and new symptoms. There are five main reasons for this situation:

- the fragmentation of work and the increasing lack of job security;
- work is more intense;
- the out-sourcing of certain risks;
- the development of new technologies and new products;
- new means of organisation of work.

The political context: The Lisbon employment summit in March 2000 established the objective of full employment through a strategy aimed at developing both the quantity and quality of employment. The Nice Council in December 2000 adopted a Social Agenda establishing the Community social policy for the next 5 years and which is an integral part of that strategy. The Stockholm employment summit in March 2001 consolidated that strategy, in particular in the area of lifelong learning. The forthcoming Belgian Presidency will place the emphasis on the quality of employment. It is therefore necessary that the Community strategy in the field of health and safety should be closely co-ordinated and integrated with this global strategy, by leaving the national and European public authorities ample room for maneouvre as regards initiatives, control and evaluation procedures, and by increasing the involvement of the social partners.

Six Action Goals

Promoting a better work environment Beyond the framework-directive, the Community policy in the field of health and safety has until now mainly been aimed at the removal of risks or hazards at the work place. The new programme should highlight the improvement of the work environment in order to better prevent risks such as stress or bullying or mobbing. The European Court judgement on the working time Directive created opportunities to establish new legislative and contractual requirements not only for better jobs but for jobs of better quality.

Evaluating, adapting and supplementing Community legislation Ten years after the transposition and application of the framework directive it is, in our view, important to review the progress achieved in implementing this directive and those which have been adopted subsequently in this area not just into national legislation but in practice at the work place level. This evaluation should focus on identifying the difficulties encountered in their implementation, checking whether an adaptation or additional legislation is necessary and examining how the social partners have been involved in the transposition process. This exercise should also allow identification of the necessary improvements to the directives, particularly concerning their aims on prevention and all workers being covered by information and consultation rights. But such an evaluation should not be any reason not to press ahead with new legislation or amendments. The CCHS should be a driving force in this evaluation process.

Reinforcing the involvement of the social partners to promote the quality of employment, improving the organisation of work and reducing social inequalities in the field of health Health and safety are key elements in the quality of employment, but they are also a way, through a good organisation of work and jobs, of improving access to employment and protecting jobs held by women, older workers, disabled people, etc. In particular, the ETUC believes that health and safety legislation and practices should be gender sensitive, rather than gender neutral. It is necessary to establish best practice benchmarks to be used to define convergence targets with an evaluation procedure. A health and safety policy should never be an exclusion policy but must, in the contrary, be a policy of adaptation, readaptation and rehabilitation leading to the development of disabled people employment. It is necessary to continue, by way of negotiations or legislation to regulate new forms of work, for example, the social partners played a key role in regulating part-time work and fixed-term contracts and the European Union must take the lead with regard to temporary work. It is primordial for the quality of the employment and health/safety of these workers to ensure equal treatment and good conditions preventing the abusive use of such contracts. As the two framework agreements signed assert "fixed-term contracts are and will continue to be the general form of work relations... and contribute to the quality of life of the workers concerned and to an improvement in their level of performance". The Community strategy in the area of health and safety must be co-ordinated with the Commission's communication on the modernisation of the organisation of work. The role of the social partners is therefore fundamental in order to create the best possible working environment over and above their involvement in health and safety policy. In this context, the role of the social partners should be enhanced at European, national, industry and work place level. Union representation over health and safety should be extended to cover all workers, especially those in small firms. In recent years, we have noticed an increase in the social inequalities in the field of health, namely in terms of life expectation. A health and safety policy must contribute to the reduction of these inequalities.

Creating the right conditions for the accession of candidate countries in the field of Community "acquis" The Community "acquis" in the field of health and safety is important and requires providing specific means to the accession candidate countries and the active involvment of the social partners in those countries. The ETUC has long advocated that observers from the social partners in the candidate countries should be associated in the work of the CCHS. This must be made effective with the new programme. The Bratislava conference on the social dialogue in the accession candidate countries, organised by the ETUC, UNICE and the CEEP on 16 and 17 March 2001, emphasised the importance of supporting and consolidating the role of the social partners in the integration process.

Developing, harmonising and co-ordinating the means of action and evaluation and establishing new ways to promote and measure success It is necessary to achieve greater synergies and complementarity at national, European and international level. In particular at European level, the work of the Dublin Foundation and the European Agency for Safety and Health at Work in Bilbao must be co-ordinated and complementary, taking into account their specific missions. This should not substitute for the central role over policy of the CCHS and the Commission itself in matter of initiative and elaboration of the Community healh and safety policy.

Ensuring the complementarity and links between the responsibilities of the public authorities as regards standards, open co-ordination and the area of the social dialogue The role of the public authorities must remain at the heart of health and safety policy in order to ensure the effectiveness of the standards introduced and their consistency with other public health, environmental and internal market policies. The open co-ordination process in concertation with the social partners can help to achieve convergence between working conditions and protection situations and precise quantitative and qualitative objectives established on the basis of common indicators. The social dialogue must provide a way of ensuring the right conditions for employment. The trade unions must be provided with the necessary ressources to be able to participate more actively in European technical standardisation, according to subjects of interest to be determined by them.

TWELVE PRIORITY PROPOSALS

Evaluating the results of the application of the directives, especially the framework directive. This evaluation must be completed in the first year of the implementation of the programme and discussed at a conference to be organised by the CCHS. Adopting, before the end of 2002, a support programme for SMEs and the social partners of the SMEs on the implementation of the Community regulations, with the contribution of the European social partners and the interested groups of the CCHS, particularly by extending, on a multi-annual basis, the SME programme adopted by the European Parliament on the 2001 budget. Developing a pragmatic approach at sectoral and territorial levels.

Ensuring the adoption of legislative proposals already submitted to the European Council, revising and supplementing the regulatory provisions and ensuring their co-ordination with the Internal Market directives (maternity, noise, asbestos, musculo-skeletal disorders, physical risks, chemical and cancer-producing risks, stress, etc.).

Extending, before 2004, the scope of legislation in the field of the health and safety to self-employed people and to domestic workers. Reinforcing immediately the participation of trade union experts in the process of fixing technical standards, according to the interest of workers. Setting up in 2003 an minimal harmonization of the systems for the recognition of occupational illnesses. Establishing a system to monitor on an ongoing basis working conditions and risks through closer co-operation and harmonisation between national and European institutions.

Establishing in 2002 common guidelines with concrete objectives, in accordance with the open co-ordination method, for the development of prevention services in order to improve employee protection to the level of the 3 best countries. Developing a social dialogue at all levels on the organisation of work, by establishing guidelines at European, sectoral and cross-industry levels. Setting up a four-year programme to provide support for accession candidate countries and the social partners in those countries on the integration of the Community "acquis" in the field of health and safety and the organisation of work.

Ratification by the Member states of the European Union of the ILO conventions 155 and 161 and their recognition in international trade agreements.

Reinforcing the role of the CCHS in accordance with the proposals put forward by the social partners in October and increasing the means of the Commission's internal services. The Executive Committee asks the Secretariat to prepare a European awareness Campaign on a theme of Trade Union action with the support of the TUTB and the ACHS Workers group.

VOLUNTARY AND COMMUNITY ORGANISATIONS

Government remains committed to reforming public services and to enabling the voluntary and community sector (VCS) to take on a greater role in public service delivery. The aim must be to achieve a genuine, lasting and positive transformation in the public services that people receive. However, if government continues to focus on strengthening procurement processes to achieve transfer rather than the more wide ranging changes needed to achieve transformation, then these objectives are unlikely to be met.

Public sector commissioners and procurers need to develop a more sophisticated understanding of how public services needs can be met and delivered, and ensure that contracting processes, and the funding available to deliver public services, properly reflect this better understanding. If this does not happen, the real failure will not be that VCOs cannot take on a greater role in public service delivery but that citizens and communities will fail to get the services they need and deserve.

The Issue of Public Services

NCVO has played a leading part in the debate about the role of voluntary and community organisations (VCOs) in the reform of public services. We have argued that many VCOs can play a crucial role in delivering public services that better meet the needs of individuals and communities. But, if they are to do so, it must be on their own terms: public service delivery should contribute to the delivery of their own mission; it must be undertaken in ways that respect the independence of the organisation and the expertise and knowledge that they contribute; and the services they provide must be properly costed and paid for.

However, there is a real danger that the current debates about public services are not addressing the real issue. Attention has focused on the barriers to VCOs taking on public service delivery and on the practical steps needed to facilitate the transfer of public services to the voluntary and community sector (VCS)-i.e. improving the process of contracting. Attention in this area is needed. But it is at least as important that we do not lose sight, and have a clear understanding, of why the government wants the sector to take on public service delivery, and equally importantly (for both the government and VCOs) why it is that many VCOs do want to take on public service contracts. If government is not clear about what it wants to achieve by working with the sector and if it does not properly understand what benefits the sector can bring, then it is unlikely to put in place the right mechanisms to achieve the real transformation in public services that everyone wants to see.

THE LIMITATIONS OF TRANSFER

Politicians on all sides constantly refer to the need to make services more consumer driven and to segment beneficiaries into markets. However, little progress has been made to truly reform and transform public services because the agenda has been dominated by a flawed approach. All too often, rather than creating services which are tailored to the needs and preferences of the full range of users, commissioners in the public sector have prized economic savings and throughput. Such an approach tends to focus on delivery by a few large service providers, excluding smaller, specialist or locally based organisations.

At best, the most this model has achieved is to provide consistent services for the majority, but this may well be at the expense of vulnerable, harder to reach users who need more specialist or different services. It is also unlikely to lead to the development of more holistic services, which understand and meet the whole needs of individuals. And there is little scope, within a model concerned with throughput, to invest in researching and developing new solutions, supporting innovation and piloting new services.

Instead, there is an apparent belief that simply transferring existing services out of the public sector to another provider will achieve more efficient and effective services-through the market mechanisms of competition and choice. If government simply wants to transfer services out of the public sector, to open up a market in public service delivery, then VCOs are undoubtedly one option for helping to achieve this. Many VCOs have been prepared to take contracts on this basis-because they believe that even within the constraints of a standard public sector contract they can still provide a better service to users. But although transferring services from the public sector to the VCS may have some marginal benefits to users and communities, it is unlikely to achieve a real transformation of services. To achieve a real transformation there needs to be a wider review of how service needs are defined, and how services to meet those needs are designed and commissioned.

How do we Transform Public Services?

Not all public services are inefficient or ineffective: many are very good. That should serve to remind us that where public services are inefficient or ineffective it is not simply because they are in the public sector, it is because the wrong model of delivery is driving them. If the public sector continues to design and commission public services in the same ways that it always has done, and simply offers contracts to VCOs that ask them to replicate the practices and models utilised by either public sector or private sector delivery, then it will be difficult for VCOs to bring additional benefits to those services and nothing will really change for users. Markets and contestability have their place in the public sector and should be processes that VCOs can operate effectively within. But many in the VCS express frustration that conventional approaches to commissioning and procurement limit the extent to which services can actually be changed to better meet public need. Commissioners need to review what it is they value in service delivery, and how that is recognised and rewarded through the procurement process, if they are not to drive out many of the very characteristics and benefits that VCOs at their best can bring to service delivery.

In order to achieve transformation a radical approach is needed, one that:

- Places the agenda of citizens and communities, not just individual consumers, at the heart of the reform process.This is an important distinction.Public services provide not just a private benefit to individual consumers, but also a public good.It is not sufficient to ensure that a service meets the needs of the majority of the community, it must also be available to citizens who need an adapted or even a quite different service, which may have less scope for economies of scale and therefore tend to be more expensive to provide.

- Ensures public services are designed and delivered in a way that enables the *voice* of citizens and communities to be heard and acted upon, as well as providing them with a market *choice*. This will require putting in place processes to engage with and listen to the widest possible range of service users (and potential users). In addition, where choice is offered, service providers should ensure that users have the information and support they need to be aware of and access the range of choices available to them.
- Recognises the need for a holistic approach, which provides effective, joined up services to citizens. This will require developing a full understanding of the needs of citizens and communities, listening to their preferences and building services around the way they live, rather than around organisational structures and silos. For example,at present there is no incentive for a statutory funder to support a project or service if all of the cost falls to one department whilst some of the benefits accrue to another, or indeed to another public sector body. If real change and reform is being sought then government (at all tiers) needs to get better at sharing costs and benefits, through effective joint commissioning.
- Applies a more sophisticated understanding of the efficiency agenda, which gives as much weight to effectiveness as it does to cost savings. Government needs to move away from short term quick fix solutions: real transformation may need up front investment, and some patience, to achieve lasting and meaningful benefits. And there should be a greater willingness to value and invest in preventative services. This would require better modelling of the likely cost savings of prevention, so that a clear funding case can be made.

What Role can the VCS play?

Commissioners need to understand and take account of the transforming principles for public services set out above-so that the design, commissioning and management of public service contracts reflects a more sophisticated understanding of the needs of users and communities and the various ways of meeting those needs. Those commissioning and procuring services also need to better understand and value the range of skills and strengths that different partners can contribute to public services. In particular, if the VCS is to play a full role, then there needs to be a greater appreciation of what it can bring and how it operates.

Putting Citizens and Communities

Many VCOs have a greater ability to engage with and understand the needs of users and communities than statutory agencies are able to do. There are many and varied reasons why this may be the case. These include, amongst others:

- the way a particular organisation is set up-for example many VCOs are founded by people with direct experience of the issue they are seeking to address;
- the way they operate-such as having users on their board, or amongst their staff;
- because the organisation is based in the local community;
- because the organisation specialises in a particular issue; or
- higher levels of trust, confidence and credibility than the statutory sector, in some cases simply because a VCO is independent and not part of the state.

As a result, there are many VCOs that have a strong track record in generating innovative learning about people's real needs and in creatively designing and delivering services that reflect those needs. This has particularly been the case with the needs of diverse and disadvantaged communities.

SUPPORTING VOICE AND CHOICE

Government wants individuals and communities to become more engaged as active citizens within public services. But it is not sufficient to give people the opportunity to engage, they also have to be given the skills and support to take on new roles. This includes empowering users to be able to make choices and to express their preferences at the point where services are being designed, as well as at the point of delivery. - In some cases government agencies can directly providc the support and capacity building to enable people to engage more effectively, but in many cases VCOs are often better placed to provide this support. Advocacy and advice and information giving have always been as much a part of the role of VCOs as direct service delivery. Through these roles VCOs enable individuals and communities to have their voice heard when decisions are being made about what services are needed and how they should be provided. And by providing information, advice and support, VCOs can support people to understand and make the most of the choices available to them: if one of the mechanisms to achieve transformation is the provision of greater levels of choice, it will only be effective if all service users are capable of expressing their preferences and of making informed choices.

It is important that commissioners understand that the VCS' roles of advocacy, support and advice giving contribute directly to public service delivery. Some argue that there is a conflict of interest if a VCO wants to both advocate for a certain approach, or be consulted on or contribute to decisions about how a service should be designed and delivered, and then bid for the contract to deliver that service. However, many VCOs argue that the type and quality of services they provide is directly influenced by their knowledge of their users and the information they receive from them. Equally, they argue that their campaigning and advocacy work is strengthened and has legitimacy because they also have direct service delivery experience. Where there may be issues of conflict of interest and competitive advantage this should be acknowledged and managed through the commissioning and procurement processes. However, this needs to be done in ways that enable knowledge and experience from user engagement to inform and lead public service transformation.

Providing Effective

Whilst a VCO may specialise in a particular field, it is

likely to focus around a particular client group or community and to provide its services to that group in a joined up way. As a result, VCOs are often able to deliver joined-up services across governmental boundaries. In the voluntary sector,-'outcomes-based collaboration'-is already emerging as an important concept and government is well placed to benefit from this.

In many cases services provided by VCOs have been developed in areas where neither the state nor the market have been able or willing to operate. VCOs provide specialist knowledge, of an issue or client group, to help fill niche markets. VCOs have also pioneered services, by being the first to identify and meet a need and then successfully arguing that the state should take responsibility for making those services universally available.

Balancing Professionalism and Mission

The efficiency agenda is also important for the VCS. VCOs are not driven by shareholder value. However that does not mean that VCOs are not as keen as those in the private sector to promote efficiency. The bottom line for VCOs is how effectively their work achieves their mission, within a given budget. Where the private sector has shareholders, the VCS has stakeholders, and it is important for VCOs to demonstrate a return on stakeholder investment. That return is judged on the impact they achieve.

VCOs have, rightly, endeavoured to become more professional in the way they deliver services. But this has resulted in some confusion. Government and statutory funders need to understand that being more business-like in the way an organisation is managed does not mean being more like business in all respects. VCOs are different from both the public and the private sectors. Whilst prudent use of resources is important, they are not seeking a return on shareholder value. Instead, VCOs are mission driven: their objective is to achieve a social, environmental or economic impact. This difference is reflected in their governance structure and the roles and responsibilities of trustees. They do and should operate differently because they are operating with different objectives and different stakeholders. If we want to see new approaches to public service delivery, then our statutory partners need to understand and value these differences because they are an important part of the reason why VCOs can play a crucial role in helping to achieve the transformation of public services.

What do we need to enable VCOs to really transform public services? VCOs have the potential to play three different, and equally important, roles in the reform of public services:

- Identifying service need, as a result of gaps in service provision, or poorly designed or delivered services;
- Helping to design solutions to meet a need; and
- Delivering services.

Individually, some VCOs will want to contribute to all three roles, others to only one or two of them. However it is this combination of the three roles across the sector that means that the VCS as a whole can help to truly transform public services. If VCOs are not involved in service definition and design, including those who have no interest in subsequently taking on a contract to deliver the service, then the scope for transformation could be extremely limited. And if the commissioning and procurement process does not recognise and reward the wider contribution VCOs can make to public service reform, public service delivery will, for many VCOs, continue to be of limited interest.

It is equally important that voluntary and community organisations of all sizes are encouraged and supported to engage in the process of public service reform. There is an important role here for infrastructure bodies within the VCS to advise, support and encourage their members who can contribute to this agenda. But it is at least as important that public sector bodies do not put in place processes to design and commission services which effectively exclude smaller or more specialist organisations.

Enable VCOs to contribute fully to decision making processes about service needs. Government needs to develop an approach that recognises the broad range of roles that VCOs play, how these broader roles are inherently related to the provision of good public services, how VCOs can be enabled to contribute to discussions about what services are needed and how they can best be provided. The primary aim must be to ensure that the opinions and concerns of users, and the wider community, inform the debate.

For this to happen, public sector commissioners need to engage with and provide support to organisations that give a voice to communities at an early stage in their decision making process. This engagement should be both formal and informal. The Compact codes on consultation and funding both provide some guidance on these issues-for example the expectation that VCOs should be consulted on issues that can be expected to directly affect them or those they work with. However, a more direct and deeper engagement in the commissioning process is needed. This could include:

- Putting in place open and transparent consultation and decision making processes that actively encourage those with an interest or expertise in an issue to contribute, and make it straightforward for them to do so.
- Commissioning or grant funding VCOs to play a representative or consultative role in relation to the development of specific services or activities. This could include commissioning an organisation to undertake a consultation exercise, or to hold discussion or focus groups.
- Commissioning or grant funding VCOs that provide support to individuals or communities to enable them to have their voice heard.
- Entering into a consultancy relationship with VCOs specialising in a particular field to benefit from their knowledge or expertise of an issue.

Enable VCOs to help design and commission solutions to meet those needs. Commissioning and procurement are separate processes, and often in the public sector they are carried out by different people in different parts of the organisation. - It is therefore essential that those commissioning services are clear about what it is they want to purchase and what selection criteria should be applied at the procurement stage: all too often procurement is ineffective because commissioners have not properly specified the service and the outcomes they want.

VCOs have a wealth of knowledge and experience of working with users to design and, where appropriate deliver high quality public services. Some of this knowledge and expertise comes from direct experience of service delivery, but some also comes from the role of VCOs as advocates or advisors. Making best use of this expertise requires a different approach to commissioning services, one that understands and values the distinctive contribution VCOs can offer and seeks to enable them to fulfil their potential. If government wants to transform public services, then it is the wider roles of advocacy, support and advice that it needs to utilise and build on.

It is also the case that, in some circumstances, VCOs need to be clearer about their objectives in service delivery. For example, a wider engagement with VCOs in the designing and commissioning of services may mean that the solutions designed and piloted by VCOs may become funded as part of the mainstream, and will not remain within the VCS.

Whilst there are issues about how such investment in service development is funded, it is equally true that if it results in a better service for a larger number of people, then it is still a successful outcome for both the VCO and those with whom it works.

Commissioning also needs to develop in ways that cut across traditional public sector 'silos'. There needs to be more thought to joint commissioning by the various statutory partners that require and/or benefit from a particular service. Joined up commissioning (and recognition and reward) should enable services to be provided that better meet the needs of users and communities. And joined up commissioning should also reduce the burden of bureaucracy and duplication, and the associated costs, experienced by many service providers-in the VCS and elsewhere.

- VCOs could be paid to help design a service solution-effectively acting as consultants.
- VCOs may choose to 'sell' what they do to the public (or private) sector to enable it to be implemented more widely-for example by taking a contract to train staff in another sector, or producing guidance or best practice material.
- VCS specialists in a particular field should be invited to comment on draft specifications.

- Large projects with an advisory panel should be expected to include experts from the VCS (either in service delivery or community engagement).
- Public sector bodies should consider investing in research and development undertaken by VCOs.

Where VCOs do deliver public services, ensure that those services are commissioned and procured in ways that:

- do not drive out the reasons for working with the sector in the first place
- are properly negotiated and managed
- are sustainably funded.

Government policy statements have recognised the 'added value' that VCOs can bring. To an extent this concept of 'added value' has muddied the waters because it has led many, particularly those working in procurement and audit, to try and quantify 'added value'. The real point is that commissioners need to be clear what value it is they are seeking for a particular service, and which potential providers are best able to provide that value. This needs to be properly specified in the commissioning process. For example, commissioners should include in contracts an expectation that communities and users will inform the delivery of a service; and service providers will need to demonstrate how they listen and respond to their users. The contract should include the costs of this engagement.

The issue of better procurement processes comes into play once service needs have been properly identified and a solution designed and commissioned. - The reforms needed for procurement processes have already been identified in the Treasury's 2002 cross cutting review, and reiterated by the NAO and PAC reports, but there remains the need for a stronger commitment to implementation. This includes funding the full cost of providing a properly defined service, ensuring that risk is fairly shared, providing longer term funding where appropriate and ensuring that monitoring requirements are proportionate. It is to be hoped the Action Plan that government is due to publish in the autumn will help truly embed these reforms at both the national and local level.

However, in order to achieve reform we also need to address the issue of funding. Firstly, there is the need to create capacity.

If government really wants change, it has to create the environment and drive the agenda, including making available resources to increase capacity-as it did with foundation hospitals. In some cases short term and up front investment will be needed to enable VCOs to increase their capacity to achieve long term gains. Futurebuilders clearly has a part to play here, but as has been pointed out elsewhere, Futurebuilders' success depends on VCOs being able to win longer term, fully funded contracts.

Which leads directly to the more fundamental issue: the need to fund the work of VCOs in relation to existing services properly. The VCS should be engaged in decision making processes, designing solutions and delivering services because doing so will result in better services and better outcomes for users and communities. But it would be wrong to assume that this has no cost: VCOs are not a free good that government can use to implement its reforms. The VCS cannot engage properly in the commissioning and delivery of public services because adequate funding is not made available.

ORGANIZATION INVOLVEMENT IN WELFARE REFORM

Community-based organizations (CBOs), such as community action agencies and the local affiliates of Volunteers of America, the YMCA, Boys & Girls Clubs of America, and the Salvation Army, have always provided certain services to low-income children and families, particularly in the areas of child welfare and adoption, family preservation, special needs child care, transportation, and youth development. However, with the emphasis the Personal Responsibility and Work Opportunity Reconciliation Act (PRWORA) of 1996 place on "work first" and the time limits it imposes on cash assistance, the impetus for CBOs to address additional family needs, such as career counseling, employment training, and job retention, has grown. CBOs are becoming integral partners in state and local governments' welfare-to-work and workforce development policy and planning processes and service delivery. As welfare reform progresses, it is likely that CBO involvement in providing work supports and services to low-income families will continue, if not increase.

This *Issue Note* examines the role CBOs have played and will likely continue to play in supporting families that have left or are taking steps toward leaving the welfare rolls. It describes some of the emerging challenges CBOs face as they vie for government contracts, improve their organizational capacity and accountability, and attempt to meet the needs of low-income families and, increasingly, hard-to-employ individuals. Finally, it discusses policy implications, offers program examples, and provides additional resources for state and local policymakers and CBOs as they make further decisions under welfare reform.

Policy Questions

What factors and specific welfare reform and related legislation have expanded opportunities for CBO involvement in welfare reform? The welfare reform law's devolution of program authority to state and local governments, as well as its shift to a time-limited, "work-first" approach to cash assistance, are key driving forces for greater CBO involvement in welfare reform. Work first transformed the nature of the TANF eligibility worker's job from one of determining eligibility and cutting checks to one of counseling on career opportunities and providing wrap-around service planning. This welfare office culture change, in part, enables CBOs to offer more of the counseling and benefit planning services they have been providing to low-income families for years. Some of the other provisions in TANF and related legislation that give CBOs more opportunity to participate in welfare reform include the following. "Charitable choice" provision. Section 104 of PRWORA enables faith-based organizations (FBOs) to compete for state and federal welfare funds on the same basis as other social service providers. Although FBOs cannot use government funds for religious missions or to screen the religious backgrounds of potential clients, they can deliver publicly funded programs that contain religious messages. However, states opting to contract with FBOs must provide TANF participants with a secular program alternative should they choose not to seek services from the FBO.

"Contracting out" of services by state and local welfare agencies. PRWORA also allows states to contract with other private providers, such as nonprofit organizations, for-profit consulting agencies, and community colleges, to determine eligibility and make use of contracts, certificates, or vouchers in providing services to eligible low-income clients. Some states have made their workforce development agencies responsible for welfare-related employment services, and many of those agencies have added the provision of welfare-to-work services to their existing contracts under the former Job Training Partnership Act. These factors, along with freezes in public-sector hiring in some states and growing political acceptance of privatization, have led to an expansion in contracting for welfare-related services (Yates, November 1998).

Increasingly, CBOs have received performance-based welfare-to-work contracts from state and/or local governments. The welfare reform law's work participation rate requirements, as well as financial bonuses for decreases in out-of-wedlock births and increases in job placement and retention prompted states to structure contracts that compensate providers based on their performance in achieving certain program outcomes.

Designation of CBOs as qualified recipients of Welfare-to-Work competitive grants. Administered by the U.S. Department of Labor, the Welfare-to-Work (WtW) competitive grant program identifies CBOs, local governments, and private industry councils as qualified applicants for these grants and emphasizes the importance of responding to community needs as families make the transition from welfare to work. Nearly 200 WtW competitive grants have been awarded to a single CBO or coalitions of CBOs to provide postemployment services to hard-to-serve welfare recipients and noncustodial parents. WtW formula grants awarded to states and local workforce investment boards (WIBs) may also be distributed to CBOs at state or WIB option. States are now requesting federal waivers to spend WtW funds for an additional two years.

How are CBOs serving low-income families who have left or are trying to leave welfare? In addition to child welfare, family preservation, and related services, CBOs are offering services more directly related to helping individuals achieve employment outcomes and meet basic needs. Some organizations, such as the Wildcat Service Corporation in New

York City, operate job-readiness or "soft-skills" training programs that prepare clients to successfully adapt to workplace demands and responsibilities. Other groups sponsor mentoring programs in which welfare recipients pair up with a former welfare recipient, a colleague at work, or another individual who can help them pursue employment and training opportunities, manage their finances, improve their parenting skills, and find quality child care. Community development corporations and local chapters of Habitat for Humanity are some of the CBOs that help low-income families secure affordable housing or obtain emergency assistance.

Some of PRWORA's provisions related to convicted drug felons, domestic violence, and the maintenance of two-parent families have also contributed to increased caseworker referrals to CBO-operated substance abuse and mental health treatment programs, domestic violence shelters, and fatherhood programs. The DeKalb Economic Opportunity Authority, Inc., a WtW competitive grantee and community action agency, partners with the DeKalb County Government, the public housing authority, the DeKalb College, Goodwill Industries of Atlanta, DeKalb County Chamber of Commerce, and other organizations to provide educational training, employment assistance, and substance abuse services to noncustodial fathers.

Other CBOs offer multiple services on-site to address family needs more holistically. For example, the SHIELDS for Families Project in Los Angeles is a community-based, non-profit organization that provides job training, substance abuse and mental health treatment, and child abuse and domestic violence services to low-income mothers and their children in order to address interrelated and cross-generational barriers simultaneously.

What are some of the barriers CBOs confront in getting involved with welfare reform? Many CBOs have proven track records in identifying and addressing the needs of low-income families, with some organizations having operated since the early nineteenth century. Nevertheless, CBOs face several challenges to participating in welfare reform given the multiple infrastructure needs of their organizations and PRWORA's strict requirements. For example, states must meet comprehensive TANF caseload data collection and reporting requirements, so the burden often falls on CBOs to collect the information and submit it to the state or county. Some CBOs, particularly small service providers do not have the data collection systems needed to track and report detailed information on each program participant and some cannot finance information system upgrades. The TANF block grant also gives states more flexibility to contract with CBOs than under the Aid to Families with Dependent Children (AFDC) program, and this flexibility has increased competition for government funds. Service providers with greater capacity and other financial resources to leverage are typically in a better position to win contracts, placing smaller CBOs at a disadvantage.

Limited staff and service capacity are other factors inhibiting CBO participation in welfare reform. Staff may be lacking in numbers, knowledge about welfare reform requirements, and requisite skills to meet the needs of certain low-income clients. For example, individuals with more serious barriers to employment may need specialized counseling and treatment services that cannot adequately be assessed and addressed by some CBOs, particularly those that rely heavily on lay volunteers to provide services. In other cases, CBOs do not have the space or facilities needed to serve additional clients or provide specialized services for the hard-to-employ.

CBOs may have difficulty providing services to low-income families under welfare reform because of a lack of sustainable funding. To remain effective and able to meet contract obligations, CBOs need access to long-term funding sources, as well as high-quality financial management and accounting systems. Some CBOs find they are less likely to secure grants and contracts if they fail to show funders they already have resources to leverage and match any new funding sources. Funders also often like to see positive program outcomes before renewing a CBO's contract or awarding it any new funds. This can be problematic, however, for programs that do not experience significant changes in client behavior or employment during the initial period of program implementation.

Program outcomes, whether they are positive or negative,

may not materialize until the program has operated for a few years. Finally, CBOs that lack a solid understanding of the political environment and relationships with key players also find it difficult to participate in welfare reform. CBOs that are used to working within traditional service provider networks must be willing to reach out to governments, businesses, and other nontraditional partners to become familiar with these groups' agendas as well as identify opportunities for collaboration.

What are some promising approaches CBOs can consider implementing to overcome these barriers? Given the barriers some CBOs face in participating in welfare reform, they may want to consider the following options.

- Partner with other organizations to obtain the necessary expertise or specialized services for certain populations, such as hard-to-employ individuals. Collaboration can also help CBOs expand their capacity for providing services and potentially broaden their delivery area. These partnerships, in turn, may give smaller CBOs a competitive edge for receiving government funds and other contracts.
- Ensure staff understand TANF work requirements, time limits, and other restrictions that affect how they serve TANF participants. Staff who are inadequately informed about the welfare reform policies of a state or county are less likely to meet performance contract measures, and they will be less effective in addressing client needs.
- Enhance data collection and reporting systems and use the outcome data to improve the CBO's performance. Such actions can improve the organization's ability to satisfy contract reporting requirements as well as improve service delivery for clients. Increasingly, CBOs are developing web sites to provide service and referral information. CBOs with less capacity for information systems management could hire a staff person who is specifically tasked with managing these databases.
- Identify sustainable funding sources to ensure the CBO's solvency and help leverage interest among other funders. Securing matching funds from community foundations

and other private funders is one way CBOs can better position themselves to compete for state and local government contracts. Many national organizations representing CBOs also provide technical assistance to their members on fundraising strategies, board development, cultural competency, leadership development, and other areas that contribute to an organization's ability to raise capital.

What opportunities exist for state and local policymakers to reduce barriers to CBO participation in welfare reform? State and local governments that offer services to low-income families through CBOs may want to assess whether their policies inhibit current and potential contract arrangements. State and local policymakers may want to consider using these strategies to reduce barriers to CBO participation.

- Allow CBOs to commingle and use state and federal funds in a more flexible way whenever this is permitted by state or federal law. Policymakers may also want to streamline funding sources to ease CBOs' program management and data tracking burdens.
- Offer, or continue to offer, grants to CBOs for welfare-related direct service and infrastructure-building activities. State and local policymakers may want to provide grants for services and supports, as well as grants to help CBOs retrain staff, upgrade data collection and reporting systems and other organizational technology, and meet other capacity improvement needs.
- Conduct special outreach efforts to inform CBOs of funding and other opportunities to serve low-income families. State and local governments can identify gaps in service delivery and then, through direct marketing campaigns, community forums, and other activities, make CBOs aware of opportunities to fill those gaps.
- Train CBO staff in TANF program requirements. In many cases, state and local governments may be able to include CBO staff in existing government-sponsored training sessions to minimize duplication of effort and communicate standardized messages regarding TANF policies and procedures to all providers.

How can CBOs continue to be involved as welfare reform evolves? As states continue to implement welfare reform and assist low-income working families, there will likely be a steady need for CBO involvement in providing services that promote employee retention and advancement and target hard-to-employ individuals. States are gaining information from pilot programs they have implemented during the past few years and are considering options for spending TANF funds in light of these results and other factors. CBOs will continue to play a key role in delivering substance abuse and mental health treatment, domestic violence services, special needs child care, after-school programs, and long-term support services. Several studies suggest multiple employment barriers affect a considerable portion of both welfare "leavers," who may still be struggling to make ends meet, and TANF "stayers" who may still be experiencing problems in leaving the welfare rolls. CBOs also have a continued role to play in conducting outreach activities to ensure eligible families receive such employment supports as food stamps, Medicaid, and child care. States that received TANF high performance bonuses and financial awards for reducing out-of-wedlock births may want to consider using the new funds to support community-based service delivery. States, the federal government, researchers, and other interested parties are also beginning to look ahead to the congressional reauthorization of the TANF program in 2002. Many CBOs and their national affiliates are now developing policy recommendations for reauthorization. Others are helping their members organize grassroots lobbying efforts and are tracking other CBOs' positions on TANF reauthorization.

Recent White House action will also likely provide additional opportunities for CBO participation in welfare reform. In January, President George W. Bush established an Executive Office of Faith-Based and Community Initiatives (OFBCI) and parallel branches of this office in five federal departments—Labor, Education, Health and Human Services, Justice, and Housing and Urban Development. OFBCI will "promote a policy of respect for and cooperation with religious and grassroots groups. It will identify barriers to such groups in federal rules and practices, propose regulatory and statutory relief, and coordinate new federal initiatives to empower and partner with faith-based and community-based problem-solvers." The president also released policy proposals designed to increase funding and reduce bureaucratic barriers for FBOs and CBOs. These proposals seek to allow non-itemizers to deduct charitable contributions from their federal income tax, expand charitable choice to include other federal programs, encourage states to create charitable tax credits, create a capital fund to expand FBO and CBO service capacity, and offer new competitive grants for specific social programs.

Research Findings

Research on CBO involvement in welfare reform tends to focus on assessing organizational capacity to provide services and the types of partnerships being formed among CBOs, government, and the private sector. Launched in 1995, the Annie E. Casey Foundation Jobs Initiative is an eight-year demonstration project providing funding and support for community-based initiatives in six cities—Denver, Milwaukee, New Orleans, Philadelphia, St. Louis, and Seattle. The projects aim to help young, low-income workers find and advance in meaningful jobs and to identify national employment and training models. Part of the initiative involves providing technical assistance to CBOs to help them build organizational capacity. Following four years of program planning and implementation, some key lessons for CBOs include the following.

- Newly placed enrollees must be closely monitored and provided with support and followup services, including support groups and telephone calls, as well as financial, housing, and child care assistance, to ensure they stay on the job.
- CBOs must be provided with adequate financial support, technical assistance, networking opportunities, and other resources that enable them to design more effective, accountable, and outcomes-oriented programs.
- CBOs need funds that can be allocated quickly and efficiently so they can respond to employers' training and hiring needs in a timely manner.

The Manpower Demonstration Research Corporation Project on Devolution and Urban Change is tracking the implementation of welfare reform in four large urban counties—Cuyahoga (Cleveland, Ohio), Los Angeles, Miami-Dade, and Philadelphia—between 1997 and 2001. The project seeks to understand how state and local welfare agencies, poor neighborhoods, and low-income families are affected by the changes to the income support system in response to PRWORA. It includes an institutional study examining how new policies and funding mechanisms are affecting nonprofit organizations. Its most recent report includes early findings on welfare reform's impact on CBO involvement at the sites. For example, in Miami-Dade, the new local WAGES Coalition's performance-based contracts posed difficulties for smaller nonprofit service providers who could not maintain operations under the more demanding contract terms. Welfare reform in Los Angeles saw the emergence of CBOs to provide domestic violence and counseling services and substance abuse and mental health treatment, as well as their rise to become potentially important players in the policymaking process (Quint et al., April 1999). Results from the institutional study are expected in March 2001.

Researchers with Indiana University examined the impact of welfare reform on the receipt of social services from FBOs using data from Indiana's welfare reform evaluation. They also analyzed cross-sectional data from Indiana social service agencies; cases from faith-based and non-faith-based organizations were matched to compare how these two types of organizations were serving welfare recipients. Recipients seeking assistance from FBOs were more likely to be disadvantaged than those seeking services from CBOs—23 percent of FBO clients were sanctioned cases and 35 percent were individuals with disabilities. FBOs were also slightly less likely (29.1 percent) than non-FBOs (34 percent) to provide employment and educational services. However, the study's authors suggest this discrepancy could be because FBOs receive less public financial support than non-FBOs (Reingold et al., October 2000).

ROLE OF COMMUNITY BASED ORGANISATION IN RURAL DEVELOPMENT

The two case studies were taken up as a part of the thrust

area group under the Role of Community Based Organisation and Non-Governmental Organisation. The first case study was done by a team consisting of four members who visited a Water User Association (WUA) in Edulabad village at Ghatkesar Mandal Ranga Reddy district. The details pertaining to its functioning were collected from the WUA members and discussion with villagers helped us to understand its role vis-a-vis Panchayti Raj Institutions. The second one was conducted in Tarnil Nadu.

Objectives

(a) To understand the role of WUAs as a self-help group community based organisation involved in promoting people's participation in development;

(b) To highlight the role of such CB0s vis-a-vis PRIS. Are there any strategies that were adopted by these 11 institutions to synergise their efforts for people's development?

(c) To examine the role of NG0s in rural development;

(d) To suggest a few policy measures (be it in a small way) that can sustain and promote these institutions to play an effective role in development.

Metodology

Both primary and secondary data were collected from department of irrigation, Research Institutions (WALAMTARI), and also NG0s Ue IDIRAS were consulted. Field visit was taken up in Edulabad village of Ghatkesar Mandal, Ranga Reddy district in Andhra Pradesh. Team members visited the gram panchayat and also the WUA at Edulabad village. A checklist was prepared to collect data from the members. This helped us in getting their perceptions. Interview with some of the elected representatives was carried out to understand their role. This was taken up because the hypothesis was that community based institutions are basically trying to scuttle the existing powers of local institutions or they are parallel institutions of power. Likewise secondary data were gathered from an NG0s-Rural Community Trust located in one of the districts in Tamil Nadu. Wherever necessary, information was also gathered from the executives of the Trust.

Findings

1. The tank is filled with pollutants because of the feeder channel carrying industrial and urban waste from the Musi river and filling the tank. The foul smell is emitted in and around the area. The earlier drinking water wells and bore wells are now yielding polluted water. Even the irrigation wells in the surroundings of the village are polluted and coloured water is pumped out. It is said earlier that lots of birds were found in and around the tank, which are not seen now-a-days. It is told that some animals died by drinking the water from the tank. Now the piped water supply is provided to the village through a well located at a distant place through ovehead reservoir (OHSR).
2. The villagers told that since the pipeline carrying Manjira water to Hyderabad city is laid through the village, they are making a request, rather demand, to provide drinking water from the same source and restore the tank from pollution. They need not bear the brunt of pollution, as they did not cause it.
3. A farmer centered non-directive approach is most appropriate for institution building. Use of this approach means leaving the initiative for mobilising action for improving the irrigation system to farmers. Progress may be slow but it is both effective and replicable.
4. One of the major problems, which are found both in the structural and operational level was the participation of the PRI functionaries in the WUAS. In our village, we found that one of the members is the village sarpanch who is actively participating in the WUAs activities. Although this being a minor irrigation tank, it does not come under the purview of the PRIS, hence, the role of the local sarpanch is limited in nature. As a farmer and elected representative, his participation needs to be evaluated. The sarpanch stated that, he personally feels that the WUAs of this nature need to he given a special status and it caters to a large section of farming community. His participation in the body has helped to understand the nitty gritty pertaining to several village

problems. It was possible to visualize the village problems and find a holistic view to the issue.

5. The rural leadership takes time, more so the PRI functionaries do not seem to have any direct role with the WUA except as one of the members. The use of the approach means that the agency has respect for village 'people and has faith in their ability to reconcile conflicts and work with consensus.

RURAL COMMUNITY TRUST

Rural Community Trust (RCT) as a non-governmental, charitable organisation is located in Villupuram district and Thirvannamalai district covers scheduled caste people of fifty villages. Since 1985 RCT decided to help people for creating unity and independence among the rural community. All projects were initiated in response to the needs of the people. RCT believed in self-reliance, local leadership and concrete act ion and expected change to emerge form people out of their own efforts.

To begin their activity RCT conducted a mass compaign from village to village for developing rapport with the villagers. Village survey was conducted to analyse the felt needs of the people. Lack of transport services, non-existence of school and hospitals, lack of drinking water, lighting, housing, roads and land were identified by the people. While addressing the problem RCT plunged into action with the identification of animators in the villages and formed women's group. These women's groups were accomplished the formidable task of challenging the socioeconomic problems such as prohibition and dowry. Subsequently, RCT also ran credit unions, day care centres for the aged, preschool education and home for the rural boys. Despite skill training provided to rural girls for tailoring, mat weaving and greeting cards making, typing and vocational guidance for coaching students for engineering courses are also being taken up. Capacity building is being encouraged for all its staff members through various institutions at national and state. level.

In essence, RCT's efforts in Mugiyur village established an illustration for a model village by having collaboration with the Panchayati Raj Institutions. Fortunately the founder of RCT

is an elected member of the panchayat. This provided him an opportunity to experience himself with both govern-mental and voluntary organisations. Besides, these experiences crystallized for mutual understanding. RCT therefore has set-up perfect partnership along with the local level institutions to bring greater growth and sustainable development.

Policy Implications

The results of the two case studies are indicative of the fact that closer cooperation between Panchayats and the bodies in the informal sector can go a long way in providing useful services to the people in a given community. It is therefore necessary that strategies have to be worked out to forge appropriate linkage between Panchayats and the other village based organisations so that they can take up activities concerning welfare of the people in close cooperation.

COMMUNITY DEVELOPMENT AND SOCIAL CAPITAL

This set of papers on social capital collectively raises very interesting theoretical, methodological, and applied questions about the concept and its application. Not surprisingly, they do not resolve those questions, although they provide some useful directions for future research and for applied community development work.

Bridger and Alter, in the lead article in this issue, examine the state of both urban and rural communities and the potential for progressive community development outcomes in those communities by enveloping political economy analysis within Wilkinson's interactional framework. They examine the effects of global capitalism on U.S. communities and neighborhoods, identifying growing spatial, class, and ethnic inequalities, as well as the contrasting leveling effect of the telecommunications revolution. All of these patterns, they argue, militate against community social capital as an engine of change for place-based community development. In effect, Bridger and Alter answer the question, "Do communities act?," in the negative, as does Wilkinson, who provides inspiration for their work:

> *[C]ommunity development, when it occurs, is one part of the larger process of community change. Ecological,*

> *organizational, situational, and other forces converge to structure and alter the relationships among people in a local setting, and random events also bring turbulence to the local arena. Given this it would be an error to say that "the community acts" in any literal sense, even in situations where community actions might occur. Instead, people act, and their actions connect with the acts of others to form action [social] fields (1991, p. 92).*

Bridger and Alter argue that an interactionist perspective provides a better basis for understanding efforts to promote community development than does a perspective focusing on social capital, and that, given all the cross-cutting loyalties of community residents and the openness of community boundaries, such perspective provides the basis for progressive change without the necessity of trust (a central feature of social capital, since at least a minimal level of trust must exist to achieve higher degrees of social capital). Another way of stating the question is as follows: is progressive community development (what Wilkinson, 1991, calls the community field, a special case of the social field) a result of enduring patterns of relationships (trust, stable although changing networks, norms of reciprocity) or does it usually arise from structures of shifting interaction involving local and extra-local actors responding primarily to external forces on the community? Or does progressive generalized community and neighborhood development sometimes fit one of these perspectives and other times the other?

The other three social capital articles in this issue suggest that communities can and sometimes do act. Agnitsch et al., state it this way: "Although the question 'Do communities act?' has long been of great interest to community sociologists, the answer today is, 'They better act,'" citing the declining support for community-level improvement from state and federal sources (p. 37, this volume). Emery and Flora agree with Bridger and Alter that social capital is not the key to explaining why community development is successful in certain communities and not in others; nor do they believe that financial capital is the key. Rather, it is the combination and integration of different kinds of capital that is central for understanding community change. Social capital is indeed an important link in that chain, but not the only one. They argue that it is important to address political capital separate from social capital to insure that political power is treated explicitly. They introduce the idea of an upward or downward spiral of capitals, reminiscent of Myrdal's concept of cumulative causation, but they see social capital as a glue or ligament for holding the other kinds of capital together in a purposeful chain.

Bridger and Alter conclude that bridging social capital (particularly those ties between community-based and external actors) is more central to locality development than is bonding social capital, and that bonding social capital is only relevant in isolated or more homogeneous geographic communities. Flora et al.'s 1997 analysis of a national sample of non-metropolitan communities supports Bridger and Alter's conclusion: communities with a larger number of formal organizational ties to the outside were more likely to have developed successful economic development projects than those communities with fewer such ties. Bonding type indicators were less effective in predicting economic development. In this volume, Agnitsch et al., using a sample of Iowa communities, test the hypothesis that bridging social capital is more strongly related to community action than is bonding social capital, but find no significant difference between the two kinds of social capital. They do find that the combination of bridging and bonding social capital provides more explanatory power than does either alone, and that to a degree one can substitute for the other.

Sturtevant's case study of the Applegate Partnership concludes that bonding social capital is a prerequisite for collective action in an economically declining community with a deep cleavage between environmentalists and those who are strong advocates of keeping jobs through natural resource development. In this instance, she argues that community and economic redevelopment cannot take place without first building trust. The Applegate Partnership brought together these two factions to work on new approaches to community economic development, focused almost entirely on building trust before tackling "substantive" projects related to economic development.

Sociologists can trace the emergent properties of social interaction, and therefore of social capital, as far back as Durkheim; for other social scientists, this recognition has awaited the popularization of social capital. In other words, sociologists could get along without the term social capital and still do good community development research, but interdisciplinary research and cross-disciplinary dialogue that affect practice-community development practice, in particular-has been given a great boost by the surge of interest in social capital.

The problem is that social capital means different things to different people-even within the same discipline. We believe that by separating social capital into two parts-bridging and bonding-the World Bank group has done a great service to social capital researchers, offering potential conceptual clarity through the distinction between homogeneous and heterogeneous ties.

Sturtevant also makes a strong plea for careful conceptualization and measurement of social capital; she argues specifically that researchers should carefully separate indicators of social capital from its outcomes. This sounds easier than it is, because social capital can be both a prerequisite and an outcome of community action. In different ways, the articles in this collection that favor social capital point the way for more rigorous conceptualization and measurement. For the near future at least, the watchword in social capital research should be "It's the measurement, stupid!" How well we measure social capital by linking our indicators tightly to meaningful conceptual sub-dimensions and to outcomes may determine whether social capital becomes another quaint sociological dichotomy or spawns exciting interdisciplinary research and community development practice.

The authors of all of the papers in this collection agree that the embedded or emergent character of social interaction is central to understanding and explaining community development. Although the authors of the other three papers argue for better measurement and more careful empirical testing of the relationship between different kinds of social capital, on the one hand, and community and economic development, on the other, the theoretical conundrum raised by Bridger and Alter remains important: will a strict political economy perspective, a strict interactionist approach, or a more collective, culturallyoriented approach such as that taken by Bourdieu take us farther in understanding and ultimately in practicing community development?

Are there useful ways of combining the three, such as the capitals approach presented by Emery and Flora, which incorporates political power into a framework that also includes the cohesive elements of social and cultural capital-and guides communities in participatory contextual measurement of progress along the various capitals dimensions.

Or are Bridger and Alter more correct in arguing that community development most often occurs through opportunistic combinations of local and extra-local structure and interactional fields that form and reform according to the particular issue or external pressure facing the community, rather than there being a major role for more enduring networks, patterns of reciprocity, and trust in generating community development. These papers do not tell us definitively which choices to make, either theoretically or methodology, but they definitely get us thinking about those choices.

DISABILITY AND COMMUNITY DEVELOPMENT

Worldwide, 600 million people live with disability, 80% of whom live in developing countries (World Health Organization, 2005). But the idea of disability is controversial, influenced by culture and competing conceptual systems. Fujiura and Rutkowski-Kmitta (2001) argue that industrialized Western nations tend to emphasize a restricted-activity approach to estimate the rate of disability within their populations, including: Australia (14.2%), Canada (13.2%), New Zealand (19.0%), and Spain (14.9%).

Using this approach, the U.S. Census Bureau estimates that about 49 million U.S. citizens over the age of five years experience a disability, with about 38 million living in urban and 11 million living in rural communities (Enders, 2005). About half of these experience significant disability. Historically, regardless of the approach to defining disability, society reacted to people with disability by stigmatizing, institutionalizing, criminalizing, marginalizing, and medicalizing them.

During the past 30 years, a new, ecological paradigm of disability has emerged, one that focuses attention on the environment's contributions to disability rather than placing the cause of disability solely within the individual. This view—a social rather than a medical model of disability—supported the de-institutionalization movements of the 1960s and 1970s, and led to the development of the Americans with Disabilities Act of 1990.

More recently, the World Health Organization revised its International Classification of Function, Disability, and Health (World Health Organization, 2001) to emphasize disability as the product of the interaction between an individual and his or her environment.

In this ecological framework, the environment is generally taken to mean the community. The outcome of the interaction between the individual and the environment may be measured by the degree of participation in community life. Under this framework, there are new opportunities for partnerships between people with disabilities, disability advocates, and community development researchers and practitioners.

The articles in this collection touch on the intersection between disability and community development. They report on studies of disability advocacy, accessible and affordable housing, economic development, community planning, transportation, and access to faith communities. They report studies that involve people with disabilities associated with a wide range of impairments, including mobility as well as cognitive, psychiatric, and sensory impairments. The authors in this issue describe how theories of independent living and community development overlap, and how methods from both are being applied by disability advocates to achieve their dreams and aspirations for equity, freedom, and dignity.

O'Day introduces readers to independent living philosophy and the national network of Centers for Independent Living (CIL) that promote the empowerment of people with disabilities from all causes through advocacy at the local, state, and national levels. Her national study shows that CILs and their consumers focus a great deal of advocacy efforts on changing community environments and systems of service such as housing, transportation, and employment. She argues that CILs may be good partners for broader community development agencies.

Hernandez and her colleagues describe an example of participatory action research and advocacy conducted by citizens with disabilities in a large city. They emphasize how advocacy by people with disability achieves the two defining aspects of community—solidarity and agency—described by Bhattacharyya (2004). They also demonstrate the changes in the environment that local advocacy can achieve. In the process, they highlight the fact that people with disability can be a minority within a minority group.

Maisel introduces the concept of "visitability" in housing—a growing movement across the country to achieve a minimal level of accessible housing so that people with mobility impairments—some 6.8 million people—can enjoy the simple pleasures of visiting friends and family. This concept, again, emphasizes the role the designed community environment can play in facilitating or inhibiting the experience of solidarity by people with disability.

Housing is a central element to people with disability related to many impairments. Sylvestre and his colleagues remind us that people with mental illness are often among the homeless, and that poverty and disability are often associated. These authors describe efforts in Canada to organize affordable and dignified living options for those with serious and persistent mental illness. Similarly, Feinstein and her colleagues report on their efforts to promote home ownership among adults with intellectual, developmental, and other disabilities in the United States.

People with disabilities experience a high rate of unemployment, and rural economies struggle to produce employment opportunities. Ipsen and her colleagues bring these two problems together into a solution that involves placing people with disabilities in the role of leaders of small town community economic development. This program highlights the contributions people with disabilities can make to the entire community.

Nisbet and her colleagues provide a history of the evolution of the field of disability from de-institutionalization to community inclusion. In the process, they highlight the critical concepts implied by the social model of disability and universalistic approaches to social policy, in describing a case study of community development planning in a small rural community in Northern New Hampshire that operationalizes those concepts.

Similarly, Guillory and her colleagues describe a model for applying principles of community development to increase community connections of people with disabilities and report on their efforts to implement that model in four communities in the Southern United States.

Some people would assume that participation in religion might play a large role in the lives of people with disabilities. Evanson and her colleagues report, however, that people with disabilities are much less likely to attend religious services than their non-disabled counterparts because of architectural, communication, and attitudinal barriers. They describe the development of the Faith Inclusion Forum to increase the integration of people with disabilities in faith communities.

Finally, as with housing, public transportation is a critical element of community environments for people with disabilities. Gonzales and her colleagues report on the evaluation of a national demonstration of a voucher model for rural transportation. By putting resources into the hands of people with disabilities, this transportation model promotes both agency and solidarity.

ADVOCACY

Advocacy by an individual or by an advocacy group normally aim to influence public-policy and resource allocation decisions within political, economic, and social systems and institutions; it may be motivated from moral, ethical or faith principles or simply to protect an asset of interest. Advocacy can include many activities that a person or organization undertakes including media campaigns, public speaking, commissioning and publishing research or poll or the 'filing of friend of the court briefs'. Lobbying (often by Lobby groups) is a form of advocacy where a direct approach is made to legislators on an issue which plays a significant role in modern politics.

Forms of Advocacy

There are several forms of advocacy, which each represent a different approach in the way change is brought into society. One of the most popular forms is social justice advocacy.

Although it is true, the initial definition does not encompass the notions of power relations, people's participation and a vision of a just society as promoted by social justice advocates. For them, advocacy represents the series of actions taken and issues highlighted to change the "what is" into a "what should be", considering that this "what should be" is a more decent and a more just society. Those actions, which vary with the political, economic and social environment in which they are conducted, have several points in common. They:

- Question the way policy is administered
- Participate in the agenda setting as they raise significant issues
- Target political systems "because those systems are not responding to people's needs"
- Are inclusive and engaging
- Propose policy solutions
- Open up space for public argumentation.

Some of the other forms of advocacy include:

- Budget advocacy: Budget advocacy is another aspect of advocacy that ensures proactive engagement of Civil Society Organizations with the government budget to make the government more accountable to the people and promote transparency. Budget advocacy also enables citizens and social action groups to compel the government to be more alert to the needs and aspirations of people in general and the deprived sections of the community.
- Bureaucratic advocacy: people considered "experts" have more chance to succeed at presenting their issues to decision-makers. They use bureaucratic advocacy to influence the agenda, however at a slower pace.

- Health advocacy: Health advocacy supports and promotes patient's health care rights as well as enhance community health and policy initiatives that focus on the availability, safety and quality of care.
- Ideological advocacy: in this approach, groups fight, sometimes during protests, to advance their ideas in the decision-making circles.
- Interest-group advocacy: lobbying is the main tool used by interests groups doing mass advocacy. It is a form of action that does not always succeed at influencing political decision-makers as it requires resources and organisation to be effective.
- Legislative advocacy: legislative advocacy is the "reliance on the state or federal legislative process" as part of a strategy to create change.
- Mass advocacy: is any type of action taken by large groups (petitions, demonstrations, etc.)
- Media advocacy: is "the strategic use of the mass media as a resource to advance a social or public policy initiative" (Jernigan and Wright, 1996.) In Canada for example, the Manitoba Public Insurance campaigns illustrate how media advocacy was used to fight alcohol and tobacco-related health issues. We can also consider the role of health advocacy and the media in "the enactment of municipal smoking bylaws in Canada between 1970 and 1995." (Asbridge, 2004)

Different contexts in which advocacy is used:

- In a legal/law context: An 'advocate' is the title of a specific person who is authorized/appointed (in some way) to speak on behalf of a person in a legal process.
- In a political context: An 'advocacy group' is an organized collection of people who seek to influence political decisions and policy, without seeking election to public office.
- In a social care context: Both terms (and more specific ones such as 'independent advocacy') are used in the UK in the context of a network of interconnected organisations and projects which seek to benefit people

who are in difficulty (primarily in the context of disability and mental health).

- In the context of inclusion: Citizen Advocacy organisations (citizen advocacy programmes) seek to cause benefit by reconnecting people who have become isolated. Their practice was defined in two key documents: CAPE, and Learning from Citizen Advocacy Programs.

Advocacy Groups

Advocacy is led by advocates or, when they are organized in groups as is the case most of the time, advocacy groups. Advocacy groups as defined by Young and Everritt (2004, 5) are different from political parties which "seek to influence government policy by governing." They are "any organization that seeks to influence government policy, but not to govern." This definition includes social movements, sometimes network of organizations which are also focused on encouraging social change. Social movements try to either influence governments or, like the environmental movement, to influence people's ideas or actions.

Today, advocacy groups contribute to democracy in many ways (ib., 2004.) They have five key functions:

- Assist in the development of better public policy
- Ensure governments' accountability to citizens.
- Give a voice to (misrepresented) citizen interests
- Mobilize citizens to participate in the democratic process
- Support the development of a culture of democracy

In comparison to other countries and other the last thirty years, an increasing number (40 percent) of the Canadian population is member of an organization which has had an advocacy role and has tried to achieve political change. Such a level of participation is a positive indicator of the health of the democracy in Canada (ib., 2004.)

Transnational Advocacy

Advocates and advocacy groups represent a wide range of categories and support several issues as listed on WorldAdvocacy.com. The Advocacy Institute, a US-based global organization, is dedicated to strengthening the capacity of political, social, and economic justice advocates to influence and change public policy.

The phenomenon of globalization draws a special attention to advocacy beyond countries' borders. The core existence of networks such as World Advocacy or the Advocacy Institute demonstrates the increasing importance of transnational advocacy and international advocacy. Transnational advocacy networks are more likely to emerge around issues where external influence is necessary to ease the communication between internal groups and their own government. Groups of advocates willing to further their mission also tend to promote networks and to meet with their internal counterparts to exchange ideas.

8

Cultural Competence in Social Work

SOCIAL WORK PRACTICE

Therefore, cultural competence in social work practice implies a heightened consciousness of how clients experience their uniqueness and deal with their differences and similarities within a larger social context.

Definitions

The NASW Board of Directors, at its June 2001 meeting, accepted the following definitions of *culture, competence, and cultural competence* in the practice of social work. These definitions are drawn from the NASW *Code of Ethics* and *Social Work Speaks.*

Culture

"The word 'culture' is used because it implies the integrated pattern of human behavior that includes thoughts, communications, actions, customs, beliefs, values, and institutions of a racial, ethnic, religious, or social group" (NASW, 2000b, p. 61). Culture often is referred to as the totality of ways being passed on from generation to generation. The term culture includes ways in which people with disabilities or people from various religious backgrounds or people who are gay, lesbian, or transgender experience the world around them.

The Preamble to the NASW *Code of Ethics* begins by stating: The primary mission of the social work profession is to enhance

human well-being and help meet the basic human needs of all people, with particular attention to the needs and empowerment of people who are vulnerable, oppressed, and living in poverty.

And goes on to say, "Social workers are sensitive to cultural and ethnic diversity and strive to end discrimination, oppression, poverty, and other forms of social injustice" (NASW, 2000a, p. 1). Second, culture is mentioned in two ethical standards:

Value: *Social Justice* and the Ethical Principle: *Social workers challenge social injustice.* This means that social workers' social change efforts seek to promote sensitivity to and knowledge about oppression and cultural and ethnic diversity.

Value: *Dignity and Worth of the Person* and the Ethical Principle: *Social workers respect the inherent dignity and worth of the person.*

This value states that social workers treat each person in a caring and respectful fashion, mindful of individual differences and cultural and ethnic diversity.

Competence

The word competence is used because it implies having the capacity to function effectively within the context of culturally integrated patterns of human behavior defined by the group.

In the *Code of Ethics* competence is discussed in several ways. First as a value of the profession: Value: *Competence* and the Ethical Principle: *Social* workers practice within their areas of competence and develop and enhance their professional expertise. This value encourages social workers to continually strive to increase their professional knowledge and skills and to apply them in practice. Social workers should aspire to contribute to the knowledge base of the profession. Second, competence is discussed as an ethical standard:

Competence

- Social workers should provide services and represent themselves as competent only within the boundaries of their education, training, license, certification, consultation received, supervised experience, or other relevant professional experience.

- Social workers should provide services in substantive areas or use intervention techniques or approaches that are new to them only after engaging in appropriate study, training, consultation, and supervision from people who are competent in those interventions or techniques.
- When generally recognized standards do not exist with respect to an emerging area of practice, social workers should exercise careful judgment and take responsible steps (including appropriate education, research, training, consultation, and supervision) to ensure the competence of their work and to protect clients from harm.

Cultural competence is never fully realized, achieved, or completed, but rather cultural competence is a lifelong process for social workers who will always encounter diverse clients and new situations in their practice. Supervisors and workers should have the expectation that cultural competence is an ongoing learning process integral and central to daily supervision.

Cultural Competence

Cultural competence refers to the process by which individuals and systems respond respectfully and effectively to people of all cultures, languages, classes, races, ethnic backgrounds, religions, and other diversity factors in a manner that recognizes, affirms, and values the worth of individuals, families, and communities and protects and preserves the dignity of each.

"Cultural competence is a set of congruent behaviors, attitudes, and policies that come together in a system or agency or among professionals and enable the system, agency, or professionals to work effectively in cross-cultural situations" (NASW, 2000b, p. 61).

Operationally defined, *cultural competence* is the integration and transformation of knowledge about individuals and groups of people into specific standards, policies, practices, and attitudes used in appropriate cultural settings to increase the quality of services, thereby producing better outcomes (Davis & Donald,

1997). Competence in cross-cultural functioning means learning new patterns of behavior and effectively applying them in appropriate settings.

Gallegos (1982) provided one of the first conceptualizations of ethnic competence as "a set of procedures and activities to be used in acquiring culturally relevant insights into the problems of minority clients and the means of applying such insights to the development of intervention strategies that are culturally appropriate for these clients.". This kind of sophisticated cultural competence does not come naturally to any social worker and requires a high level of professionalism and knowledge.

There are five essential elements that contribute to a system's ability to become more culturally competent. The system should (1) value diversity, (2) have the capacity for cultural self-assessment, (3) be conscious of the dynamics inherent when cultures interact, (4) institutionalize cultural knowledge, and (5) develop programs and services that reflect an understanding of diversity between and within cultures. These five elements must be manifested in every level of the service delivery system. They should be reflected in attitudes, structures, policies, and services.

The specific Ethical Standard for culturally competent social work practice is contained under *Section 1. Social workers' ethical responsibilities to clients.*

CULTURAL COMPETENCE AND SOCIAL DIVERSITY

- Social workers should understand culture and its functions in human behavior and society, recognizing the strengths that exist in all cultures.
- Social workers should have a knowledge base of their clients' cultures and be able to demonstrate competence in the provision of services that are sensitive to clients' cultures and to differences among people and cultural groups.
- Social workers should obtain education about and seek to understand the nature of social diversity and oppression with respect to race, ethnicity, national origin, color, sex, sexual orientation, age, marital status, political

belief, religion, and mental or physical disability. Finally, the Code reemphasizes the importance of cultural competence in the last section of the Code, *Section 6. Social Workers Ethical* Responsibilities to the Broader Society.

Social and Political Action

Social workers should act to expand choice and opportunity for all people, with special regard for vulnerable, disadvantaged, oppressed, and exploited people and groups. Social workers should promote conditions that encourage respect for cultural and social diversity within the United States and globally. Social workers should promote policies and practices that demonstrate respect for difference, support the expansion of cultural knowledge and resources, advocate for programs and institutions that demonstrate cultural competence, and promote policies that safeguard the rights of and confirm equity and social justice for all people.

Social workers should act to prevent and eliminate domination of, exploitation of, and discrimination against any person, group, or class on the basis of race, ethnicity, national origin, color, sex, sexual orientation, age, marital status, political belief, religion, or mental or physical disability.

Goals and Objectives of the Standards

These standards address the need for definition, support, and encouragement for the development of a high level of social work practice that encourages cultural competence among all social workers so that they can respond effectively, knowledgeably, sensitively, and skillfully to the diversity inherent in the agencies in which they work and with the clients and communities they serve. These standards intend to move the discussion of cultural competence within social work practice toward the development of clearer guidelines, goals, and objectives for the future of social work practice.

The specific goals of the standards are

- to maintain and improve the quality of culturally competent services provided by social workers and programs delivered by social service agencies

- to establish professional expectations so that social workers can monitor and evaluate their culturally competent practice
- to provide a framework for social workers to assess culturally competent practice
- to inform consumers, governmental regulatory bodies, and others, such as insurance carriers, about the profession's standards for culturally competent practice
- to establish specific ethical guidelines for culturally competent social work practice in agency or private practice settings
- to provide documentation of professional expectations for agencies, peer review committees, state regulatory bodies, insurance carriers, and others.

ETHICS AND VALUES OF SOCIAL WORKERS

Social workers shall function in accordance with the values, ethics, and standards of the profession, recognizing how personal and professional values may conflict with or accommodate the needs of diverse clients.

Interpretation

A major characteristic of a profession is its ability to establish ethical standards to help professionals identify ethical issues in practice and to guide them in determining what is ethically acceptable and unacceptable behavior (Reamer, 1998). Social work has developed a comprehensive set of ethical standards embodied in the NASW *Code of Ethics* that "address a wide range of issues, including, for example, social workers' handling of confidential information, sexual contact between social workers and their clients, conflicts of interest, supervision, education and training, and social and political action" (Reamer, 1998). The Code includes a mission statement, which sets forth several key elements in social work practice, mainly the social workers' commitment to enhancing human well-being and helping meet basic human needs of all people; client empowerment; service to people who are vulnerable and oppressed; focus on individual well-being in a social context; promotion of social justice and social change; and *sensitivity to cultural and ethnic diversity*. Social workers clearly have an ethical responsibility to be culturally competent practitioners. The Code recognizes that culture and ethnicity may influence how individuals cope with problems and interact with each other.

What is behaviorally appropriate in one culture may seem abnormal in another. Accepted practice in one culture may be prohibited in another. To fully understand and appreciate these differences, social workers must be familiar with varying cultural traditions and norms. Clients' cultural backgrounds may affect their help-seeking behaviors as well. The ways in which social services are planned and implemented need to be culturally sensitive to be culturally effective. Cultural competence builds on the profession's valued stance on self-determination and individual dignity and worth, adding inclusion, tolerance, and respect for diversity in all its forms. It requires social workers to struggle with ethical dilemmas arising from value conflicts or special needs of diverse clients such as helping clients enroll in mandated training or mental health services that are culturally insensitive. Cultural competence requires social workers to recognize the strengths that exist in all cultures. This does not imply a universal nor automatic acceptance of all practices of all cultures. For example, some cultures subjugate women, oppress persons based on sexual orientation, and value the use of corporal punishment and the death penalty. Cultural competence in social work practice must be informed by and applied within the context of NASW's *Code of Ethics* and the United Nations Declaration of Human Rights.

SELF-AWARENESS

Social workers shall develop an understanding of their own personal and cultural values and beliefs as a first step in appreciating the importance of multicultural identities in the lives of people.

Interpretation

Cultural competence requires social workers to examine their own cultural backgrounds and identities to increase awareness of personal assumptions, values, and biases. The workers' self-awareness of their own cultural identities is as fundamental to practice as the informed assumptions about clients' cultural backgrounds and experiences in the United States. This awareness of personal values, beliefs, and biases inform their practice and influence relationships with clients. Cultural competence includes knowing and acknowledging how fears, ignorance, and the "isms" (racism, sexism, ethnocentrism, heterosexism, ageism, classism) have influenced their attitudes, beliefs, and feelings.

Social workers need to be able to move from being culturally aware of their own heritage to becoming culturally aware of the heritage of others. They can value and celebrate differences in others rather than maintain an ethnocentric stance and can demonstrate comfort with differences between themselves and others. They have an awareness of personal and professional limitations that may warrant the referral of a client to another social worker or agency that can best meet the clients' needs. Self-awareness also helps in understanding the process of cultural identity formation and helps guard against stereotyping. As one develops the diversity within one's own group, one can be more open to the diversity within other groups. Cultural competence also requires social workers to appreciate how workers need to move from cultural awareness to cultural sensitivity before achieving cultural competence and to evaluate growth and development throughout these different levels of cultural competence in practice.

Self-awareness becomes the basis for professional development and should be supported by supervision and agency administration. Agency administrators and public policy advocates also need to develop strategies to reduce their own biases and expand their self-awareness.

CROSS-CULTURAL KNOWLEDGE

Social workers shall have and continue to develop specialized knowledge and understanding about the history, traditions, values, family systems, and artistic expressions of major client groups served.

Interpretation

Cultural competence is not static and requires frequent relearning and unlearning about diversity. Social workers need to take every opportunity to expand their cultural knowledge and expertise by expanding their understanding of the following areas: "the impact of culture on behavior, attitudes, and values; the help-seeking behaviors of diverse client groups; the role of language, speech patterns, and communication styles of various client groups in the communities served; the impact of social service policies on various client groups; the resources (agencies, people, informal helping networks, and research) that can be used on behalf of diverse client groups; the ways that professional values may conflict with or accommodate the needs of diverse client groups; and the power relationships in the community, agencies, or institutions and their impact on diverse client groups" (Gallegos, pp. 7–8).

Social workers need to possess specific knowledge about the particular providers and client groups they work with, including the range of historical experiences, resettlement patterns, individual and group oppression, adjustment styles, socioeconomic backgrounds, life processes, learning styles, cognitive skills, worldviews and specific cultural customs and practices, their definition of and beliefs about the causation of wellness and illness or normality and abnormality, and how care and services should be delivered. They also must seek specialized knowledge about U.S. social, cultural, and political systems, how they operate, and how they serve or fail to serve specific client groups.

This includes knowledge of institutional, class, culture, and language barriers that prevent diverse client group members from using services. Cultural competence requires explicit knowledge of traditional theories and principles concerning such areas as human behavior, life cycle development, problem-solving skills, prevention, and rehabilitation. Social workers need the critical skill of asking the right questions, being comfortable with discussing cultural differences, and asking clients about what works for them and what is comfortable for them in these discussions. Furthermore, culturally competent social workers need to know the limitations and strengths of current theories, processes and practice models, and which have specific applicability and relevance to the service needs of culturally diverse client groups.

CROSS-CULTURAL SKILLS

Social workers shall use appropriate methodological approaches, skills, and techniques that reflect the workers' understanding of the role of culture in the helping process.

Interpretation

The personal attributes of a culturally competent social worker include qualities that reflect genuineness, empathy, and warmth; the capacity to respond flexibly to a range of possible solutions; an acceptance of and openness to differences among people; a willingness to learn to work with clients of different backgrounds; an articulation and clarification of stereotypes and biases and how these may accommodate or conflict with the needs of diverse client groups; and personal commitment to alleviate racism, sexism, homophobia, ageism, and poverty. These attributes are important to the direct practitioner and to the agency administrator.

More specifically, social workers should have the skills to

- work with a wide range of people who are culturally different or similar to themselves, and establish avenues for learning about the cultures of these clients
- assess the meaning of culture for individual clients and client groups, encourage open discussion of differences, and respond to culturally biased cues
- master interviewing techniques that reflect an understanding of the role of language in the client's culture
- conduct a comprehensive assessment of client systems in which cultural norms and behaviors are evaluated as strengths and differentiated from problematic or symptomatic behaviors
- integrate the information gained from a culturally competent assessment into culturally appropriate intervention plans and involve clients and respect their choices in developing goals for service
- select and develop appropriate methods, skills, and techniques that are attuned to their clients' cultural, bicultural, or marginal experiences in their environments

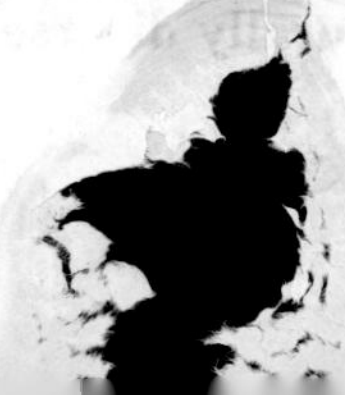

- generate a wide variety of verbal and nonverbal communication skills in response to direct and indirect communication styles of diverse clients
- understand the interaction of the cultural systems of the social worker, the client, the particular agency setting, and the broader immediate community
- effectively use the clients' natural support system in resolving problems—for example, folk healers, storefronts, religious and spiritual leaders, families of creation, and other community resources
- demonstrate advocacy and empowerment skills in work with clients, recognizing and combating the "isms", stereotypes, and myths held by individuals and institutions
- identify service delivery systems or models that are appropriate to the targeted client population and make appropriate referrals when indicated
- consult with supervisors and colleagues for feedback and monitoring of performance and identify features of their own professional style that impede or enhance their culturally competent practice
- evaluate the validity and applicability of new techniques, research, and knowledge for work with diverse client groups.

SERVICE DELIVERY OF SOCIAL WORKERS

Social workers shall be knowledgeable about and skillful in the use of services available in the community and broader society and be able to make appropriate referrals for their diverse clients.

Interpretation

Agencies and professional social work organizations need to promote cultural competence by supporting the evaluation of culturally competent service delivery models and setting standards for cultural competence within these settings. Culturally competent social workers need to be aware of and vigilant about the dynamics that result from cultural differences and similarities between workers and clients. This includes monitoring cultural competence among social workers (agency evaluations, supervision, in-service training, and feedback from clients). Social workers need to detect and prevent exclusion of diverse clients from service opportunities and seek to create opportunities for clients, matching their needs with culturally competent service delivery systems or adapting services to better meet the culturally unique needs of clients. Furthermore, they need to foster policies and procedures that help ensure access to care that accommodates varying cultural beliefs.

For direct practitioners, policymakers, or administrators, this specifically involves

- actively recruiting multiethnic staff and including cultural competence requirements in job descriptions and performance and promotion measures
- reviewing the current and emergent demographic trends for the geographic area served by the agency to determine service needs for the provision of interpretation and translation services
- creating service delivery systems or models that are more appropriate to the targeted client populations or advocating for the creation of such services
- including participation by clients as major stakeholders in the development of service delivery systems
- ensuring that program decor and design is reflective of the cultural heritage of clients and families using the service
- attending to social issues (for example, housing, education, police, and social justice) that concern clients of diverse backgrounds
- not accepting staff remarks that insult or demean clients and their culture
- supporting the inclusion of cultural competence standards in accreditation bodies and organizational policies as well as in licensing and certification examinations
- developing staffing plans that reflect the organization and the targeted client population (for example, hiring, position descriptions, performance evaluations, training)

- developing performance measures to assess culturally competent practice
- including participation of client groups in the development of research and treatment protocols.

EMPOWERMENT AND ADVOCACY OF SOCIAL WORKERS

Social workers shall be aware of the effect of social policies and programs on diverse client populations, advocating for and with clients whenever appropriate.

Interpretation

Culturally competent social workers are keenly aware of the deleterious effects of racism, sexism, ageism, heterosexism or homophobia, anti-Semitism, ethnocentrism, classism, and xenophobia on clients' lives and the need for social advocacy and social action to better empower diverse clients and communities.

As first defined by Solomon (1976), *empowerment* involves facilitating the clients' connection with their own power and, in turn, being empowered by the very act of reaching across cultural barriers. Empowerment refers to the person's ability to do for themselves while advocacy implies doing for the client. Even in the act of advocacy, social workers must be careful not to impose their values on clients and must seek to understand what clients mean by advocacy. Respectful collaboration needs to take place to promote mutually agreed-on goals for change.

Social workers need a range of skills and abilities to advocate for and with clients against the underlying devaluation of cultural experiences related to difference and oppression and power and privilege in the United States. The empowerment tradition in social work practice suggests a promotion of the combined goals of consciousness raising and developing a sense of personal power and skills while working toward social change. Best practice views this as a process and outcome of the empowerment perspective (Gutiérrez, 1990; Simon, 1994). Social workers using this standard will apply an ecosystems perspective and a strengths orientation in practice. This means that workers consider client situations as they describe needs in terms of transitory challenges rather than fixed problems.

According to Gutiérrez and Lewis (1999), empowerment is a model for practice, a perspective and a set of skills and techniques. The expectation is that culturally competent social workers reflect these values in their practice.

DIVERSE WORKFORCE OF SOCIAL WORKERS

Social workers shall support and advocate for recruitment, admissions and hiring, and retention efforts in social work programs and agencies that ensure diversity within the profession.

Interpretation

Increasing cultural competence within the profession requires demonstrated efforts to recruit and retain a diverse cadre of social workers, many of whom would bring some "indigenous" cultural competence to the profession as well as demonstrated efforts to increase avenues for the acquisition of culturally competent skills by all social workers. Diversity should be represented at all levels of the organization, and not just among direct practitioners.

The social work profession has espoused a commitment to diversity, inclusion, and affirmative action. However, available statistics indicate that in the United States social workers are predominantly white (88.5 percent) and female (78.0 percent). The proportion of people of color has remained relatively stable in the social work membership of the National Association of Social Workers over a period of several years: 5.3 percent identify themselves as African American; Hispanics, including Mexican Americans, Puerto Ricans, and other Hispanic groups constitute about 2.8 percent of the membership; Asians and Pacific Islanders 1.7 percent; and American Indians/First Nations People 0.5 percent (Gibelman & Schervish, 1997). Social work client populations are more diverse than the social work profession itself. In many instances, service to clients is targeted to marginalized communities and special populations, groups that typically include disproportionately high numbers of people of color, elderly people, people with disabilities, and clients of lower socioeconomic status.

Matching workforce to client populations can be an effective strategy for bridging cultural differences between social worker and client, although it cannot be the only strategy. The assumption is that individuals of similar backgrounds can understand each other better and communicate more effectively (Jackson & López, 1999). Yet an equally compelling fact is that "the majority of clinicians from the mainstream dominant culture will routinely provide care for large numbers of patients of diverse ethnic and/or cultural backgrounds. Clearly increasing the numbers of culturally diverse social workers is not sufficient. Even these professionals will need to be able to provide care for patients who are not like themselves" (Jackson & López, 1999, p. 4). In addition, culturally competent social workers who bring a special skill or knowledge to the profession, like bicultural and bilingual skills, or American Sign Language (ASL) skills, are entitled to professional equity and should not be exploited for their expertise but should be appropriately compensated for skills that enhance the delivery of services to clients.

PROFESSIONAL EDUCATION OF SOCIAL WORKERS

Social workers shall advocate for and participate in educational and training programs that help advance cultural competence within the profession.

Interpretation

Cultural competence is a vital link between the theoretical and practice knowledge base that defines social work expertise. Social work is a practice-oriented profession, and social work education and training need to keep up with and stay ahead of changes in professional practice, which includes the changing needs of diverse client populations. Diversity needs to be addressed in social work curricula and needs to be viewed as central to faculty and staff appointments and research agendas.

The social work profession should be encouraged to take steps to ensure cultural competence as an integral part of social work education, training and practice, and to increase research and scholarship on culturally competent practice among social work professionals. This includes undergraduate, master's and doctoral programs in social work as well as post-master's training, continuing education, and meetings of the profession. Social agencies should be encouraged to provide culturally competent in-service training and opportunities for continuing education for agency-based workers. NASW should contribute to the ongoing education and training needs for all social workers, with particular emphasis on promoting culturally competent practice in continuing education offerings in terms of content, faculty, and auspice.

In addition, the NASW *Code of Ethics* clearly states, "Social workers who provide supervision and consultation are responsible for setting clear, appropriate, and culturally sensitive boundaries" (p. 14). This highlights the importance of providing culturally sensitive supervision and field instruction, as well as the pivotal role of supervisors and field instructors in promoting culturally competent practice among workers and students.

LANGUAGE DIVERSITY OF SOCIAL WORKERS

Social workers shall seek to provide and advocate for the provision of information, referrals, and services in the language appropriate to the client, which may include the use of interpreters.

Interpretation

Social workers should accept the individual person in his or her totality and ensure access to needed services. Language is a source and an extension of personal identity and culture and therefore, is one way individuals interact with others in their families and communities and across different cultural groups. Individuals and groups have a right to use their language in their individual and communal life.

Language diversity is a resource for society, and linguistic diversity should be preserved and promoted. The essence of the social work profession is to promote social justice and eliminate discrimination and oppression based on linguistic or other diversities. Title VI of the Civil Rights Act clarifies the obligation of agencies and service providers to not discriminate or have methods of administering services that may subject individuals to discrimination.

Agencies and providers of services are expected to take reasonable steps to provide services and information in appropriate language other than English to ensure that people with limited English proficiency are effectively informed and can effectively participate in and benefit from its programs.

It is the responsibility of social services agencies and social workers to provide clients services in the language of their choice or to seek the assistance of qualified language interpreters. Social workers need to communicate respectfully and effectively with clients from different ethnic, cultural, and linguistic backgrounds; this might include knowing the client's language. The use of language translation should be done by trained professional interpreters (for example, certified or registered sign language interpreters). Interpreters generally need proficiency in both English and the other language, as well as orientation and training. Social agencies and social workers have a responsibility to use language interpreters when necessary, and to make certain that interpreters do not breach confidentiality, create barriers to clients when revealing personal information that is critical to their situation, are properly trained and oriented to the ethics of interpreting in a helping situation, and have fundamental knowledge of specialized terms and concepts specific to the agency's programs or activities.

CROSS-CULTURAL LEADERSHIP OF SOCIAL WORKERS

Social workers shall be able to communicate information about diverse client groups to other professionals.

Interpretation

Social work is the appropriate profession to take a leadership role not only in disseminating knowledge about diverse client groups, but also in actively advocating for fair and equitable treatment of all clients served. This role should extend within and outside the profession.

Guided by the NASW *Code of Ethics*, social work leadership is the communication of vision to create proactive processes that empower individuals, families, groups, organizations, and communities. Diversity skills, defined as sensitivity to diversity, multicultural leadership, acceptance and tolerance, cultural competence, and tolerance of ambiguity, constitute one of the core leadership skills for successful leadership (Rank &

Hutchison, 2000). Social workers should come forth to assume leadership in empowering diverse client populations, to share information about diverse populations to the general public, and to advocate for their clients' concerns at interpersonal and institutional levels, locally, nationally, and internationally. With the establishment of standards for cultural competence in social work practice, there is an equally important need for the profession to provide ongoing training in cultural competence and to establish mechanisms for the evaluation of competence-based practice. As the social work profession develops cultural competencies, then the profession must have the ability to measure those competencies. The development of outcome measures needs to go hand in hand with the development of these standards.

UTILIZATION OF SOCIAL SERVICES

Effective utilization of social services by the poor and the needy is not just determined by the supply side. Social disadvantages associated with these people, such as disability, lack of ways and means and socio-economic status, often make accessibility to services difficult. Countries in Asia and the Pacific are modelling their social services after those provided in the more developed countries, and there are many similarities in the philosophies, definitions and provision of social services in developing countries as compared to developed countries. Likewise, such services have been intended primarily to serve as a safety net in supporting the poor. There are differences, however, in the actual delivery of services when regional and cultural characteristics are taken into account. In exploring the issues in access to social services for the poor and the disadvantaged in Asia and the Pacific, it is necessary to understand, using the experiences of the more developed countries as a reference frame, similarities and differences right from the concept of social services, definition of service targets, the measurement of needs, service supply, delivery and accessibility, and finally, quality and the measurement of outcomes.

Perspectives on Social Services

In a broad sense, theories of economy, society, social problems, social policy and social services are interrelated. The subject of social welfare came into being after the Second World War. It denoted the policy of the government to combat poverty and the problems associated with it, and to aid economic growth while containing poverty. The concern at that time sprang from many basic philosophies centring around the issues of social equality, resources redistribution, universal or selective provision, individual freedom or social control. The many debates on social welfare theories in the 1970s represented efforts to align the many fractions into a more unified and coherent view of social welfare, with an added dimension of feminism upon the focus on social inequality. Prompted by the limited resources held by the government in the 1980s, attention focused on the shared responsibility of the government, non-governmental organizations (NGOs) and citizens in providing welfare. From this premise, market consumerism and user accountability have been brought into the discussion of social welfare in the 1990s.

To simplify the arguments, one could look at the dichotomy in responsibility in providing care between the Government and the individual (George and Wilding 1985). Theoreticians proposing more individual responsibility including family responsibility, are referred to as the anti-collectivists. These people believe in the free market mechanism and take poverty as an individual problem, that it is only the government who is responsible for taking care of the needy and the sick (i.e. the deserving poor). The reluctant collectivists are those who believe in the free market while maintaining that the government has more responsibility in ensuring the rights and choices of the individual. Hence, their willingness to provide a safety net for those in need (for example, social security, education, health care and housing). The collectivists believe in a socialist economy and hence a total redistribution of wealth in society. Social welfare such as education, health care and personal social services are means of resources redistribution, thus making welfare-for-all a mandatory responsibility of the government. George (1985) further takes in perspective dichotomizing social inequality-social equality and has produced a rather neat summary of the range of typologies for social services. Alongside the development of these ideologies for social services are the more practical concerns, such as providing an environment conducive to care and social rehabilitation, user or consumer choices, quality of services and affordability. In addressing these issues, governments in the developed countries have moved from providing care and services through massive institutions to encouraging family and volunteers to share in providing care in the community. There is a consensus that community care, as an attempt to replicate extended family care, should be brought back (Heginbotham 1990). Countries in Asia and the Pacific have the advantage of short-cutting the social services path by selecting the desirable outcomes from the experience of more developed countries for adoption or adaptation in their own countries. As a result, voluntary care in and by the family and the community is being actively preserved by governments in Asia and the Pacific (except for several countries, such as Australia and New Zealand).

Types and Range of Social Services

The types of social services provided by countries in Asia and the Pacific are invariably the same as those in developed countries. The organization of these services within a Government modelled after a Western bureaucratic structure would inevitably produce the same categories of services. In a modern society-organized government rationality, government policy is expected to deal with social needs and social problems. Thus, public policy governs services to meet needs or to eradicate social problems. From this stance, social services are seen to have a broad coverage and serve different aspects of lives in modern society. These include education, health care, social security and personal social services, housing, law and order, social recreation, sewage and hygiene, transport and environment, and others. However, with the prevailing ideologies of community care, shared responsibility and market consumerism in social services, Governments often tend to focus on their responsibility principally in health, education, social security and social care (personal social services). Other areas are, in general, considered to be more or less the responsibilities of the community, family and individuals.

Health services can be broadly classified into primary, secondary and tertiary services. In the region, most are curative (medical) rather than preventive services. Primary care includes those services provided in the community, close to and generally accessible by potential patients. Secondary services such as clinics and other facility-based services provide somewhat higher quasi-hospital services, while the tertiary/quaternary hospital services provide increasingly specialized ranges of general and specialist medical and surgical care (Phillips 1990). In many ways, primary health-care services have the greatest relevance as a basic social service.

In terms of prevention, primary prevention refers to a situation where health can be promoted and therefore illnesses prevented. The range of services include health promotion, such as healthy eating, home safety, health screening, healthy lifestyle and avoidance of health hazards such as smoking. Secondary prevention means avoidance of hospital admission. In realizing this, a country would need a good curative medical support networks, such as an adequate number of family medicine practitioners and specialist clinics so that illnesses can be dealt with in the community without the need for hospitalization. Tertiary prevention occurs when hospitalization becomes necessary, making the stay and recovery as short as possible, and avoiding re-admissions.

This involves the provision of good hospital, rehabilitation and postdischarge care. Many of the rural parts of the Asian and Pacific countries are ridden with inadequate primary care and primary prevention programmes, especially in environmental health, leading to many casualties jamming up the already very inadequate curative care. For instance, malaria can be prevented effectively by a good drainage and clean environment, and it can be easily treated with early diagnosis. These services are normally organized under the environmental health and hygiene departments of the local government. Social security and personal social services are usually organized under a department of social development or social welfare services. Social security entails the provision of basic security, usually supplied either in cash or in kind, or some combination, to secure people's daily living. Social security, in a broad sense, also includes social insurance, pensions and a central provident fund or other social security systems. These benefits are generally given free, but means tests are usually required. The names and range of these services vary a great deal from country to country, but benefits in cash normally include weekly or monthly living allowances, disability allowances, and other supplements (for example, meals for diabetes) if necessary, and/or one-off emergency payments to temporarily needy persons. The in-kind benefits include clothes, meals-on-wheels, emergency help with accommodation, furnishings, and others. Personal services are a final and important provision, which aim to provide a range of support and assistance (often domiciliary-based) varying from simple domestic help to highly skilled psychological and social interventions (such as counselling, psychotherapy and advocacy). Most Asia and the Pacific countries have, to date, tended to have little in the way of comprehensive social security safety nets and provide cash benefits cautiously, leaving the distribution of in-kind benefits to voluntary efforts. However, in most countries, the provision of professional personal social services is gradually increasing alongside a conscious government preservation of traditional extended family inputs in social care. Such services often include family services (for example, case and family crises interventions), drop-in or neighbourhood centres, child and youth development activities and public education on issues such as citizens' responsibilities and good neighbourhood programmes.

Education is another key service that is gaining importance in developing countries. Governments in these countries increasingly take serious pride in the responsibility for the provision of a basic level of education, normally up to secondary school levels. Education is perceived as a long-term social investment by the government, and usually occupies a core part of government expenditure. Free or partial assistance is provided in forms of scholarship or block grants for university education (for example, Australia; Hong Kong, China; and Japan). However, provision is often linked to the economic situation of the country. Free education or loans can be found in better-off countries for compulsory or universal basic education, while education remains a private business in countries with a lower national income (for example, rural parts of China and Indonesia). A formal education system, mainly school-based with a pyramidal structure, from pre-primary to university levels, has been established in most

Asian and Pacific countries. Both the public and the private sectors are involved in the provision of education, ranging from basic literacy purposes to higher education or vocational training, which is normally geared towards professional and specialized training in relation to the labour demand of the country. As a compromise to universal and more specialized university education, many countries in the region have developed vocational or industry-specific training as an alternative for students who could not get into tertiary education because of the very keen competition. The organization of the educational system is similar to that in developed countries, except that examinations are the commonly adopted mechanism in assessing and screening students for the next stage.

NEED FOR SOCIAL WORK INTERVENTION

Social work operates in an environment of competing professions and there has been a longstanding difficulty in defining and expressing its unique contribution and expertise. The reasons for this vary from a reluctance to claim its own slice of professional territory and the authority derived from special knowledge not available to the lay person that often goes with that claim. In part the concern has been that asserting its professional authority could further dis-empower people requiring its services.

Skill and knowledge shifts within and between professions routinely take place over time. A characteristic of social work is that it's knowledge base is multi disciplinary and social workers have the capacity to move into territories of skill and knowledge that 'belong' to other professions and occupations. At times this is part of assessing the need for specialist expertise, at other times it is part of journeying (Care Journeys) with the person using services.

In a world where professionalism is seen territorially, this capacity to travel into and out of other people's territory is not seen as flexibility, but as social work 'being a Jill of all trades but mistress of none' (Williams 2004). At the same time social work feels threatened by claims from nurses, police and other professions to be able to do what social work does. This paper starts with the assumption that social work takes a holistic view of a person's life and situation whether this is in assessment of need, in direct work with them, or through accessing support from social care staff, other organisations, professionals and other workers in related fields.

The key characteristics of social work are:

* the focus on the whole of the person's life, their social context, and environment
* the capacity, in circumstances that are often difficult:
    - o to engage quickly with people to establish trust,
    - o to persist in efforts to engage even when this has proved difficult and others have given up
* consciously to move into situations that would be avoided by most people because they are complex and high risk
* the relationship established between the social worker and the service users involved is integral to achieving quality
* the capacity to manage situations where risks are very finely balanced so that 'you are damned if you do and damned if you don't'

We have assumed that there is a generic base for social work and that this means that newly qualified workers 'enter the social work world with the core knowledge and skills necessary to begin professional practice across the required range of settings' (Williams, 2004). Earlier specialisation can lead to tunnel vision that hinders social worker being able to keep an holistic perspective on their work and to 'indefensible divisions of responsibility' (Williams, 2004). This is particularly important given the structural divisions such as those between services and within for adults and children. If the key feature of social work is its holistic approach, retaining a generic foundation is essential. Specialist areas of practice will emerge because existing knowledge and skills have to be transferred and built on for the social worker to function effectively in a specific set of circumstances. These include the legal, organisational and inter-professional and inter-organisational arrangements involved. The stage at which these specialist areas of practice are introduced is debatable. In the view of the authors at least at post qualification levels they are likely to include the following:

* direct practice, of various types and techniques
* management and development:
    o of practice, including work based learning for students and staff
    o of service provision and development, including commissioning
    o policy and strategic developments within the organisation or the field
* working within a range of organisations to contribute to promoting policies and practice that support social and personal well-being
* research and development.

We are not suggesting an exclusive focus, but that the majority of the social worker's time will be spent on one of these areas. All will be operating in a multi-organisational and multi-professional context whether in the statutory, private or voluntary and community sector.

The term 'social work intervention' usually describes work undertaken with individuals, families, groups and communities. In looking to the future we have also used the term to cover the use of social work knowledge and skills when using any of these methods of intervening:

1. within a social care organisation to facilitate the provision of services and practice consistent with the Codes of Practice and with standards of service and practice
2. to promote the social inclusion and life opportunities of people using services
3. between organisations, where the objective is to promote partnerships that are required on a short, medium or longer term basis to provide integrated services, or to personalise a particular package of support e.g. when working with dual diagnosis in mental health and alcohol abuse, or learning disabilities and sensory impairment
4. as part of a multi-professional or multi-disciplinary team to promote effective integrated working with people with dementia and their carers, rehabilitation following strokes or brain injury, or neighbourhood and community

development

5. in organisations such as businesses and industry, corporate governance, the media, and the political arena, to bring the social work perspectives and skills into organisational development and management.

Successful social work includes the capacity to work effectively within organisations and across organisational boundaries. In the vast majority of instances social work intervention is a collective activity not an individual activity whether as an employee or an independent social worker. This aspect of social work intervention should be given the status of an intervention rather than as an adjunct to direct work with people using services. The Framework for Social Work Education in Scotland emphasises:

The significance of interrelationships with other social services, especially education, housing, health, criminal justice, income maintenance, and other services provided by partners (p32)

And the competence to:

Develop, maintain and review effective working relationships within and across agency boundaries (p42).

The most common forms of methods of social work intervention are:

Community Development

Where problems such as environmental poverty, high unemployment rates and poor housing, are affecting a community, social work intervention at the individual, family or group level will not address the problems and a community development approach is necessary. Social work intervention with individuals and families may, however, assist people to survive coping with the impossible, foster resilience or enable them to begin to build platforms of support that could improve their lives.

Social workers were key in the UK in undertaking community development in the early 1970s, and the values, skills and expertise recommended in neighbourhood renewal programmes are consistent with those of social work. However, the documentation on social exclusion in England is singularly and deliberately silent on the role of social workers. In Scotland the role of social services in community development is embedded in legislation and pioneered much of the work underpinning the development of community social work (Smale and Bennet 1989).

Group work is an appropriate form of intervention where people share difficulties and want, or are required, to find ways of resolving them.

The most common forms of group work are with people who abuse alcohol and drugs, with mental health difficulties, young carers, children and young people who are accommodated, teenage mothers, children who are unaccompanied asylum seekers, and offenders. They use the collective experience and expertise to share effective solutions, provide mutual support, promote self esteem, confidence and identity. They are a powerful resource in facilitating the empowerment of people using services and in reducing isolation for example of disabled young people from black and minority ethnic groups and women who have survived domestic violence. Many of these groups take place outwith social work departments in the voluntary and community sector, in hospitals, in youth work or the health service. The workers may or may not be social work trained. The generic expertise and skills are those required for setting up, running and ending groups, understanding and using group dynamics. Specialist skills relate to understanding the needs and issues facing the particular group of services users and how these may impact on group process and dynamics.

In recent years there has been a growing number of groups and organisations run by people using services. They are based on structuring the experience and expertise of a particular service user group to form a resource for others facing similar issues. The philosophy that shared personal experience is a valuable and essential resource in achieving change is in direct contradiction to the ethos in the organisations in which most of social work is practised. Here staff are fearful of managers knowing about personal difficulties as this is deemed likely to affect views about their competence as a worker and their potential for promotion (Turner and Evans 2004). Similarly, the expertise of the 25% of staff with responsibilities for caring for an adult family member is not seen as a resource for the organisation, but often an impediment to its operation (Balloch, McLean and Fisher, 1999).

Traditionally residential care has been thought of as 24 hours a day and 365 days a year, but in supported living support can range from intensive to minimal. A different conception of residential care that recognises the diversity of 'collective', 'group living' or 'communal living' arrangements should be developed (Residential Forum, 2004). Similarly, extra care and Direct Payments can offer intensive support in people's homes as part of community based support. Group work and communal living arrangements are likely to involve individual or family casework or therapy where a personalised programme is combined with other sources of support. In a minority of cases the communal living itself is used as a continuous therapeutic experience rather than being a periodic event within it. The main interventions are likely to be undertaken by social care staff and managers, with support from a range of professionals including psychologist, psychiatrists. Social workers may be involved on a regular or ad hoc basis or as external or internal managers.

Individual or Family Casework

Here social work is the intervention. It supports the individual or family to identify, and use, their own and their social network's experience and expertise as a resource for:

* releasing potential that has been blocked by past experiences
* problem solving where there are current relationship or parenting difficulties
* devising the service user's/s' preferred way of coping with intractable problems or difficulties
* promoting self esteem and confidence to adopt different approaches to existing problems
* surviving living with high risks or uncertainty
* learning new approaches to existing, new or emerging difficulties
* accessing and using information, new skills and knowledge

* devising ways of influencing organisations, groups or individuals that are blocking the achievements of preferred outcomes.

Problems or difficulties may have resulted from the effects of social exclusion, lack of skills or knowledge, or, self-defeating or self-damaging behaviour that achieves the very result that the individual or family most dreads.

The purpose of the intervention is diverse and ranges from:

* increasing life skills or changing behaviour to increase life options
* promoting independence and inter-dependence
* working with conflicts of interest or in relationships
* stabilising or slowing down deterioration and loss of independence
* coping with changed life situations and transitions
* learning new skills, for example in parenting or as a family carer
* loss, bereavement and trauma,
* balancing expectations, needs and responsibilities that involve ethical and moral dilemmas
* supporting individuals' development to enable them to participate in groups, use local community resources or to move to mainstream services.

Bibliography

A K Rizwi : *Social Policy and Social Work*, Mohit Pub, Delhi, 2008.

Akash Gulalia : *Social Work Practice : With Mobile Population Vulnerable to HIV/AIDS,* Mohit, Delhi 2008.

Ankit Prasad: *Social Welfare and Social Action in Community: YMCA at Work*, Mittal, Delhi, 2005.

Barnes, Bob.: *Social Survey Division in the 1990s*, Population Trends, 1991.

Batliwala, Srilatha: *Population Policies Reconsidered: Health, Empowerment and Rights*, Cambridge, Harvard University Press, 1994.

Bedi, M.S. : *Social Development and Social Work with Society* , Himanshu, Delhi, 1994.

Bhaskaran, Vanila : *Research Methods for Social Work* : Rawat, Delhi 2008.

Bhatia, S.C.: *Education and Social Cultural Disadvance,* Delhi Xeres Publication, 1982.

Bhattacharya, Sanjay : *Social Work : An Integrated Approach*, Deep and Deep, Delhi, 2003.

Carol Kemelgor : *Athena Unbound: The Advancement of Women in Science and Technology*, Cambridge, Cambridge University Press, 2000.

Carr, Marilyn: *Speaking Out: Women's Economic Empowerment in South Asia,* London, 1996.

Chhaya Patel: *Social Work Practice : Religio Philosophical Foundations : Essays in Honour of Professor Indira Patel*, Rawat, Delhi, 1999.

Devi, Ranjna K. : *Social Work, Philosophy, Concepts and Dimensions*, Omega, Delhi, 2009.

Elisabeth Relchert: *Social Work and Human Rights : A Foundation for Policy and Practice*, Rawat, Delhi, 2003.

Frederic G. Reamer : *Social Work Values and Ethics,* Rawat, Delhi, 2005.

Gorhe, Neelam: *Social Development and Working with Community*, Gyan Pub. House, New Delhi, 1995.

Jacob, K.K. : *Social Work Education in India*, Himanshu, Delhi, 1994.

Khan, M A : *Social Work and Social Policy, Concepts and Methods*, Book Enclave, Delhi, 2007.

Kumar, Ajit : *Social Work Concerns and Challenges in the 21 Century*, APH, Delhi, 2009.

Kumar, I.S. : *Social Mobility and Caste Violence: A Study of the Gujarat Riots*, Delhi, Adjanta Publications, 1985.

Maeda J Galinsky: *Handbook of Social Work With Groups*, Rawat, Delhi, 2007.

Mishra, Brijesh : *Glimpses of Social Welfare in India : Problems and Perspectives*, ABD Pub, Delhi, 2006.

Murugesan, P : *Social Welfare Programmes and Fertility Decline*, Abhijeet Publication, Delhi, 2009.

Naqi, Mohammad : *Social Work for Weaker Sections*, Anmol, Delhi, 2005.

Nussbaum, Martha: *Women and Human Development: The Capabilities Approach*, New York, Cambridge Press, 2000.

Prasanta K. Pattanaik: *Essays on Individual Decision-making and Social Welfare*, Oxford University Press, London, 2009.

Sen, S K : *Social Work Practices in Society*, Book Enclave, Delhi, 2007.

Sinha, Debotosh : *Aspects of Industry and Occupational Social Work*, Abhijeet Pub, Delhi, 2007.

Steve Max: *Organizing for Social Change: A Manual for Activists in the 1990s*, Midwest Academy, Seven Locks Press. 1991.

Subheda, I.S. : *Fieldwork Training in Social Work in Community,* Rawat, Delhi, 2001.

Wendy Bowles : *Research for Social Workers : An Introduction to Methods*, Rawat, Delhi, 2003.

Index

S

T

U

W

Y

❑❑❑